# DECLINE OF
# AMERICA AND ISRAEL:

## THE LAST TWO RACIAL APARTHEID WHITE COLONIAL NATIONS

Dr Deshay David Ford, Ph D.

ISBN

Paperback: 979-8-90190-112-0

Hardcover: 979-8-90190-111-3

# Dedication

To my sons

Daniel Deshay Ford and Edward Maurice Ford

# Acknowledgment

I would like to thank my foster brother, Mr. Robert W. Lewis, for his encouragement and support throughout my writing projects.

I would also like to thank my parents, Maurice Harold Ford and Juanita Robinson Ford. They taught me the importance of a good education and the value of hard work.

I wish to pay tribute to my beloved brothers who have passed: Harold Maurice Ford, Glenn Bonnet Ford, Robert Lewis Ford, and Philip Jewel Ford.

My heartfelt thanks go to Elizabeth W. Minor, my foster mother, a great African-American woman and a true asset to our race and culture.

I would also like to thank Graham Root Hall and Louise Boaz Hall for their support, encouragement, affection, and kindness. Dr. Graham Root Hall, a former employee of the United States Department of State, encouraged and supported my love and research in American foreign policy.

# Table of Contents

# Introduction:
# America and Israel – Two British Colonies Built to Fail

Empires, like all human constructs, rise with ambition and collapse under the weight of their contradictions. This book begins with a single, haunting premise: that both the United States and the State of Israel, nations born of colonial ambition, constructed upon occupied land, and driven by myths of divine destiny, were never built to last. They were built to dominate, to expand, to exploit. But they were never built to endure.

To understand their decline, we must first tell the truth about their origins—not the sanitized versions found in schoolbooks, nor the patriotic hymns sung at parades, but the raw, bloody, inconvenient truth buried beneath centuries of denial.

Let us begin with America.

The story often begins in 1776, with men in powdered wigs signing a declaration beneath the blazing sun of a new republic. We are told they were freedom fighters, champions of liberty, standing against the tyranny of a British crown. But the roots of this rebellion stretch further back—back to 1603, when a different kind of conquest began under the banner of the Virginia Charter Company.

This company, established by British investors and sanctioned by the monarchy, was not created to promote religious freedom or noble ideals. It was a business venture. Its mission was profit, and its currency was land, labor, and blood. The settlers it sent to Virginia were not pilgrims escaping persecution; they were employees tasked with extracting wealth from the so-called "New World." (Zinn, 1980)

From the very beginning, the foundations of the American project were soaked in the logic of exploitation. The English settlers launched a campaign of annihilation against the Indigenous peoples of the land.

They saw native tribes not as fellow humans but as obstacles to resource extraction. Lands were seized, villages burned, and bodies piled high to make way for plantations and profit.

Then, in 1619, came another defining moment. The arrival of enslaved Africans on the shores of Virginia. Human beings were auctioned into a system that would become the economic spine of the American South. This was not freedom. It was racial capitalism in its purest form. A new kind of empire was being born, one cloaked in the language of liberty but baptized in genocide and slavery.

When the American colonies declared their independence from Britain between 1776 and 1781, they simply replaced one empire with another. The young republic wasted no time in continuing its expansionist agenda, waging war against Native nations, driving them from their ancestral lands, and forcing survivors into internment zones called "reservations." These were the United States' own concentration camps, long before that term would be etched into human memory by Nazi Germany.

In the 1920s, German officials came to America to study these camps. They learned. They adapted. And they built their own system of genocide on American blueprints. (Zinn, 1980; Brown, 1970)

Now shift your gaze to 1948. A year often celebrated, yet rarely interrogated. That year, under the protective wing of the British Empire and with the backing of Western powers, the modern State of Israel was declared. But Israel, like America, was born not in peace but in displacement.

Its ideological roots trace back to the Balfour Declaration of 1917, in which Lord Arthur James Balfour promised British support for a "national home for the Jewish people" in Palestine. This promise was not made out of empathy, but geopolitics. European Zionist leaders had backed British efforts in World War I, and the imperial ledger demanded payment.

But that promise was written on someone else's land.

Decline of America and Israel: The Last Two Racial Apartheid White Colonial Nations

When Jewish survivors from Europe, bearing the trauma of the Holocaust, began arriving in Palestine, they did not enter a barren wasteland. They arrived in towns and villages, among orchards and mosques, beside centuries of Palestinian life. And soon, a campaign of forced expulsion, massacres, and occupation began. In 1948 alone, over 700,000 Palestinians were driven from their lands in what they call the *Nakba*, or "catastrophe." The aim was clear: to clear the land for a Jewish ethnostate. (Jacques, 2009)

Poles, Germans, Russians, Austrians, and new Jewish settlers from Europe flooded into the Levant, supported by Western military and political power. And just like the American settlers three centuries prior, they deemed the existing population disposable.

Two nations. Two mythologies. One blueprint.

Both Israel and America were born of colonial ambition wrapped in religious justification. Both were built upon the backs of murdered Indigenous peoples. Both clothed themselves in the language of freedom while practicing domination. And both now face internal decay, haunted by the ghosts of their foundations.

This pattern is not unique to these two nations. France slaughtered millions in Algeria and Indochina. Belgium cut off the hands of African laborers in the Congo. Germany committed genocide in Namibia long before it turned inward on its own Jewish citizens. Australia and Canada built their modern nations on the bodies of Indigenous children. These are not isolated incidents; they are the operating logic of colonial whiteness.

And in 2024, history tried once again to demand accountability.

South Africa, standing at the gates of the United Nations, filed charges of genocide against the State of Israel for its assault on Gaza. The court at The Hague convened. The evidence was laid bare. And still, every white-majority nation—America, Canada, Australia, and their European allies—voted against the charge. They voted to protect themselves. Because to condemn Israel would be to condemn themselves. Their history is Israel's mirror.

# Decline of America and Israel: The Last Two Racial Apartheid White Colonial Nations

The Global South, the post-colonial nations, the peoples of color whose ancestors had been pillaged, enslaved, and silenced, cast their votes in favor. They saw in Palestine the same story they knew all too well.

And this is not just an international tale. It is deeply American. In 1950, African-Americans, led by civil rights leaders and global allies, filed charges of genocide against the United States itself. They documented the lynchings, the mass incarceration, the racialized violence of police, the denial of education and housing, and health care. They named it what it was: genocide, not just in the act of killing, but in the destruction of a people's ability to live free. (Janken, 2003)

So here we are.

The nations that call themselves the world's great democracies—those who preach freedom, human rights, and justice—have never extended those ideals to their non-white populations. Their moral claims are hollow when their histories remain buried. Their democratic facades cannot hide the foundations of theft, genocide, and racial apartheid.

America and Israel, two settler colonies built on Indigenous graves, upheld by white supremacy, now buckling under the weight of their own myths.

This is their story.

And this is their reckoning.

# The New American Country

America, they say, is where dreams come true. But in 1968, standing barefoot on the red dust fields of Scott, Arkansas, opportunity felt like a faraway myth, something read about in library books, not lived by those who tilled the soil from sunup to sundown. We were Black sharecroppers. We didn't inherit opportunity. We inherited the land, not in title, but in toil.

My parents were peasants in the truest sense of the word. They lived on a large Southern plantation, working hands weathered by cotton and sun, laboring for a man who owned the land, the tools, and our time. Their labor was never recorded in the pages of American progress, yet it was their hands that built the country beneath the stories, quiet, unrecognized, but essential.

That year, I graduated high school, one of the few from our plantation to do so. My diploma did not hang in a golden frame. It sat heavy in my hand, like a promise that something different might be possible. Something beyond the cotton fields, beyond the Southern system that kept Black children yoked to the futures of their parents.

*Glenn Bonnett Ford*

And then something unexpected happened.

Mr. Robert Alexander, the plantation owner and a Harvard man, called for my mother and me. We were summoned to his house, not the way field workers are usually called, but as guests. He was elegant, soft-spoken, and well-dressed, a man who could hold a brandy in one hand and the fate of families in the other. He spoke about a friend, another Harvard man, who had returned to Arkansas and needed help maintaining his estate. This friend, he said, had been a United States Consul-General. A diplomat. A man who had served his country in faraway places like India and Australia under the Eisenhower administration.

His name was Dr. Graham Root Hall.

Dr. Hall's resume was almost mythical. A retired figure of the U.S. State Department, appointed during the presidency of Dwight David Eisenhower, he had once stood among the elite of foreign service. His classmates included John Sherman Cooper, a towering figure who would become U.S. Ambassador to both India and Australia.

*Dr Graham Roots Hall and his wife, Louise Boax Hall*

By some stroke of grace, divine or ancestral, I was chosen to work
for Dr. Hall and his wife Louise at their estate in Little Rock. I was just
nineteen. Young, green, and still smelling of farmland. But I walked
onto that estate with a spine full of work ethic and a heart full of
purpose. They welcomed me into their world, a world of chandeliers,
quiet libraries, and global visitors. And I gave them everything I had in
return.

*Dr Deshay David Ford*

I became not just their gardener or helper. I became the caretaker of their lives, their land, and eventually, their legacy. I remained in their service until their passing. Dr. Hall died in 1981, Louise in 1987, and I still carry pieces of their stories with me.

Working at the Halls' estate became an unexpected education. It wasn't school, but it was learning. I stood in the company of ambassadors and justices, men and women whose names were inked into diplomatic histories. I met John Sherman Cooper in person, the very man who helped shape America's relations with Asia. I was introduced to Jeffrey Lewis, the U.S. Ambassador to Nigeria, and Sir Stanley, Australia's Chief Justice, alongside his wife, Lady Burberry, a woman of poise and intellect. These were names that walked through doors I once never knew existed.

And then, there were legends.

I met Ann Margaret Chowning, the world-renowned anthropologist, whose research reshaped our understanding of Pacific Island cultures. She was born in Arkansas, just like me. Her presence alone was proof that brilliance could come from overlooked places.

Decline of America and Israel: The Last Two Racial Apartheid White
Colonial Nations

I met Winthrop Paul Rockefeller, who would go on to become Arkansas's first Republican governor in the same year I graduated. He was different from many white Southern politicians, thoughtful, reserved, and curious about the stories of the people around him.

But the moment that still glows brightest in my memory came in 1970, inside the walls of Philander Smith College. I stood face to face with Muhammad Ali, The People's Champion, The Louisville Lip, the greatest to ever step into a boxing ring or onto a stage. We debated, not fists, but words. His presence was electrifying, his voice melodic and defiant. I didn't win that debate, but I walked away feeling like a champion nonetheless. To speak, to be heard, to be challenged by a man like Ali, that was worth more than a trophy.

But all of this, the ambassadors, the scholars, the legends, was a long way from the cotton fields of Scott.

My parents were born into a world that offered little and asked much. They were never offered the chance to dream beyond survival. My mother, wise and ambitious, had wanted a college education. She wanted to be more than a worker under a Southern sun. But doors were shut. Scholarships did not knock. Opportunities were not passed down to Black girls on plantations. Still, she carried a vision for us, her children, a vision drenched in sacrifice and prayer.

She told me that God always makes a way.

And He did.

My father, a man of few words but endless grit, taught me how to work. The kind of work that makes your back ache and your soul steady. My mother taught me the value of education, the kind that feeds the mind and frees the spirit. Between them, I was raised with discipline, dignity, and a hunger to rise.

And rise I did.

From a boy in the cotton fields to the caretaker of an ambassador's estate. From sharecropper roots to a lifetime pursuit of knowledge. I would go on to earn twelve college and university degrees, two master's, seven associate's, and complete coursework for two doctoral programs. Every certificate, every diploma, is a brick laid in honor of those who could not build their dreams because they were too busy picking the cotton that built someone else's.

Education was my mother's prayer. And in a way that only God could arrange, Dr. Graham Root Hall became its answer. A man shaped by diplomacy and distant capitals, he stood on the far side of the American color line. Yet, somehow, he saw my mother's dream and chose to lift it higher.

He spoke often of learning, of duty, of the power of words. But it was his wife, Louise Boaz Hall, who turned those ideals into action. Louise was gentler than Graham, warm and quiet, with the wisdom of a woman who had watched history unfold from embassy windows and foreign parlors. Her lineage was one of deep Southern power, her father, Bishop Hiram Boaz, founded Southern Methodist University in Dallas, Texas. But she chose to use that privilege to plant seeds in others.

She paid for every step of my education, unconditionally. Whether it was a class, a certificate, or a degree, Louise stood behind me like a second mother with open hands and unwavering faith.

Their children, Donald Roots Hall and Lee Boaz Hall, carried their own legacies. Donald was a professor at the University of Arizona, a scholar with a tender voice and sharp mind. Lee had retired from the Central Intelligence Agency, his life shaped by shadows and briefings. Both men were kind, respectful, and unpretentious. Their humanity was real.

But there was another name, perhaps less known in formal history, whose impact on my life was no less monumental, Winston Elizabeth Minor.

Mrs. Minor was an extraordinary African-American woman who had served the Halls throughout their years in the U.S. Foreign Service. She had traveled the world beside them, walking through embassies in Paris, Delhi, Canberra, and beyond, always with dignity. She told stories of palaces and protests, of foreign rituals and the great Althea Gibson, the first Black woman to win Wimbledon and the Australian Open. Mrs. Minor had seen her with her own eyes, watched Gibson's serve slice through not just tennis courts but centuries of exclusion.

Winston Minor was grace in motion, resilience wrapped in modesty. And through her, I met another figure who would change me forever, her son, Robert W. "Bob" Lewis.

Robert was more than a friend. He was a mentor, a compass, and a living mirror. A Black man navigating a white world with unshakable dignity, he showed me what it meant to walk tall even when the streets were bent against you. His presence was both shield and sword. He taught me how to see the world, not just through the lens of education or diplomacy, but through the lived truth of an African-American man in a nation built to deny him his place.

Robert spoke of the battles we faced daily, racial profiling, silent exclusion, denied justice. Yet, he never surrendered to bitterness. His fight was for something greater, human rights, dignity, and the liberation of all oppressed people. He taught me how to resist with intelligence and how to endure with pride. His death in 2021 was a loss to the world, not just to me.

He reminded me constantly that America was not, and had never been, a country of justice for its non-white citizens. Not for the Indigenous peoples whose lands were stolen and children abducted. Not for the enslaved Africans who built its infrastructure with broken backs and bare hands. Not for the Asians and Latinos whose labor was exploited while their identities were criminalized.

And the truth is carved in the very parchment of the Constitution.

The American Constitution, ratified in 1787, did not grant freedom to Black people. Article IV, Section 2, Clause 3 enshrined the legality of slavery. It didn't just tolerate bondage, it protected it. The founding fathers, idolized in monuments and textbooks, were slaveowners and slave sympathizers. George Washington. Thomas Jefferson. James Madison. Pierce Butler. Their democracy was selective. Their freedom, conditional. Their wealth was measured in human lives.

That same Constitution allowed slavery to flourish for nearly a century, and its legacy persists today. The systems they built never fully collapsed, they evolved.

As of 2024, the majority of U.S. Senators and Representatives are direct descendants of slaveholders. That is not coincidence. It is continuity. Power passed down like property. Silence inherited like wealth.

And when the world looked again at the United States in the wake of Ferguson, Missouri, after the shooting of unarmed teenager Michael Brown by a white police officer in 2015, his parents did not take their pain only to a courtroom. They took it to the United Nations.

There, at the Human Rights Council, they filed a formal complaint. They called America what it refused to call itself, a violator of human rights. The UN launched an investigation into institutional racism in U.S. policing and criminal justice. Its findings? No significant progress. The racism was not accidental. It was systemic. And it remained deeply rooted.

At the global level, only two countries stood as enduring examples of state-sponsored racial supremacy in the 21st century, the United States and Israel.

These were not conclusions drawn in anger. They were findings built on data, lived testimony, and decades of historical record.

The U.S. incarcerates more of its population than any other country on earth, more than China, more than Russia, more than Iran or North Korea. It is not the freest nation. It is the most incarcerated.

And yet, through it all, I count myself among the most blessed.

I always wanted to be a writer. A storyteller. A witness. That dream, born in the shadows of cotton stalks and carried through embassies and classrooms, came true. I authored two books. They transformed me into a Chinese scholar and earned me recognition in foreign policy circles, places my younger self never even imagined.

*Dr Deshay David Ford in the President's office of Ronald Reagan's Museum in Simi Valley, California.*

But what I write now is not about accolades. It is about accountability.

Let the record show, the American Revolution was not a war for freedom. It was a war for control. It was fought by wealthy white men, men like Washington, Jefferson, Madison, and Butler, who owned hundreds of African slaves. They did not fight for liberty. They fought to protect a social and economic system that depended on forced labor and racial hierarchy.

Their revolution was about property. And we were the property.

This is the America they created.

This is the truth they buried beneath fireworks and national anthems.

But we are still here. And we are still writing, writing the unfinished story of The New American Country.

# Section I:
# U.S. Racial History,
# Slavery,
# Domestic Genocide
# & Structural Racism

# The Beginning of the English First Settlement

In 1772, a single legal decision sent a tremor through the foundations of the British Empire—one that echoed across the Atlantic and shook the moral illusion on which American slavery stood. It was not delivered on a battlefield, nor in the halls of revolution, but from the bench of Britain's highest court.

The case was Somersett v. Stewart.

At its center was James Somersett, a man enslaved by Charles Stewart, an official in the British Colonial Agency. Stewart had purchased Somersett in one of Britain's overseas colonies, and in 1771, he brought him to England. But on English soil, Somersett dared to do what so many others only dreamed—he demanded freedom.

He reached out to members of the burgeoning British Abolition Society, a group of reformers and humanitarians who had long sought a legal opening to challenge the institution of slavery. Somersett gave them that opening. They agreed to represent him in court, and together, they challenged not just one man's bondage, but the legality of slavery itself within the British Empire.

The case landed before Lord Chief Justice John Murray, also known as the Lord of Mansfield, who had the power to affirm slavery's legality or declare it incompatible with British Common Law.

In his landmark ruling, Lord Mansfield declared that slavery was unsupported by the Common Law of England, and therefore, Somersett must be set free. He refused to allow the coercive force of bondage to persist in the heart of the empire. (Zinn, 1980)

It was a quiet decision rendered in a British courtroom, but its implications thundered across continents.

The ruling struck terror into the hearts of the American planter class. If the law of the empire no longer protected their so-called property, then their entire economic foundation—built on human bondage—could collapse. George Washington, Thomas Jefferson,

James Madison, Alexander Hamilton, and Pierce Butler all owned enslaved people. Under Mansfield's ruling, they would be forced to free them. To them, this was not justice. It was a threat.

So Jefferson, ever the tactician, picked up his pen.

In 1776, just four years after the Somersett decision, Jefferson declared the independence of the thirteen American colonies. But the Declaration of Independence was not written to free the enslaved; it was written to protect the enslavers. The Revolution was not a popular uprising of the people; it was a calculated rebellion by the elite, a class of wealthy white men determined to preserve their property, their plantations, and their power.

What they called liberty was, in truth, the right to own others without imperial interference.

This agenda became even more apparent in 1787, when these same men gathered at the Constitutional Convention in Philadelphia. There, under the guise of unity and nationhood, they enshrined slavery into the republic's DNA. Article IV, Section 2, Clause 3 of the new Constitution declared that if any "person held to service or labor" escaped across state lines, their owner had the right to reclaim them.

This clause wasn't about the law. It was about chains.

It wasn't about protecting a nation. It was about preserving a caste.

Yet, for generations, Americans were taught to believe that the Constitution was colorblind and that its parchment stood for equality. Even Associate Justice Clarence Thomas has made that claim. But history knows better.

The Constitution was not written for the enslaved. Nor for Indigenous peoples. Nor for women. Nor for poor white men. It was crafted by and for the elite of the eighteenth century, its words carefully chosen to shield their interests. Native Americans would not gain the right to vote until 1924. American women would not win that right until 1920, with the passage of the Nineteenth Amendment. African-Americans were granted the right to vote in 1868 with the Fifteenth

Amendment, but in truth, they did not begin to exercise that right freely until the Voting Rights Act of 1965. (Zinn, 1980)

Even then, the ink was barely dry before the resistance began.

In 2013, Chief Justice John Roberts delivered a Supreme Court ruling that gutted a key provision of the Voting Rights Act. He claimed that the requirement for states with histories of racial discrimination to obtain federal approval before changing voting laws was outdated. In his opinion, racial discrimination in voting no longer existed.

But the lived experience of millions tells a different story.

America, according to Roberts, had evolved past its racist past. But across the country, polling stations closed in Black communities. Voter ID laws spread like wildfire. Gerrymandering drew racial boundaries with surgical precision. Disenfranchisement didn't disappear—it simply changed form.

This is the real legacy of American democracy: a system that claimed freedom while codifying exclusion.

It began not with revolution but with charters and contracts. In 1603, King James granted a group of wealthy British investors a royal charter to establish the Virginia Company. Their mission was not religious liberty or moral enlightenment—it was profit.

These early settlers, employed by the company, did not come to worship freely—they came to extract wealth. The colony of Jamestown was built not by pilgrims seeking refuge, but by agents of capital seeking returns. The land they occupied was not unclaimed. It belonged to the Indigenous peoples of North America, whose communities they decimated with violence, disease, and displacement.

The settlers saw these people not as fellow human beings, but as obstacles to be removed.

It was not a mistake. It was policy.

The colony's purpose was racial extermination for economic expansion.

Decline of America and Israel: The Last Two Racial Apartheid White
Colonial Nations

Like so many others in American history, this truth was buried beneath layers of mythology. But dig deep enough, and the blood still rises.

From Lord Mansfield's courtroom to the plantations of Virginia, from the ink of the Constitution to the protests for the ballot box, one story repeats itself: those in power will rewrite the law to protect their dominance and call it freedom.

And yet, across centuries, people like Somersett, the abolitionists, and the women and men who marched in Selma kept rising.

Because freedom, even when denied, remembers how to breathe.

History, as taught in American classrooms, is not a mirror—it is a mural. Painted by those in power, polished for the eyes of children, and framed in myths that hide the blood beneath the brushstrokes. Nowhere is this more evident than in the origin story of the United States.

We are told that the first English settlers crossed the Atlantic to flee religious persecution. That they were pious dreamers, desperate to worship freely, unmolested by kings and tyrants. But the truth, as ever, is less romantic—and far more revealing.

The settlers who arrived in Jamestown, Virginia, were not pilgrims in search of sacred soil. They were agents of the Virginia Company, a business enterprise granted a royal charter by King James I in 1603. Their mission was not spiritual—it was financial. They came not to build a kingdom of God, but to turn a profit for shareholders in London.

And yet, their survival depended on the very people they would later betray. During those first brutal winters, the Indigenous peoples of Virginia provided food, shelter, and guidance. Without them, the settlers would have perished.

But gratitude has never been a foundation of empire.

The moment the settlers gained strength, they launched a campaign of racial extermination. Armed with muskets and scriptures, they declared that God had given them this land. They believed they were

His chosen people, divinely ordained to remove the so-called savages who stood in the way of plantations and progress.

Dee Brown writes that the white colonists saw this theft and slaughter not as evil, but as a holy duty. (Brown, 1970) The same ideology would later be echoed by European Jews—white Jews from Poland, Germany, Russia, and elsewhere—who, in 1948, declared that God had promised them Palestine, and then began a systematic campaign of removal and extermination of the Palestinian people. (Brown, 1980)

History, it seems, loves to repeat itself when no one is punished the first time.

The white colonialists who rebelled against King George III in 1776 claimed they were being persecuted, taxed without representation, and denied liberty. But just over a century earlier, in 1619, these same colonists had begun enslaving Africans—ripping them from their homes, chaining them in ships, and building an economic empire on their backs.

They sought freedom for themselves, while denying it to everyone else.

This hypocrisy, rooted in the founding of America, echoes into our modern age. The very ideological foundation of the United States— white supremacy, settler colonialism, and racial capitalism—continues to define its policies both at home and abroad.

Just as the State of Israel, created in 1948 by displaced European Jews, began a campaign of racial violence and land seizure against the Palestinians, the United States waged a parallel campaign against its own Indigenous people and enslaved African population. Together, these twin settler colonies became architects of the twenty-first-century empire—one built on domination, not democracy.

The British Empire, too, played its part. Across Africa, Asia, and the Americas, it unleashed its armies on non-white populations—burning villages, toppling kingdoms, redrawing borders with no regard for the people they erased. Its goal was not enlightenment. It was control.

And with that control came something far more insidious—the weaponization of skin color.

In ancient times, slavery was often a matter of conquest, not color. When the Romans defeated the Greeks, they enslaved them. In 44 A.D., when Emperor Claudius conquered Britain, he enslaved its people—not because of race, but because of power.

But beginning with the European colonizers of the fifteenth and sixteenth centuries, race became the defining feature of bondage. Skin color became a brand. Whiteness became the marker of dominance. Blackness, the badge of servitude.

Dr. Nikole Hannah-Jones, in her groundbreaking *1619 Project*, argues that under this system, the entire globe was subdivided by color. Africans, Asians, Indigenous peoples of the Americas and the Pacific— all were marked for subjugation by the shade of their skin. (Jones, 2018)

And this logic did not die with the end of formal slavery.

In March of 2024, the nation of South Africa stood before the International Court at The Hague and filed formal genocide charges against Israel. The accusation: that Israel had carried out a sustained campaign of extermination against Palestinians in Gaza and the West Bank.

The charge was bold. And it was right.

Predictably, every white-majority power—the United States, Britain, Canada, Australia, and the European Union—condemned South Africa's filing. But their opposition was not rooted in justice. It was rooted in shared guilt. To condemn Israel would be to confront their own crimes: the Trail of Tears, the Congo, Algeria, apartheid, Hiroshima.

As I wrote in *Why Muslim People Hate Donald Trump and America* (Ford, 2024), the United States itself is guilty of genocide—against its Native nations, its African-American citizens, its immigrants from the

Global South. It has killed with bullets, with poverty, with prisons, and with the pen.

And it has done so with partners.

During Nelson Mandela's liberation struggle, when he and his comrades were fighting the racist apartheid government of South Africa, the United States and Israel both provided weapons, intelligence, and financial support to the very regime Mandela sought to overthrow. (Ford, 2022)

They chose whiteness over justice. Settler solidarity over human life.

This is not ancient history. This is our now.

Empires may dress themselves in flags and laws, but beneath every anthem is a scream. Beneath every constitution, a chain. And until those screams are heard, until those chains are broken, there can be no justice—only repetition.

In the shadows of the American dream lies a history that still haunts us—a history of conquest, betrayal, and extermination. Not just of people, but of truth itself.

Between 1846 and 1876, the United States government, in collusion with the newly formed State of California, embarked on what historian Benjamin Madley calls a campaign of state-sanctioned racial genocide. In his searing work, *American Genocide: The United States and the California Indian Catastrophe*, Madley reveals how Native Californians were systematically hunted, enslaved, starved, and massacred. (Madley, 2018)

These atrocities weren't rogue actions by frontier vigilantes. They were orchestrated, funded, and endorsed by public officials—from local militias to governors. Genocide was not the byproduct of expansion. It was the policy of it.

This blueprint of elimination did not begin or end in California. Nor was it uniquely American.

It was inherited—from empire.

## Decline of America and Israel: The Last Two Racial Apartheid White Colonial Nations

The State of Israel, too, was not born solely out of the ashes of the Holocaust. It was shaped, strategically, by the imperial interests of Great Britain. In 1917, Lord Arthur Balfour, Britain's Foreign Secretary, penned the now infamous Balfour Declaration, addressed to Baron Rothschild, promising to support "the establishment in Palestine of a national home for the Jewish people." But this declaration came not from compassion. It came from geopolitical bargaining.

During World War I, Britain needed help destabilizing its rival— Imperial Germany. In exchange for Zionist support, Britain offered a promise: Palestine.

At the Paris Peace Conference in 1919, that promise was ratified— not in principle, but in imperial interest. Palestine was handed over as a British protectorate, while behind closed doors, the betrayal of the Arab people was sealed. Despite prior commitments made to Arab leaders who had supported British forces against the Ottomans, oil and racial hierarchy won the day. (Hourani, 1991)

The West's colonial appetite was never about freedom. It was about resource control, and the belief that brown people—Arabs, Africans, Asians—could not be trusted with sovereignty.

This ideology was not an aberration. It was mainstream. Even President Woodrow Wilson, a self-proclaimed moralist and architect of the League of Nations, believed deeply in white racial superiority. According to Howard Zinn, Wilson referred to non-white populations as inferior and saw their governance as a duty reserved for white Christian men. (Zinn, 1980)

So when European Jews—many from Poland, Germany, Russia, and England—declared the independence of Israel in 1948, they were not entering a political vacuum. They were entering a land occupied by Palestinians who had lived there for over 2,000 years. And they brought with them not only trauma, but ideology—a settler-colonial logic that mirrored that of the early American colonists at Jamestown in 1603.

The settlers in Jamestown justified genocide by invoking divine destiny. The early Zionists invoked Biblical covenant. In both cases, the

Indigenous people were rebranded as obstacles, and their removal as sacred duty. (Jones, 2018)

In March 2024, South Africa—itself a former British colony and a nation forged through generations of resistance to white supremacy—filed formal genocide charges against Israel at the International Court of Justice in The Hague. The charge: that Israel had executed a sustained campaign of racial extermination against the Palestinian people.

The response from the Western world was predictable—and damning.

Every white-majority colonial power—the United States, Canada, Britain, France, Germany—voted against the charge. But this was not a judgment of justice. It was a defense of their shared reflection.

To condemn Israel would mean acknowledging their own crimes: the Trail of Tears, the Congo Free State, the Herero massacres, the stolen generations in Australia, and the forced sterilizations in Canada.

They could not point the finger without blood dripping from their own hands.

But those who stood with South Africa were not silent. They were nations long bruised by colonial bootprints—nations of the Global South, whose histories were written in chains and ashes. These countries recognized in Gaza and the West Bank not simply a tragedy, but a mirror of their own suffering.

In 1956, African-American leaders also tried to hold the United States accountable. They filed formal charges of racial genocide at the United Nations, citing lynching, mass incarceration, and the systemic denial of civil rights. The U.S. dismissed the claims. But the world remembered. (Zinn, 1980)

As Dr. Deshay David Ford argues, the United States and Israel remain the last bastions of formalized racial apartheid—nations that still codify inequality through policy, still criminalize color, and still incarcerate more people than China, Iran, North Korea, and Russia combined. (Ford, 2022)

Decline of America and Israel: The Last Two Racial Apartheid White
Colonial Nations

These are not democracies in crisis. These are empires refusing to die.

Even the American Civil War, so often romanticized as a fight for unity, reveals another buried truth. According to Robert Rosen in *The Jewish Confederates*, many Jewish Americans in the South were not only complicit in slavery—they were deeply embedded in it. (Rosen, 2006)

In New Orleans, a major hub for the slave trade, Jewish merchants, planters, and professionals played prominent roles in the buying, selling, and owning of African people. One of the most powerful figures was Judah P. Benjamin, a Jewish statesman who served as Secretary of State in Confederate President Jefferson Davis's government. Benjamin owned hundreds of enslaved people on his Louisiana plantations and helped write the legal architecture of the Confederacy.

This truth—uncomfortable, inconvenient, and often erased—complicates the narrative of Jewish history in America. It forces us to see beyond identity and into ideology. Whiteness, when wedded to power, does not discriminate among religions. It only demands loyalty to supremacy.

History does not simply unfold. It is constructed—shaped by the hands of those with power, and often written in the blood of those without it.

One such hidden chapter begins with the Monsanto family, a wealthy Jewish merchant dynasty that traces its roots to Portugal. Long before the name Monsanto became associated with modern agriculture and corporate biotech, the family's wealth was rooted in a different enterprise—the slave trade.

According to Dr. Deshay David Ford (2022), the Monsanto family owned vast plantations and enslaved thousands of African people, profiting not just from labor, but from the very machinery of human trafficking. They financed and operated slave ships that sailed from Africa to the Americas, delivering chained men, women, and children to plantations from South Carolina to Brazil—destroying generations of African families for economic gain. (Ford, 2022; Monsanto, 2021)

Slavery was not incidental. It was the business model.

In contrast, Adolf Hitler's persecution of the Jewish people in Nazi Germany—a racialized campaign of imprisonment, starvation, and extermination—was rooted in political scapegoating and ideology, not economic exploitation. Hitler viewed Jews as traitors to the German state, blaming them for its loss in World War I and the perceived betrayal through international agreements like the Balfour Declaration of 1917, in which Britain had pledged to support a Jewish homeland in Palestine.

Yet the irony remains bitter. While Hitler waged a genocidal war against Jews in the name of racial purity, some Jewish families like the Monsantos had already committed their own crimes against humanity—not for political power, but for profit.

The weight of history grows heavier.

Another chapter in this haunting legacy involves the Sackler family, a Jewish-American dynasty originally from Poland. They founded Purdue Pharma, the company that manufactured OxyContin, a highly addictive opioid that sparked a nationwide health crisis in the United States. As addiction spiraled into epidemic, millions of Americans— young and old—lost their lives and families to a pharmaceutical empire built on denial and deceit.

The Sacklers made billions while insisting their drug was safe. They later reached settlements with U.S. states, agreeing to fund addiction treatment programs—but they never served prison time, and they retained much of their fortune. The story of OxyContin is not just about addiction. It is about how wealth shields itself from accountability, even when it destroys entire communities. (U.S. Health Services, 2022)

From human trafficking to chemical dependency, the throughline is clear: profiteering at the expense of the vulnerable, whether Black, poor, or addicted.

In 1948, the State of Israel was formally declared, a project born from the British colonial imagination and solidified by the power of

Western alliances. Back in 1917, the Balfour Declaration had promised Palestine to European Jews, even while promising the same land to Arab allies who helped the British defeat the Ottoman Empire.

The betrayal was imperial and deliberate.

Today, with billions in U.S. military aid, Israel wields devastating force over the Palestinian people—its government led by Prime Minister Benjamin Netanyahu, whose war policies have drawn comparisons to Adolf Hitler's Final Solution. In this narrative, Palestinians are not citizens. They are problems to be solved. Their history is erased, their existence reduced to resistance, and their lives made expendable. (Ford, 2024)

This campaign of displacement, siege, and slaughter has been justified by an ancient claim: that God gave the land of Palestine to the Jewish people. But who are these chosen people? Many Israelis are descendants of Jews from Poland, Russia, Germany, and America— nations of cold climates, light skin, and European culture. And yet, they claim ownership of a sun-drenched land in the Levant, where the people have lived for thousands of years.

The parallel is painful.

In 1603, English settlers arrived in Jamestown, Virginia, and declared that God had given them the land. The Indigenous peoples who had lived there for 10,000 years were soon stripped of everything— their land, their languages, their children.

Now, white settlers in Tel Aviv and Jerusalem echo the same logic. They claim a divine deed to Palestine. But the desert sun does not choose sides—and history will not forget whose bones lie beneath its sands.

We often speak of race as though it were a scientific truth. But science tells a different story.

There is no such thing as a "white race." There are people with less melanin, whose ancestors adapted to colder, less sunny climates, and whose skin lightened over millennia to absorb more Vitamin D. This is not racial superiority—it is biological adaptation. Pale skin is not a badge of chosen status. It is a response to limited sunlight.

When people migrated north from Africa—into Europe's forests and tundras—their melanin levels decreased to survive the scarcity of light. But that evolutionary quirk became weaponized. Whiteness, once a shade of skin, became a structure of power.

In truth, everyone is a person of color. What we call "white" is not colorless—it is pigment deficiency, shaped by geography, not destiny.

As a security officer at the J. Paul Getty Museum, I met Italians from both ends of their country—those from the Mediterranean, with deep bronze skin, and those from the Alps, pale and freckled. Same country. Different sun.

Yet we are told to believe in a hierarchy based on hue.

I was once told by a doctor that African-American children in California can be deficient in Vitamin D because their melanin-rich skin blocks the UV rays needed to synthesize it. This is biology—not identity.

And here is the truth many cannot face: White people cannot produce color, but people of color carry the genetic potential to produce a range of hues. Whiteness is not the origin. It is the offshoot.

As documented by the American Institute of Dermatology, melanin is not just pigment—it is protection, a natural armor for those born under the equator's sun. It is not a curse. It is resilience made visible.

This chapter is not written to blame. It is written to confront.

From Monsanto's slave ships to the Sackler opioid empire, from Israeli airstrikes in Gaza to Confederate generals in New Orleans, the story is not about isolated events. It is about a pattern of power, rooted in racism, justified by religion, and perpetuated through silence.

But history is changing. Truths buried beneath centuries of denial are rising to the surface, loud and raw and undeniable.

This book is part of that reckoning.

And we are no longer asking to be heard.

We are writing the record ourselves.

There is a truth that cannot be postponed any longer: If humanity is to survive, not simply technologically or economically, but spiritually must learn to live together or face destruction.

Israel, built in 1948 on the bedrock of colonial approval and Western complicity, must accept the full humanity of the Palestinian people. Not as enemies. Not as subjects. But as equals with an unbroken claim to the land beneath their feet.

Pulitzer Prize-winning journalist Chris Hedges once warned: *"If Israel continues on this path, it will not survive."* He wasn't speaking of politics alone. He was warning of moral implosion—of what happens when a nation trades justice for dominance, and neighborly coexistence for permanent siege.

History has already delivered its verdict on empires that thought themselves invincible.

The United States Army, armed with the most advanced weapons in the world, was humbled by the Vietnamese people, who fought not with drones or satellites, but with conviction. The Afghan Taliban, with neither tanks nor fighter jets, outlasted twenty years of American occupation. Their strength came not from technology, but from unbreakable resolve.

Force can conquer—but only for a season. As Abraham Lincoln once said, "Force is all-conquering, but its victories are short-lived."

Across the Global South, from Baghdad to Bamako, there is a growing belief: that if you fight long enough, and believe deeply enough, even the mightiest war machines can be broken.

Israel, with full support from the United States and Europe's former colonial powers, is the final active settler colony conducting a campaign of extermination against its Indigenous population.

Every nation that once flew the banner of colonial empire—Britain, France, Spain, Portugal, Belgium, Germany—built their wealth on the bones of native peoples. They razed villages in Africa, plundered temples in Asia, burned fields in South America, and enslaved entire civilizations. Even in China, the British launched the Opium Wars (1839–1842), forcing an entire nation into addiction for commercial gain. (Ford, 2024)

European powers, including European Jews, profited from that suffering. The global machinery of white supremacy did not stop at borders, nor did it exclude any who could benefit from the system.

And Israel, despite its narrative of survival, has become its most recent custodian.

The foundation of the United States was not democracy. It was domination.

The Founding Fathers—men like Jefferson, Washington, Madison, and Hamilton—built a new nation while enslaving African people, working them to death on tobacco and cotton plantations. In 1619, the first enslaved Africans were brought to Jamestown, Virginia, marking the beginning of a 250-year system of racial subjugation.

In 1787, as they gathered in Philadelphia to draft the Constitution, these men did not craft a document of universal rights. They legally enshrined slavery into the new Republic with Article IV, Section 2, Clause 3—a fugitive slave provision that guaranteed slaveholders the right to retrieve "property" across state lines.

This was not liberty. It was the law used as a leash.

In 1857, Chief Justice Roger B. Taney, writing for the U.S. Supreme Court in the infamous Dred Scott v. Sandford decision, ruled that Black Americans had "no rights which the white man was bound to respect." Taney declared Dred Scott to be property, not a person—a ruling fully consistent with the 1787 Constitution.

That was not an error in American law. It was the law working exactly as designed.

What begins in chains often returns in chemicals. In the twenty-first century, the Sackler family—a powerful Jewish-American dynasty—developed and aggressively marketed OxyContin, the opioid that ignited a national epidemic. While towns were hollowed out and families torn apart, the Sacklers accumulated billions of dollars, eventually shielding their fortune behind legal settlements. (U.S. Health Services, 2022)

It is another story of profit from pain—one that echoes across centuries.

We speak of "white" people and "black" people as if those colors define us. But race is not a biological fact. It is a social invention—one built to serve the interests of empire.

There is no scientific "white race." There is light skin, a result of geographic adaptation. People in colder, less sun-drenched regions developed paler skin to better absorb Vitamin D. Melanin, which darkens skin, acts as a natural shield against ultraviolet radiation, helping those in hot climates survive and thrive.

I've seen it firsthand. Working in security at the J. Paul Getty Museum, I met Italians from the Alps, pale and freckled, and Italians from the Mediterranean, with deep bronze skin. They are not two races. They are one people shaped by two suns.

What we call white is not a race—it is a lack of pigment, not a surplus of power.

Doctors have explained to me that African-American children sometimes face Vitamin D deficiency, not because of weakness, but because their melanin-rich skin is built for sun-rich climates. This, too, is science, not superiority.

The notion that pale skin equates to divine favor is a myth of colonizers. And like all myths, it crumbles under the weight of evidence.

If we are to survive—not merely exist, but thrive as a species—we must unlearn the logic of conquest. We must see race not as a battlefield, but as a lie.

# Decline of America and Israel: The Last Two Racial Apartheid White Colonial Nations

The State of Israel must abandon the belief that domination is destiny. The United States must confront the true meaning of its founding documents. And we, the citizens of a wounded planet, must finally admit: the only chosen people are those who choose justice.

Let this chapter be our witness.

Let it speak not only of the crimes of empire, but of the possibility—still fragile, still flickering—that we can build a world beyond the color line.

On May 25, 2020, a knee pressed into the neck of George Floyd for nine minutes and twenty-nine seconds. It was more than a murder. It was a public revelation—that for Black men in America, the Constitution of 1787 does not recognize our full humanity. It never did.

And it still doesn't.

My name is Deshay David Ford, and I too stood under the shadow of institutional injustice. On September 26, 2018, I suffered a workplace injury—my Achilles tendon ruptured, a painful and debilitating tear that required surgery. That surgery failed. I was left disabled and dependent on California's Workers' Compensation System.

At the time, I was employed by Mr. Gary Lavigna, the head of a company called the Institute for Applied Behavior Analysis. During my disability period, Mr. Lavigna, a Jewish businessman, was legally obligated to report my full salary to his insurance provider, Insurance Company of the West, in order to determine my rightful compensation.

But he didn't.

Instead, Mr. Lavigna submitted fraudulent information, significantly underreporting my biweekly salary. The motive was clear: by lowering my reported earnings, the insurer would pay me less in disability benefits. It was not only unethical—it was a direct violation of California Insurance Code §11760, which defines such fraud as punishable by prison, financial penalties of up to $50,000, and exclusion from state compensation programs.

My case eventually led to a hearing scheduled for October 21, 2022, under Judge Michael Greenberg. I had incorporated §11760 into my complaint, demanding that the fraud be recognized not just as an oversight, but as a criminal act.

On the day of my hearing, I arrived at 1900 N. Rice Avenue, seeking a continuance to ensure my arguments would be fully heard. I approached Mr. Michael Avila, the information officer, and requested the delay.

He denied it.

I asked again—this time more firmly. He said he had to speak to the judge. A few moments later, Judge Greenberg emerged from his chambers, but instead of offering clarity or due process, he summoned an armed police officer into Mr. Avila's office.

The message was unmistakable.

I—a 73-year-old African-American man with no criminal record, who posed no threat to anyone—was being intimidated, harassed, and threatened with force. My only offense was insisting on my legal right to present evidence of wage fraud.

In that moment, I feared for my life. I saw the face of George Floyd in my mind. I remembered the look in his eyes as a police officer slowly robbed him of breath—while the world watched and the system shrugged.

I was profiled. I was treated not as a professional. Not as a senior citizen. Not as a man. But as a threat.

I filed a formal complaint of racial profiling in United States District Court in Los Angeles, California under case number 2-22-CV-08339, naming Judge Greenberg as the primary respondent. The case was assigned to Judge Rozella Oliver and Judge Valerie Baker Fairbank— both, to the best of my knowledge, Jewish judges.

My claim was dismissed—with prejudice.

That phrase, "with prejudice," means I cannot bring this issue before the court again. The ruling stated that my case was "without merit"—a declaration that a Black man seeking protection under the Constitution was frivolous, delusional, irrelevant.

This is the lived truth of America's justice system: Black men are presumed guilty by presence, and our claims are presumed meritless by default.

When we cry out for justice, we are silenced with legalese. When we call out injustice, we are met with a cold procedural shrug. We are told that racism must be proven beyond doubt, even while it stares the bench in the face.

George Floyd died under a knee. I stood under a gavel. But the message was the same.

The system was not made for us.

My experience is not unique. It is shared by millions of Black and Brown men whose pleas are dismissed as noise, whose trauma is filed away as irrelevant, whose dignity is systematically erased by courtroom formalities designed to shield the powerful.

But I refuse to disappear into that silence.

Like the Vietnamese people in 1975, who defeated a technologically superior U.S. military. Like the Taliban in Afghanistan, who reclaimed their land in 2021. Like the Palestinians, still resisting a regime backed by the most powerful nations on Earth.

We are not done.

The oppressed do not stay silent forever. And like the South Africans under Mandela, we remember who gave weapons to the apartheid state—who profited from the bloodshed of Black lives.

The United States and Israel, twin pillars of white-settler colonialism, have funded and armed campaigns of racial extermination from Gaza to Soweto, from Wounded Knee to Ferguson.

They have replaced old lies with new weapons. But the pattern remains.

In Palestine, children are bombed with American weapons. In America, Black men are profiled, restrained, and killed with legal impunity. The logic is the same—some lives matter more than others.

And so, as we honor the Holocaust with memorials, museums, and days of reflection, we must ask:

- Where is the Holocaust Museum for the Palestinians?

- Where is the Museum of Tolerance for the enslaved Africans, for the Indigenous peoples of this land?

- Where is the dignity for those who still carry history's shackles in the twenty-first century?

Until such spaces are built—and until such truths are recognized—we cannot speak of justice. Only of survival.

In 2023, I filed an appeal in the Ninth Circuit Court of Appeals alleging that I had been racially profiled by Judge Michael Greenberg, a sitting judge in California. I am a Black American male, seventy-six years old, and I stood before that bench not as a criminal, but as a disabled worker seeking justice after an injury.

Instead, I was met with a threat.

On October 11, 2022, during a routine court appearance, Judge Greenberg—whom I knew to be Jewish—called an armed police officer into the courtroom, not for security, but to intimidate and harass me, a man with no criminal record, no history of violence, no weapon, no crime.

My only offense was being a Black man demanding due process.

Across the United States, stories like mine happen every day. Black and Brown men are met not with fairness, but with force. Not with listening, but with loaded suspicion. The United Nations, in its investigation into the American judicial system, has documented patterns of racial profiling, discrimination, and systemic brutality—an apartheid by law, concealed in legal robes.

My original complaint—Deshay Ford v. Michael Greenberg, case number 2-22-CV-08339—was dismissed by Judges Rozella Oliver and Valerie Baker Fairbank in the United States District Court in Los Angeles. They labeled my case "frivolous" and "without merit." Not because the facts were disputed. But because the system doesn't consider a Black man's fear legitimate, even when the fear is real, immediate, and state-sanctioned.

This is not new. This is America repeating itself.

In 1857, the Dred Scott decision made clear that Black people were property, not citizens. Chief Justice Roger B. Taney, himself a slaveholder, ruled that the Constitution of 1787 did not recognize African Americans as entitled to any rights. That legacy remains intact.

It remains intact every time a judge calls the police on a Black man asking for justice.

It remains intact every time a courtroom treats racial profiling as trivial.

It remains intact every time Black and Brown people are denied employment, receive inadequate medical care, or watch loved ones die because the color of their skin determines the quality of their treatment. During the COVID-19 pandemic in 2020, it was painfully clear—people of color were systematically underserved, while white patients had better access, better hospitals, and better survival odds. (U.S. Health Services, 2020)

I was not a threat. I was not a criminal. But in the eyes of a system built on the bones of slavery, lynching, and apartheid, my very presence was treated like a crime.

Racism in America does not stop at courtroom doors. It enters universities, libraries, and lecture halls—wearing a different mask, but speaking the same language.

Decline of America and Israel: The Last Two Racial Apartheid White
Colonial Nations

In 1991, I entered the doctoral program in clinical psychology at
Pacifica Graduate Institute in Carpinteria, California—a school
founded by brilliant Jewish scholars but overwhelmingly shaped by
white culture, white standards, and a student body and faculty that were
almost entirely white. During my academic years at Pacifica, all of the
professors were white men and women. At the time of my admission,
only one other Black male had ever been enrolled in the program; I
would be the second. Two African-American women entered with me.
From the beginning, the atmosphere was heavy. We weren't just
students—we were observers and outsiders, expected to perform under
a silent but palpable scrutiny.

Not long into the program, the two African-American women
approached me quietly. They had both filed complaints against one of
Pacifica's most prominent white male professors, Dr. Robert
Romanyshyn. They told me they were receiving inexplicably low grades
and believed it was because of who they were, not the quality of their
work. I had already begun to suspect the same. While white and Jewish
students openly discussed receiving straight A's in his classes, I found
myself consistently assigned poor grades without explanation. Several
white Jewish students told me directly that Dr. Romanyshyn and Dr.
Gary Linker routinely gave them A grades.

As time went on, it became clear that Dr. Romanyshyn consistently
gave poor grades to me and the two Black female students, while white
students did not experience the same treatment. The white female
professors, by contrast, consistently gave me good grades. My academic
difficulties were limited almost entirely to Dr. Romanyshyn and Dr.
Gary Linker, the Vice President of the Institute, both of whom appeared
to be racially biased toward me as a Black student.

At one point, one of my favorite professors asked to speak with me
in private. I will not reveal his name out of fear of retaliation against him
and an unfriendly campus environment. During that conversation, he
told me that several white male professors had held a meeting and
collectively agreed that I would not be allowed to graduate with my

doctoral degree. This disclosure confirmed what I had already begun to fear—that the obstacles I faced were not incidental, but coordinated.

When the two African-American women told me what they were experiencing, I shared my own concerns and suggested that we act together—consult an attorney, file a formal complaint, and demand fair treatment. They had already brought their concerns to Dr. Gary Linker, but after that, they chose not to pursue the matter further. For me, however, the discrimination continued unabated.

Eventually, I informed my attorney, Daniel Carobine of Ventura County, California. Mr. Carobine was able to intervene on my behalf. Through negotiations between my attorney and Pacifica's legal counsel, all of the unfair and poor grades given to me by Dr. Gary Linker and Dr. Robert Romanyshyn were removed from my academic transcript. This outcome implicitly acknowledged that the grades were unjustified.

Despite this correction, the retaliation and obstruction did not end. Over the course of my three years at Pacifica, from 1991 to 1994, I was subjected to ongoing harassment and institutional resistance that made it impossible for me to complete my doctoral dissertation. Although I paid $21,000 in tuition and completed all required coursework, Pacifica ultimately refused to grant me the doctoral degree I had earned.

Throughout my time at the Institute, I was assigned five different academic advisors. One white female advisor offered genuine support, but she was forced to withdraw after a death in her family. After her departure, the instability intensified, and the targeted pressure against me increased.

My experience as a Black male at Pacifica Graduate Institute was undeniably shaped by racial discrimination—an institutional pattern that obstructed my academic progress, damaged my educational record, and ultimately denied me the doctoral degree I worked for and deserved.

The history of suffering has never belonged to one people alone; it is a ledger in which power often profits at the cost of someone else's humanity. My experience at Pacifica is part of that ledger, and it remains an essential and painful chapter in my educational narrative.

## Decline of America and Israel: The Last Two Racial Apartheid White Colonial Nations

During the transatlantic slave trade, it was not only European empires that benefited. Jewish financiers in Holland and Belgium provided insurance for slave ships, underwriting voyages that carried millions of African men, women, and children into brutal bondage. The claim that any one group was wholly innocent in this global machinery of torture, exploitation, and genocide is not just false—it erases the full scope of those who profited from our suffering.

Jewish families and institutions, like many others, participated in the slave economy, just as they did later in the Opium Wars in China between 1839 and 1842. There, too, profit was made on the backs of pain—Chinese bodies addicted, manipulated, and destroyed in service of imperial commerce. (Ford, 2024)

This history is not written to indict a people, but to clarify that victimhood in one era does not excuse participation in oppression in another.

When Lord Arthur James Balfour, Britain's Foreign Secretary, penned his now-infamous declaration to Baron Rothschild on November 2, 1917, promising a Jewish homeland in Palestine, he was not acting out of compassion. He was playing imperial chess. In exchange for Jewish assistance in undermining Germany during World War I, Britain offered up land that did not belong to them. (Ford, 2024)

President Woodrow Wilson, despite his public persona as a man of principle, stood by that decision. Like many white leaders of his time, he believed in the superiority of the European race. The founding of Israel in 1948—backed by the United States and Great Britain—was not simply about resettling survivors of the Holocaust. It was also about creating a white ally in the Middle East, a foothold to secure oil interests and regional dominance.

The echoes of colonial ambition carried across continents.

While Nelson Mandela and the African National Congress fought to dismantle the white apartheid regime in South Africa, the United

States and Israel supplied weapons and financial support to the very government that imprisoned and oppressed Black South Africans. Mandela himself, until 2008, remained on the U.S. terrorist watchlist—not because he was violent, but because he dared to challenge a racist state backed by Western power.

And today, we see the same script unfolding in Gaza.

As Israel launches assaults on the Palestinian population—targeting homes, hospitals, journalists, doctors, even United Nations aid workers—it is the United States that funds it, arms it, and defends it on the world stage. Once again, the freedom fighters are called terrorists, while the occupiers are called allies.

It happened to Mandela. It happened to the ANC. And now it is happening to Palestinians resisting occupation.

When people of color take up the struggle against racial supremacy—whether in Africa, Asia, Latin America, or the Middle East—they are too often labeled threats to democracy, when in truth, they are fighting for the democracy they've been denied.

As Howard Zinn reminds us in *A People's History of the United States*, the story of America—and of its global partners—has too often been written by those who wear the robes of justice but serve the interests of empire. (Zinn, 1980)

The oppressed are not asking for revenge. They are asking to be seen.

History will not be complete until it recognizes not only who was enslaved, but who built wealth on those shackles. Until it tells the truth about who was silenced, and who stood silent. Until it honors those who resisted—not with weapons of mass destruction, but with the courage to exist.

And in that truth, told fully and without exception, the world might finally begin to heal.

## State of Israel Established in 1948

The State of Israel declared its independence in 1948. Israel was established as a white European nation by the United States and Great Britain. The British Secretary, Lord James A. Balfour, wrote a letter to Baron Rothschild, the head of the British Jewish community, pledging that Britain would allow European Jews to settle in Palestine (November 2, 1917, Balfour Declaration, Ford, 2022; Ford, Deshay David, *Decline of America: The Last White Man's Empire and Rise of the Brown's Empire*, Dorrance Publishing, Pittsburgh, PA).

Following this, the Jews began a campaign of genocide against the native people, aiming to murder and expel the Palestinian population and seize their land (*Buried My Heart at Wounded Knee*, Brown, 1970). Similarly, American colonists initiated a racist campaign to eliminate Native American populations when they established a settlement in Jamestown, Virginia, in 1606.

The State of Israel was established by the United States and Great Britain for the specific purpose of securing the "black gold" of the Middle East, oil. In ancient times, Rome also had strategic interests in the region. Jerusalem and Palestine served as the breadbasket of the Roman Empire. Agricultural production and taxes from these areas were crucial for sustaining Rome. Without these contributions, the empire could not have thrived.

Pompey the Great conquered the Middle East and annexed it into the Roman Empire. The Jews rebelled against the Romans in 68 A.D., and in 70 A.D., the Roman general Titus Flavius Vespasian suppressed the rebellion and destroyed the Jewish temple. This marked the beginning of the Jewish dispersion throughout the world, with many Jews settling in Europe and Spain (Ford, 2022).

Titus Flavius became emperor in 72 A.D. following the death of his father, Vespasian. In 1948, Jews in Palestine began what some sources describe as a campaign for the racial extermination of the indigenous Palestinian population, who had lived in the region for over two thousand years (Rashadia, 2021). This campaign has been compared to the Holocaust initiated by Adolf Hitler against European Jews between 1940 and 1945. Some critics argue that the campaign against Palestinians mirrored the same kind of racial extermination that Jews themselves experienced during the Holocaust (*A People's History of the United States*, Howard Zinn, 1980).

In a similar vein, English settlers arriving in America in 1603 began a campaign of extermination against Native Americans. European colonial powers, including Canada, Germany, France, the United States, Australia, Belgium, Holland, and Japan, carried out genocides against the indigenous populations in their colonies.

European nations that called themselves democracies engaged in racial genocide against aboriginal populations in places like America, Israel, Canada, and New Zealand. Wherever white European settlers established colonies, they often committed acts of violence and dispossession against indigenous peoples.

The Roman Catholic Church legitimized this colonial expansion through the "Doctrine of Discovery, " which allowed European powers to claim lands occupied by indigenous peoples, seize their resources, and justify their extermination (Zinn, 1980). U.S. Supreme Court Justice Ruth Bader Ginsburg cited the Doctrine of Discovery when ruling against Native American land claims in New York. Some white American Christians argue that God gave the Jews the land of Palestine, while paradoxically refusing to return American lands to Native peoples.

Today, many Native Americans continue to live in poverty on reservations, referred to by some as "concentration camps", and endure a slow, systemic genocide (Brown, *Buried My Heart at Wounded Knee*, 1970).

The Catholic Church used the Doctrine of Discovery to justify the seizure of indigenous lands across Asia, Africa, North and South America, and Israel. The State of Israel continues to seize Palestinian land with the support of the United States government. According to some critics, Israel's presence in the Middle East serves the strategic interest of Western powers in securing Arab oil reserves.

The United States exterminated most of its indigenous population, placing the remaining tribes on reservations. Historians note that Nazi Germany studied the U.S. reservation system as a model for their concentration camps.

According to Dr. Richard D. Wolff, an economist at the University of Massachusetts at Amherst (Wolff, 2021), Israel's military efforts to eliminate the Palestinian population will ultimately fail. He argues that U.S. support for Israel will erode its influence in the Middle East, to the benefit of China, Russia, and Iran. The global balance of power is shifting, and the United States, along with other Western nations, faces new economic and military challenges in the emerging world order shaped by China, Russia, Iran, and North Korea.

The wars in Ukraine and Gaza are the current military conflicts being played out by the countries involved in a broader global power struggle. At the center of this worldwide conflict are the United States and European nations, which are attempting to preserve their philosophical doctrines and geopolitical dominance.

The Europeans and the United States have dominated much of the world for over 500 years. According to Dr. Edward E. Baptist, in his book *The Half Has Never Been Told: Slavery and the Making of American Capitalism*, capitalism was built by enslaved laborers. The American industrial and capitalist system, as well as that of the West, was constructed on the backs of enslaved people.

The United States and Britain were instrumental in the founding of the State of Israel. Their primary interest was easy access to Middle Eastern oil. U.S. oil companies were particularly focused on gaining access to the region's vast oil wealth. In 1953, the British, with the assistance of the United States, overthrew the democratically elected government of Iran in order to control Iranian oil resources.

The British-owned Anglo-Iranian Oil Company (later British Petroleum) had been profiting immensely from refining and selling

Iran's oil, while the Iranian people received little benefit. British workers lived in segregated communities, enjoying wealth generated from Iran's oil, while the local population remained in poverty.

In 1953, Mohammad Mossadegh was elected Prime Minister of Iran. He promised to secure Iran's oil wealth for the Iranian people. Influenced by the philosophies of George Washington and Thomas Jefferson, Mossadegh sought to establish a democratic republic in Iran modeled after the United States. He pledged to nationalize the Anglo-Iranian Oil Company.

The British government feared losing control over Iranian oil profits. British intelligence agency MI5 contacted the U.S. Central Intelligence Agency (CIA), and President Dwight D. Eisenhower approved a covert operation to overthrow Mossadegh. With CIA support and leadership from Station Chief Kermit Roosevelt Jr., the operation succeeded in deposing Mossadegh. He was placed under house arrest, and control over Iran's oil returned to American, Dutch, and British interests.

As a reward for his role, Roosevelt was later offered a vice presidency at Gulf Oil Company. This intervention marked the fall of Iran's first democratic government and a significant moment in U.S.-Middle East relations.

In 1948, Britain and the United States supported the creation of the State of Israel. Their aim was to establish a Western-aligned nation in the Middle East that would facilitate access to oil in Iran, Syria, Iraq, and Saudi Arabia. This move also represented a betrayal of promises Britain had made to Arab nations during and after World War I, when it pledged to support Arab independence.

The U.S. and Britain believed that a state populated by people more culturally and racially aligned with them would better serve their long-term military and geopolitical goals in the region.

European Jews, who had long faced persecution and statelessness, were allowed to settle in Palestine under the British Mandate following the Balfour Declaration of 1917. Britain had promised that Jewish settlement would not interfere with the rights of the indigenous Palestinian population.

However, like British settlers in Jamestown in 1603 who launched campaigns of genocide against Native Americans, some early Zionist settlers, and later Israeli governments, began displacing and marginalizing the Palestinian people. This has led to several violent conflicts, including the 1948 Arab-Israeli War, the 1956 Suez Crisis, and more recently, the 2024 conflict under Prime Minister Benjamin Netanyahu. Critics argue that these actions amount to a campaign of ethnic cleansing, with U.S. complicity under President Joe Biden.

Following its independence from Britain (1776–1781), the United States began a genocidal campaign against its own indigenous populations. The new republic pursued the systematic extermination and displacement of Native American tribes to seize land and natural resources.

According to Dee Brown's seminal work, *Bury My Heart at Wounded Knee* (1970), U.S. policy toward Native peoples was one of total racial genocide. Native Americans were not granted constitutional rights under the U.S. Constitution of 1787. The U.S. government signed 381 treaties with Native tribes and broke all of them.

Historian Benjamin Madley, in *An American Genocide: The United States and the California Indian Catastrophe* (2016), explains that U.S. Senator Judah P. Benjamin of Louisiana, a Jewish senator, was instrumental in securing congressional funding in 1856 for militias to carry out the extermination of Native Californians. Over $800, 000 in government funds supported these campaigns, effectively turning genocide into state and federal policy.

A century later, in 1941, Nazi officials held the Wannsee Conference to finalize their plans for the Holocaust, the "Final Solution" to exterminate Europe's Jewish population.

Judah P. Benjamin had previously been denied admission to Yale Law School, allegedly due to his sexual orientation. During the U.S. Civil War, he served as Secretary of War for the Confederacy under

President Jefferson Davis and owned a plantation in New Orleans, where he enslaved hundreds of African people.

According to Robert Rosen (*The Jewish Confederates*, 2006), New Orleans' Jewish community largely supported the Confederacy and encouraged South Carolina's secession. Rosen also suggests that Judah Benjamin may have had connections to the conspiracy that resulted in President Abraham Lincoln's assassination in 1865.

## America's Genocide Against African-American People

The origins of the American Republic are inseparable from the doctrines of white supremacy and racial capitalism. The so-called "Founding Fathers," hailed in many traditional histories as defenders of liberty, were, in reality, wealthy white men who systematically dehumanized and enslaved millions of African people. They built their personal fortunes and the nation's economy upon stolen labor, blood, and the annihilation of indigenous peoples. These men, such as George Washington, Thomas Jefferson, and James Madison, owned plantations where they worked Black bodies to death under the brutal yoke of chattel slavery.

In 1619, over a century before the American Revolution, the first African captives were forcibly brought to the British colony of Jamestown, Virginia. These African men, women, and children were not migrants, they were the foundation stones of America's racial capitalist system. The white English settlers, driven by an insatiable appetite for wealth and agricultural expansion, saw the enslavement of Africans not merely as a convenience but as a divine entitlement and economic necessity.

By 1787, the very men who enslaved Black people gathered in Philadelphia to draft the U.S. Constitution. This document, glorified as a beacon of democracy, was in truth a covenant of white power. It contained deliberate provisions to institutionalize slavery and deny personhood to the very people whose labor was enriching the American elite. Article IV, Section 2, Clause 3 of the Constitution, commonly referred to as the Fugitive Slave Clause, enshrined the return of escaped enslaved persons, solidifying the federal government's role in the maintenance of slavery.

The hypocrisy of these so-called defenders of liberty is most evident in their refusal to grant democracy to the enslaved. Their vision of freedom was restricted to white, landowning males. Black people were seen not as human beings, but as property: capital assets to be exploited, bought, sold, and inherited.

This was not just a Southern phenomenon. Northern merchants, shipbuilders, and industrialists were deeply entangled in the transatlantic slave economy. The cotton harvested in the South powered Northern textile mills; the sugar cultivated in the Caribbean sweetened the tables of Europe; and the bodies of Black men and women became currency in an empire built on genocide.

In 1857, the U.S. Supreme Court exposed the true nature of the American legal system in the infamous Dred Scott v. Sandford decision. Chief Justice Roger B. Taney, himself a product of elite white privilege, declared that Dred Scott, a man born into slavery who had sued for his freedom, had no rights under the Constitution. In one of the most shameful rulings in American judicial history, Taney wrote that Black people, whether free or enslaved, "had no rights which the white man was bound to respect."

Taney's opinion was not an aberration. It was a faithful interpretation of the 1787 Constitution, a document that codified white supremacy, protected the economic interests of slaveholders, and denied legal personhood to people of African descent. The Dred Scott decision affirmed what African Americans had always known: the law was never neutral; it was designed to preserve white power and Black subjugation.

This legal precedent, combined with centuries of violence, terror, and racial dehumanization, laid the groundwork for future policies of systemic racism, segregation, and mass incarceration. The foundations of the American nation were not laid in the ideals of equality and freedom, but in the brutal reality of genocide and enslavement. To understand America, one must confront its true origin story, one written in the blood of Native peoples and African bodies, and perpetuated by legal instruments that disguised tyranny as democracy.

## THE DEATH OF GEORGE FLOYD AFFIRMED THAT AFRICAN-AMERICANS POSSESS NO RIGHTS UNDER THE WHITE SUPREMACIST 1787 CONSTITUTION

### Deshay D. Ford v. Institute of Applied Behavior Analysis
### Case No: 11994903
### California Workers' Compensation Appeals Board

On September 26, 2018, I, Dr. Deshay David Ford, an African-American professional, scholar, and laborer, suffered a workplace injury. My right Achilles tendon was ruptured and required invasive surgery. That surgery ultimately failed, leaving me permanently disabled. I became a beneficiary of California's state disability system. But like so many Black workers before me, I quickly discovered that America's judicial and labor institutions are structured by systemic fraud, white racial solidarity, and anti-Black hostility.

I had been employed by the Institute for Applied Behavior Analysis, a company operated by Mr. Gary Lavigna, a white man of Jewish descent. During my medical leave, Lavigna and his corporate network were legally obligated to report my actual salary to the Insurance Company of the West so I would receive appropriate disability compensation. Instead, in a calculated act of deception, Lavigna submitted fraudulent salary data, falsely underreporting my income to ensure I received less than I was legally owed.

This constituted insurance fraud under California Insurance Code Section 11760, a criminal offense punishable by prison, fines, and exclusion from the Workers' Compensation Program. But in the plantation logic of American capitalism, white employers break the law with impunity as long as their victims are Black.

I sought justice through legal channels. A hearing was scheduled for October 21, 2022, before Judge Michael Greenberg. I went to the hearing location at 1900 North Rice Avenue and asked Mr. Michael Avila, the information officer, for a continuance so that the insurance fraud violations under Section 11760 could be formally addressed. Mr. Avila refused. I explained again. He said no. Then he claimed he had to speak with his superior, Judge Greenberg.

What happened next was judicial abuse and racial terror. Instead of hearing my request or engaging in legal dialogue, Judge Greenberg ordered an armed police officer into the room, not to serve justice, but to intimidate and threaten me. I am a 73-year-old Black man, and at that moment, I feared for my life. The image of George Floyd, murdered in 2020 beneath the knee of a white officer, flashed through my mind. Floyd's lynching was not an aberration. It was America.

I filed a federal complaint in the U.S. District Court in Los Angeles, naming Judge Greenberg for racially profiling me. My complaint landed before Judge Rozella Oliver and Judge Valerie Baker Fairbank, both white-presenting women of Jewish descent, embedded in the same institutional architecture as the accused. They dismissed my case "with prejudice," permanently silencing my claims and labeling them "frivolous."

This is what it means to be a Black man in the United States. The Constitution of 1787, crafted by white enslavers, was never written for people like me. Racial profiling, police brutality, judicial corruption; these crimes vanish into the white abyss of a system that was built to uphold white power.

My story is not an outlier. It reverberates through American history: through the genocide of Native peoples, the enslavement of Africans, the segregation of the Jim Crow South, and the carceral warfare of today. And like every colonized people from the Vietnamese under American bombs, to the Afghan Taliban resisting imperial occupation, to the Palestinians rising against Zionist apartheid, we are told that our lives, our truths, our pain have no merit.

But I reject that lie. History shows that empires fall. In 1975, the Vietnamese defeated the world's most powerful military. The Taliban, against all odds, forced out a nuclear superpower. The Palestinian people continue to resist settler violence in Gaza and beyond.

And while the United States and Israel, the twin pillars of modern settler-colonialism, arm themselves with lies and weapons, they cannot erase our memory or our resistance. During apartheid in South Africa, the U.S. and Israel backed the white regime. Today, they fund Israel's genocidal war machine, which massacres brown children in Gaza.

Let us speak truth to genocide. Let us build a Palestinian Holocaust Museum to chronicle Israeli state violence. Let us honor George Floyd, Breonna Taylor, and Emmett Till, not as footnotes in whitewashed history but as martyrs of an ongoing freedom struggle.

## UNITED STATES COURT OF APPEALS – 9TH CIRCUIT

### Deshay Ford v. Judge Michael Greenberg
### Case No. 23-55699

I, Dr. Deshay David Ford, a 76-year-old African-American man and lifelong laborer in the service of an ungrateful nation, brought my case before the United States Court of Appeals for the Ninth Circuit. On September 18, 2023, I filed my Opening Brief, alleging that Judge Michael Greenberg, a white-presenting man of Jewish heritage, racially profiled me in a public courtroom in violation of my most fundamental rights. My crime was not violence, theft, or deception, it was existing as a Black man in America.

Judge Greenberg's response to my procedural request was neither grounded in legal reasoning nor guided by principles of fairness. On October 11, 2022, he ordered an armed law enforcement officer into the courtroom, not in pursuit of justice, but as an instrument of intimidation. The presence of that officer, summoned solely to threaten and humiliate me, affirmed the same brutal logic that governs every racial encounter between Blackness and American law: control through terror, silence through force, death through normalization.

Black and Brown people in America live beneath a persistent threat of state-sanctioned violence. Our blood saturates the roots of this nation.

Our lives are discarded, our grievances deemed "frivolous," and our pain met with bureaucratic indifference. The United Nations has investigated this systemic racism and declared what we already knew: that the United States judicial and criminal justice system functions as a racialized apparatus, a modern apartheid regime designed to target, detain, and devastate Black and Brown men under the illusion of lawful order.

My federal case, **Deshay Ford v. Michael Greenberg, 2-22-CV-08339**, was dismissed by two U.S. District Court Judges in Los Angeles: Judge Rozella Oliver and Judge Valerie Baker Fairbank, both white-presenting women whose allegiances aligned not with truth, but with institutional preservation. They did not question the act of racial profiling. Instead, they labeled my complaint "frivolous" and "without merit," as they have with every Black man who has dared to speak his truth before them.

This is not a new tactic. In **Dred Scott v. Sandford** (1857), U.S. Supreme Court Chief Justice Roger B. Taney, a slaveholder himself, declared that Black people were "not citizens," but property. He invoked **Article IV, Section 2, Provision 3** of the 1787 Constitution to cement the legal status of African Americans as non-beings. That same Constitution, praised by white historians and judges alike, was authored by men like George Washington, a man revered as a founding father but also a perpetrator of genocide, a slaveholder, and a settler-colonialist who enshrined racial violence within the foundations of national policy.

This is the historical thread that binds the murder of George Floyd to my own courtroom experience. The same logic that knelt on Floyd's neck commands armed officers into legal hearings when Black men dare to raise their voices. In America, racial profiling is not an aberration; it is the procedure.

And what of medical care? In 2020, during the COVID-19 pandemic, Black and Brown communities in America were systematically denied adequate healthcare while white communities received better services, faster testing, and prioritization in vaccine distribution. The U.S. Health Services data confirms what we lived through: a public health system as racially tiered and deadly as the justice system.

On that October morning, I was not treated as a citizen. I was treated as a threat. My only crime was my Blackness, my refusal to disappear, my unwillingness to bow. I had no weapon, no history of violence, no record of criminality. I was simply a 75-year-old Black man in a courtroom, and for that, Judge Greenberg deployed the same terror that haunts every Black man in this nation.

This is not simply my case. It is the case of every man of color who has ever been told that his pain is not real, that his life is not sacred, that his rights are not guaranteed. We carry these wounds together, not as marks of defeat, but as living proof of a truth this nation refuses to acknowledge: that its justice is racialized, its democracy divided, and its Constitution a deception.

I guarantee you that if you are people of color fighting against white racist apartheid, segregationists, the U.S. will place you on their terrorist list ( Zinn, 1980), Zinn, Howard (1980), People's History of the United States, Harper and Rowe, New York, N.Y.).

## TULSA RACE MASSACRE

From May 31 to June 1, 1921, in Tulsa, Oklahoma, the United States committed one of the most egregious acts of racial violence in its modern history. Known as the Tulsa Race Massacre, this atrocity saw a white mob, armed and incited, launch a coordinated assault against the Black residents of the Greenwood District, the wealthiest African-American community in the nation at the time. The massacre was not spontaneous rage. It was a premeditated act of racial warfare executed on the ground and from the air using private aircraft. Over 35 square blocks were reduced to ash. Homes, businesses, churches, and the very infrastructure of Black prosperity were obliterated.

A 2001 official commission confirmed 36 deaths, with at least 26 of the victims being African-American. But eyewitnesses and survivors long contested this number, citing mass graves and systemic underreporting. The truth, as always in American racial history, lies buried beneath layers of state-sanctioned silence.

The violence was sparked over the Memorial Day weekend after Dick Rowland, a 19-year-old Black shoeshiner, was accused of assaulting a young white elevator operator named Sarah Page. No evidence was presented. No trial occurred. But white newspapers stoked hysteria, and local law enforcement, under the pretense of protecting Rowland, prepared for a lynching.

When armed Black men arrived at the jail to defend Rowland's life, they were met by an armed white mob. Tensions erupted. Shots were fired. The ensuing chaos provided white citizens and local authorities with the pretext they needed to unleash a massacre. The National Guard was summoned, not to protect the Black community, but to contain and disarm it. White mobs looted, torched, and murdered. Women, children, and the elderly were slaughtered. Greenwood, the symbol of Black self-sufficiency and resistance, was annihilated.

In the aftermath, the state of Oklahoma undertook an orchestrated effort to suppress all documentation of the massacre. Insurance claims were denied. Records were altered or destroyed. Textbooks erased the atrocity. America looked away. This suppression was not incidental; it was part of a broader strategy to protect white innocence and white supremacy.

This massacre was not an anomaly. It was one node in a vast network of genocidal policy, one that stretched from slave ships to courtrooms, from cotton fields to public housing, from lynching trees to police chokeholds. The founders of this empire, George Washington, Thomas Jefferson, and James Madison, are venerated in marble and myth, yet each was a white supremacist, a slaver, a man who profited from the theft of African bodies. Their version of democracy was never intended to include the enslaved.

The United States has long waged internal and external wars rooted in white dominance. Its racial violence mirrors the genocidal tactics of other empires. Hitler's Holocaust against the Jews during World War II is rightly condemned as an atrocity, but America's own project of racial extermination preceded it by centuries. The destruction of Native nations, the commodification of Black bodies for over four hundred years, and the persistent legal and social subjugation of nonwhite people are all parts of America's unbroken genocidal continuum.

This empire perfected racial capitalism, using human suffering as the fuel for wealth accumulation. Its global violence continues: from the napalm-scorched villages of Vietnam to the bombed-out ruins of Iraq; from the jungles of Korea to the deserts of Afghanistan. Whether under the guise of democracy or counterterrorism, the American military machine has murdered millions, most of them Black and Brown.

Like every empire before it, the United States believes itself eternal. But it, too, is subject to history. The Egyptian, Babylonian, Persian, Greek, Roman, Mongolian, Ottoman, Spanish, British, French, and Soviet empires all fell beneath the weight of their contradictions and cruelty. America will be no different.

The collapse has already begun. The American Empire is projected to fall by 2040, undone not by foreign invasion, but by the rot within: its racism, its greed, its moral bankruptcy. We are now living in the Chinese Century. As I argued in *Decline of America: The Last White Man's Empire and the Rise of China: The Brown's Empire* (Ford, 2022), the future no longer belongs to the white imperial order.

## Majority Of American Senators And House Members Are Descendents Of Slave Owners

The United States of America is a nation still ruled by the descendants of its original enslavers. This is not a poetic metaphor, it is a historical fact. Multiple studies conducted by major American universities have traced the genealogical backgrounds of U.S. senators and congressional representatives, revealing that a majority of white lawmakers in both chambers are directly descended from slaveowners. The bloodline of oppression has not disappeared; it has simply moved from the cotton fields to the marble halls of power.

## Decline of America and Israel: The Last Two Racial Apartheid White Colonial Nations

These are the inheritors of the American Empire. They preside over laws, budgets, and wars. They speak of liberty while standing on the graves of those their ancestors chained, raped, whipped, and sold. The American republic, born from rebellion against the British monarchy in 1781, wasted no time becoming an imperial power in its own right, its expansion fueled not by freedom, but by genocide and enslavement.

As historian Dee Brown documented in *Bury My Heart at Wounded Knee* (Brown, 1970), the United States initiated its first imperial campaign not overseas, but against the Indigenous peoples of North America. The new white settler government systematically exterminated Native nations, stripping them of land, resources, and culture. This genocide was not incidental, it was foundational. Land was wealth, and blood was the currency used to purchase it.

The same violence extended to Black Americans, who, though no longer legally enslaved after 1865, were subjected to racial terror and systemic repression for the next century. On June 1, 1921, in Tulsa, Oklahoma, a thriving Black community in Greenwood was reduced to ashes in what became known as the Tulsa Race Massacre. White mobs, armed, deputized, and aided by police and the National Guard, murdered an estimated 300 Black men, women, and children. Their homes were burned. Their businesses were looted. Their legacy was erased. And for decades, the state did everything in its power to bury the truth. There were no prosecutions. No reparations. Only silence.

From 1870 to 1970, over 6,000 Black Americans were lynched, often in public spectacles attended by cheering white crowds. Lynchings were not random acts of violence; they were tools of racial control, designed to terrorize entire communities. Yet not a single perpetrator was convicted in a court of law. The legal system, the very one that descendants of slaveholders still dominate, remained indifferent to the slaughter of Black lives.

During the presidency of Woodrow Wilson (1912–1920), lynchings surged. Wilson, a proud segregationist and academic elite, did nothing to halt the murders. On the contrary, he empowered them. His administration resegregated the federal government and aligned ideologically with the Ku Klux Klan, which had resurged during his tenure. When D.W. Griffith released the film *The Birth of a Nation* in 1915—a vile celebration of white supremacy and racial violence—Wilson screened it at the White House, calling it "like writing history with lightning." The film depicted Black men as monsters and the Klan as noble saviors. Hollywood gave white America a new language of hate, and the government gave it a platform.

Racism in America was not just cultural, it was institutionalized.

As Richard Rothstein exposed in *The Color of Law* (Rothstein, 2009), racial segregation in housing was not the product of individual prejudice but the result of deliberate U.S. government policy. Federal agencies provided home loans to white families while denying Black Americans the same access, effectively locking them out of wealth-building for generations. These policies—redlining, restrictive covenants, zoning laws—were crafted in partnership with white mortgage lenders, real estate agents, and local officials. Segregation wasn't just tolerated. It was engineered.

While white families accumulated generational wealth in federally subsidized suburbs, Black families were confined to overcrowded, underfunded neighborhoods, then blamed for the poverty they had been forced into. The American Dream was never universal. It was designed with a color-coded key.

And in 2024, America is more segregated than it was in 1950, according to data from the U.S. Department of Education. Schools are racially and economically divided. Neighborhoods remain separated by invisible borders of history and policy. Access to clean water, quality healthcare, and even grocery stores continues to be stratified along racial lines. The faces on the dollar bills may be different, but the system is the same.

This is not a story of the past. It is the architecture of the present.

When the majority of lawmakers are descended from those who owned people as property—when their family fortunes were built on unpaid labor, state-sanctioned murder, and stolen land—what kind of legislation do we expect them to pass? What justice do we expect them to pursue?

As a reminder, the American empire was never dismantled, it was handed down.

From the plantations to the presidencies. From slave auctions to Senate hearings. From chains to charters. From bloodlines to ballots.

The same hands that once cracked whips now write laws.

And the people they once owned are still fighting to breathe.

## Black Sailors Charged In July 17,1944 Blasted Cleared

On the night of July 17, 1944, the California coast lit up with a fireball so bright it could be seen for miles. At the Port Chicago Naval Magazine, a munitions depot northeast of San Francisco, a ship packed with explosives erupted in a chain reaction that shook the ground and shattered lives. In seconds, more than 320 sailors and civilians were dead, another 400 wounded. The majority of those killed—nearly three out of every four—were Black.

The Navy called it an accident. For the Black sailors who survived, it was more than that. It was the inevitable result of a system that treated them as expendable labor, denied them proper training, and ignored their warnings about unsafe conditions. Port Chicago was not just a workplace; it was a racial powder keg.

The war in the Pacific was at its height, and Port Chicago was a vital supply point. Day after day, Black enlisted men loaded bombs, shells, and ammunition under the orders of white officers. These officers had been trained in management, but not in the physical dangers of ordnance handling. The Black sailors had neither formal training nor safety equipment—just the relentless pressure to move faster, to load more, to keep the war machine fed.

Before the explosion, the men had voiced concerns. The pace was reckless. The oversight was careless. Their fear was not abstract—they worked with thousands of tons of explosives in sweltering heat, under supervisors who pushed quotas as if they were stacking boxes, not live bombs. But those in command brushed it off. Orders were orders. Warnings went unheeded.

When the disaster struck, it was the survivors, almost all of them Black, who were ordered to return to the same dock, to resume the same dangerous work, without changes, without training, without even the dignity of grief. White officers were given leave to recover. Black sailors were given shovels and ordered to clean up the remains of their shipmates.

Some refused.

They were not refusing the war effort. They were not rebelling against the Navy. They were demanding the basic right to be trained before risking their lives again. But in the segregated military of 1944, a Black man who demanded fair treatment was not seen as a serviceman; he was seen as a threat.

Fifty of those men were singled out, charged not with disobedience, but with mutiny—one of the most serious crimes in military law, carrying the possibility of death. Tried as a group, they were convicted and sent to prison. Not one was given the full measure of legal due process. Not one was treated as an equal before the law.

Thurgood Marshall, then a young attorney for the NAACP, took up their case. He recognized the trial for what it was: a racially charged railroading. The evidence was weak, the charges inflated, the proceedings tainted by prejudice. He argued that justice demanded the complete reversal of their convictions. History would prove him right, though justice would take 80 years to arrive.

On the 80th anniversary of the disaster, Navy Secretary Carlos Del Toro signed an order vacating the convictions of all 256 Black sailors who had been punished in the aftermath, including the fifty mutiny defendants. "The whole episode was unjust," Del Toro admitted, acknowledging that the legal process was riddled with inconsistencies and violations. The exonerations came too late for the men themselves—all of them have since passed away—but not too late for history to record the truth.

For the families, the moment was bittersweet. Thurgood Marshall Jr., son of the late Supreme Court justice, accepted the first ceremonial pen used in signing the order. "They are all gone," he said. "And that's a painful aspect, waiting so long for that kind of fairness and recognition."

President Joe Biden called the decision "righting a historic wrong." He echoed Marshall's original appeal from the 1940s: only a complete reversal could restore justice.

Yet even as their names are now cleared, the Port Chicago case remains a stark reminder of the racism that ran through the veins of the U.S. military in World War II. The Navy at that time was rigidly segregated. Black sailors were often relegated to the most dangerous, least desirable jobs. The official inquiry into the explosion exonerated every white officer, praising them for their "great effort" in managing the pier, while leaving open the insinuation that the Black sailors were at fault. That was the moral reflex of the era: when disaster struck, whiteness was innocence, Blackness was guilt.

The injustice at Port Chicago did not end when the war did. Black veterans returned home to a country that paraded its democracy abroad while denying it to its own citizens. In the South, Jim Crow laws strangled voting rights and opportunity. In the North and West, discrimination in housing, education, and employment was no less real, only less openly codified. White veterans received GI Bill benefits that funded college educations, business loans, and homeownership. Black veterans were routinely denied those same benefits through discriminatory administration.

Some returned from fighting fascism overseas only to be lynched in their own towns. Others faced police harassment, racial profiling, and economic exclusion. The democracy they had risked their lives for existed in name only.

Japanese Americans, too, were subjected to mass injustice during the war, rounded up into internment camps, stripped of property, and told it was for "national security." The racism was not episodic—it was systemic, woven into every policy and practice.

By the 1950s, the United States presented itself as the leader of the "free world," yet people of color lived in a nation that more closely resembled an apartheid state. In 1951, African American leaders filed a petition with the United Nations, charging the United States with genocide against its Black population. The U.S. government suppressed the petition, using its power in the UN to bury the charge. The lynchings continued. Segregation continued. And white supremacy was not confined to the South—it existed everywhere white America carried its flag.

As a child in that era, I saw the consequences firsthand. My parents endured the daily humiliations and limitations imposed by the color of their skin. They were denied access to quality schools, fair wages, decent housing, and the vote. In every corner of life, opportunity was reserved for others. America's promise was for white people. For people of color, America was a land of barriers, a place where service in uniform did not buy respect, and where sacrifice did not earn equality.

The men of Port Chicago fought two wars, one against an enemy across the ocean, and one against an enemy embedded in the country they served. Their exoneration, eight decades later, cannot erase the pain. But it can ensure that their names are no longer bound to the lie that they were mutineers.

They were sailors. They were patriots. And they were victims of the same system they swore to defend.

# Springfield Race Riot Of 1908

In August 1908, Springfield, Illinois—the city most associated with Abraham Lincoln, the so-called "Great Emancipator" became the site of a massacre that shocked the nation. For two days, from August 14 to 16, a white mob of nearly 5,000 people rampaged through the city, targeting Black residents in one of the worst racial pogroms in Northern history.

The violence began when two Black men were arrested as suspects in the alleged rape and murder of white women. The men were taken into custody, but the local sheriff, fearing mob violence, secretly transferred them out of the city. When the crowd discovered this, they did not disperse. Instead, they redirected their fury onto Springfield's Black community.

What followed was a wave of terror. White rioters stormed into Black neighborhoods, killing indiscriminately. Men, women, children, and the elderly were attacked in their homes and on the streets. Businesses were looted, homes set ablaze, and families forced to flee. Black Springfield was left in ruins. Seventeen people were killed in the violence, nine African Americans and eight whites—though, as historians note, most of the white deaths came from clashes within the mob itself. The riot destroyed Black property and instilled fear that lingered for generations.

The Springfield Race Riot was a turning point in American history. It occurred not in the South, where racial violence was expected, but in the North, in the very hometown of Abraham Lincoln. For many, it shattered the myth that the North was a safe haven for African Americans. Springfield revealed that racism was national, not regional.

The riot also exposed the intersection of race, class, and law in America. White immigrants, especially from Europe, joined native-born whites in the mob. Their violence was not only an expression of racial hatred but also of resentment toward the economic successes of Black citizens. In Springfield, as in Tulsa years later, white mobs destroyed Black progress rather than allow equality.

More than a century later, the memory of Springfield remains. On August 16, 2024, President Joe Biden visited Springfield to commemorate the riot's 116th anniversary. His presence marked a rare moment when an American president publicly acknowledged the nation's history of racial terror. Biden had previously commemorated the Tulsa Race Massacre of 1921, and under his leadership, Juneteenth was recognized as a federal holiday, honoring the announcement of emancipation to enslaved people in Texas on June 19, 1865, two and a half years after the Emancipation Proclamation of 1863.

These acts of recognition, though symbolic, carry weight. As Dr. Deshay David Ford observed, President Biden attempted to do for America what Nelson Mandela's Truth and Reconciliation Commission sought to do for South Africa: confront the sins of racism and apartheid in order to heal a divided nation. It is a difficult task, but necessary. Without truth, there can be no reconciliation.

The Springfield riot was not isolated. In Duluth, Minnesota, in June 1920, another white mob lynched three young Black circus workers after a white teenager, Irene Tusken, falsely accused them of rape. Years later, Tusken admitted that no rape had occurred; the accusation had been invented. The story recalls countless others, like the case of Emmett Till in 1955, a 14-year-old boy lynched in Mississippi for allegedly whistling at a white woman. Again and again, the mere suggestion of Black male sexuality directed toward white women ignited white mobs, exposing the deep sexual anxieties that underpinned racial violence in America.

Robert P. Jones (2023) in *The Hidden Roots of White Supremacy* reminds us that these riots and lynchings were not random explosions but part of a broader system of white dominance. They were tools of terror, used to remind Black communities that no matter how prosperous or law-abiding they were, they could be destroyed overnight by white rage.

The Springfield Race Riot of 1908 is therefore not simply a historical footnote. It stands as a lesson: racism is not confined to regions, decades, or political parties. It is woven into the fabric of American life. In Springfield, the city of Lincoln, America revealed its truth that freedom and equality are ideals often betrayed by the realities of white supremacy.

Today, remembering Springfield is an act of resistance against forgetting. Commemorations by leaders like President Biden are a start, but justice requires more. As long as Black communities remain vulnerable to violence, whether at the hands of mobs in 1908 or police in 2020, the story of Springfield continues.

## 1951 African-Americans Charged Americans With Racist Genocide In The United Nations

In 1951, long before social media could amplify a cry for justice, long before the phrase "Black Lives Matter" echoed across the globe, a coalition of African-American leaders took the boldest step possible: they charged the United States government with genocide.

This was no metaphor. It was a formal petition to the United Nations, entitled *We Charge Genocide*, submitted by two of the most formidable Black intellectuals and activists of the 20th century, Paul Robeson and W.E.B. Du Bois. The document meticulously detailed the crimes committed against Black Americans, crimes not only of slavery and segregation, but of systemic, state-sponsored murder. Lynching, police brutality, economic starvation, forced labor, and mass incarceration—each outlined as evidence that the U.S. had violated the U.N.'s own *Convention on the Prevention and Punishment of the Crime of Genocide*, adopted in 1948.

Under international law, genocide is defined as any act intended to destroy, in whole or in part, a national, ethnic, racial, or religious group. Robeson and Du Bois argued truthfully that the U.S. government had long practiced this against its Black population.

The petition was a political earthquake. It did not just accuse individual racists or rogue police departments—it named the state itself. The American state. The same state that claimed to be the global defender of democracy while burning crosses lit up its South and the blood of Black children stained its streets.

The United States responded with fury. Du Bois was harassed, surveilled, and ultimately silenced. Robeson was blacklisted, his passport revoked. The petition was buried under Cold War paranoia, but it was never forgotten. In fact, it remains one of the most powerful indictments ever leveled against American hypocrisy.

More than seventy years later, the echo of *We Charge Genocide* has returned—this time in solidarity with the Palestinian people.

As the Israeli Defense Forces waged a campaign of destruction in Gaza from October 7, 2023, through the summer of 2024—killing over 40,000 civilians, including women, children, and the elderly—many African-Americans immediately recognized the pattern. It was not unfamiliar. It was not distant. It was not foreign. It was the same logic that had governed the plantations, the chain gangs, the ghettos, and the police stations in America. Dehumanize. Displace. Destroy.

Black Americans, already survivors of a slow genocide, recognized the fast one unfolding before them. They stood, not as observers, but as comrades.

As *Dr. Deshay David Ford* writes in *Why Muslim People Hate Donald Trump and America* (2024), the connection between African-Americans and Palestinians is not symbolic, it is historical. The struggle against white supremacy is global. It does not change form when it crosses borders. It simply changes uniforms.

President Joseph Biden made a catastrophic political and moral error by aligning himself fully with Israel's military machine. By sending weapons instead of warnings. By writing checks instead of checks on power. The Arab world now views the United States as a Nazi-like war machine, enabling genocide under the guise of democracy. And African-

Americans, long excluded from the benefits of U.S. foreign policy, feel no allegiance to this betrayal.

The roots of Israel's founding were never about Jewish safety, they were about Western strategy. In *Why Muslim People Hate Donald Trump and America, Dr. Ford* explains how, on November 2, 1917, British Foreign Secretary Arthur Balfour signed an agreement with Baron Rothschild. In exchange for Jewish support against Germany during World War I, Britain promised to hand over Palestine as a "homeland" for European Jews. But it was never about the homeland. It was about outposts. Colonial ones.

Just as Britain used South African Boers to occupy Indigenous lands, it used Jewish settlers to colonize Palestine. Both groups were European transplants imposed on brown-skinned nations. Both were supported by white military empires. Both engaged in racial hierarchy, expulsion, and violence. The Palestinians, like Black South Africans, were cast as aliens in their own homeland.

And now, as the United States approaches another presidential election, it finds itself at a crossroads not only of leadership, but of identity. The nonwhite population is growing. The myth of a white-majority America is dying. And with it, the illusion that whiteness alone can hold the reins of political and economic power.

African-Americans, Latinos, Asians, and Indigenous peoples are awakening to their collective power. They no longer see Israel as a "partner in democracy." They see it as a settler project mirroring their own histories of exploitation. They do not mourn the fading dominance of white nations. They celebrate the global tide turning toward justice.

And that tide is turning fast.

China, once treated as a peripheral player in global affairs, now speaks boldly about America, not as a democracy, but as a *corporation*. According to Chinese scholars, America is not a country. It is a multinational business empire. Its Congress are its employees. Its Constitution is a set of bylaws. Its military? Corporate security, deployed not for freedom, but for resource acquisition.

The Chinese don't say this to flatter themselves. They say it to clarify the truth.

And history supports them.

As *Edward E. Baptist* demonstrates in his groundbreaking work *The Half Has Never Been Told* (2010), America's capitalist system, its banks, railroads, stock markets, and cotton industries were all built on the labor of enslaved Africans. Wall Street grew fat on auction blocks. Southern plantations were industrial death camps. Slavery was not an economic side note, it was the engine that drove the supremacist business.

As Baptist writes, African slaves "made America rich." Not free men. Not white men. Not democracy. Slavery.

The United States has never truly reckoned with that origin. Instead, it has doubled down on the myth of freedom while global empires crumble around it. Now, as it supports Israel's genocide in Gaza, as it arms apartheid in real time, and as it ignores its own citizens crying out for justice, the empire begins to rot from the inside.

This is what happens when a nation forgets its history.

This is what happens when genocide goes unpunished.

And once again, just like in 1951, the oppressed are charging genocide.

But this time, the world is listening.

And justice will not be buried.

It will rise.

# 1950 Charge Of Genocide Against America By Black People At The United Nations, December 1951

African American support for South Africa's legal action against Israel at the International Court of Justice is not sudden or incidental. It is the echo of centuries of lived history. Black people in America have endured a sustained campaign of racial genocide since their forced arrival on these shores in 1619. For more than four centuries, they have borne the weight of systemic oppression, violence, and erasure. This historical memory of suffering explains why African Americans instinctively recognize the reality of genocide when they witness it inflicted upon Palestinians today. Their solidarity with South Africa's charge is born from blood memory.

In March 2023, South Africa formally accused the State of Israel of committing racial genocide against the Palestinian people in the Gaza Strip. Israel dropped thousand-pound bombs on densely populated civilian areas, targeting entire neighborhoods, not to eliminate combatants but to destroy a people. The intent was clear: to erase Palestinians as a national and cultural group.

Israel is not a natural nation-state rooted in the soil of Palestine. It is a settler colony, created by white Europeans from Germany, Russia, Poland, America, Ukraine, and other parts of Eastern Europe. These settlers were planted in Palestine through the colonial designs of Britain and the United States, heirs of the imperial strategies of the nineteenth and twentieth centuries.

The Balfour Declaration of November 2, 1917, stands as the original blueprint. In the midst of World War I, when Britain was faltering against the German Empire, Foreign Secretary Lord Arthur Balfour wrote a letter to Baron Rothschild, a leading Zionist in Britain, promising a "Jewish homeland" in Palestine. This was not an act of compassion but of calculation. In exchange for Zionist support in undermining Germany's war effort and rallying American involvement, Britain pledged to deliver Palestine to European Jews. President Woodrow Wilson, motivated not only by political pressures but also by the rising demand for Middle Eastern oil, lent his support.

The British and Americans coveted the oil reserves of the region. Their strategy was to reward allies, punish enemies, and secure long-term access to energy that fueled the empire. Oil, as much as religion or politics, determined the fate of Palestine. By planting European settlers there, Britain created an outpost of whiteness in the heart of the Middle East.

Decline of America and Israel: The Last Two Racial Apartheid White Colonial Nations

This strategy has repeated itself across centuries. From 2003 to 2008, President George W. Bush launched wars in the Middle East under the false banners of democracy and freedom. In reality, those wars were designed to seize control of Arab oil, enriching American oil companies and their investors—many headquartered in Texas. Yet, while America expended lives, resources, and credibility, China pursued the same objective with shrewd restraint. Without firing a single shot, without losing a single soldier, China secured access to Iraq's oil reserves through contracts and diplomacy. The contrast is telling: America bleeds and declines as an empire; China rises and secures its future.

For African Americans, the charge of genocide is not an abstract legal matter. In 1951, they themselves presented such a charge to the world. A coalition of activists, including Paul Robeson and W.E.B. Du Bois, submitted the petition We *Charge* Genocide to the United Nations. They argued that the United States government was guilty of genocide against Black people, citing systemic lynchings, state-sanctioned violence, economic oppression, and the denial of basic human rights. This petition rooted its claims in the United Nations Genocide Convention, which defines genocide as acts intended to destroy, in whole or in part, a racial, ethnic, national, or religious group.

Though ignored by white powers at the time, the petition established a moral precedent: America, built on slavery and Indigenous genocide, stood guilty in the court of history. The crimes were not merely past but ongoing. From the Middle Passage to Jim Crow, from lynch mobs to police executions, the Black experience in America testifies to a pattern of racial extermination.

Therefore, when African Americans look upon Gaza, they see Selma. When they see Palestinians bombed in their homes, they recall Tulsa in 1921. When they watch children buried in rubble, they think of the children sold on auction blocks or gunned down in American streets. The parallels are visceral.

Solidarity, then, is not charity. It is recognition. African Americans support South Africa's charge against Israel because they know the

architecture of genocide: the lies of empire, the propaganda of
"security," the endless justifications for killing brown and Black bodies.
They have lived it.

As historian John Hope Franklin (1956) wrote in *From Slavery to
Freedom*, the struggle of Black people in America has always been part
of a larger global fight against white supremacy. The same forces that
enslaved Africans built apartheid in South Africa and constructed the
settler state of Israel. To stand with Palestine is to stand in continuity
with the struggle for liberation everywhere.

The evidence is overwhelming. From the genocide of Native
Americans (Myrdal, 1944; Madley, 2016), to the Tulsa Massacre
(Ellsworth, 1982), to the systemic violence faced by Black people today,
the United States has never been innocent. Israel, as its protégé, has
inherited both its weapons and its ideology.

Thus, African American solidarity with Palestine has become an
essential initiative that history demands. Having endured four centuries
of genocide in America, African Americans stand with Palestinians
against the apartheid state of Israel. The struggle is one, the oppressor is
shared, and the path to justice is collective.

## The Mass Killings In America By A Majority Of White Men Are Occurring As A Result Of America's History Of Genocide, Slavery, And Racist Hate

All of the killing and murdering that has marked the United States
is rooted in the nation's original sins: racism, slavery, and the genocidal
destruction of its Indigenous peoples. Dee Brown's classic work *Bury My
Heart at Wounded Knee* (1970) documents how America was built not
as a sanctuary of liberty, but as a graveyard for Native nations. From the
colonial era forward, racial violence has been the foundation of
American identity.

The so-called Founding Fathers, celebrated as champions of
democracy, were in reality wealthy slaveholders whose fortunes rested

on the bondage of Africans. At the Constitutional Convention of 1787 in Philadelphia, men such as Thomas Jefferson, James Madison, George Washington, James Monroe, and Pierce Butler of South Carolina all arrived as masters of enslaved populations. The Constitution they drafted enshrined their wealth and power, not liberty. Article IV, Section 2, Clause 3, the Fugitive Slave Clause, ensured that slavery remained a legally protected institution, binding the republic to the chains of human bondage.

This stood in sharp contrast to developments in Britain. In the 1772 case of *Somerset v. Stewart*, Lord Mansfield ruled that English common law prohibited slavery on English soil. The American Founders knew this precedent, and they knew that the expanding abolitionist movement in Britain threatened their wealth. Their 1776 Declaration of Independence, then, was not only a cry for self-determination, it was an act of class protection, a bid to preserve slavery as the backbone of their new nation (Zinn, 1980).

The fear of Black resistance haunted the American ruling class. In 1811, a massive slave rebellion erupted in New Orleans, the largest in U.S. history. Terrified of what emancipation might mean, slave-owning President Thomas Jefferson deployed the army and local militias to crush the uprising with brutal force. The revolt confirmed white anxieties: the oppressed would not remain silent forever.

Slavery in America was not solely the enterprise of Christian planters. Jewish populations in New Orleans also owned significant numbers of enslaved Africans. The Monsanto family, wealthy Jewish planters, were among the largest slaveholders in Louisiana. Judah Philip Benjamin, a Jewish senator from Louisiana, not only held hundreds of enslaved Africans but also operated several plantations worked by slave labor. As historian Robert Rosen details in *The Jewish Confederates* (2002), Jewish communities in the South were deeply enmeshed in the institution of slavery. They did not merely participate economically; they also provided soldiers for the Confederate Army during the Civil

War (1861–1865), aligning themselves with white supremacy against Black freedom.

Thus, from its inception, America revealed itself as a cruel nation built on Indigenous genocide, African slavery, and racial violence. This pattern of brutality did not end with the nineteenth century. It continues into the twenty-first, as the U.S. provides weapons to white European settlers in Palestine, aiding Israel's campaign of genocide against Palestinians in 2024. As Dr. Deshay David Ford (2022) argues, America has long been an "evil empire" whose global policy has consistently involved the killing of Black and brown people.

History offers grim parallels. The Assyrian Empire, infamous for its brutality, was ultimately destroyed in 612 B.C. by a coalition of Babylonians and Medes. For centuries, the Assyrians had terrorized their neighbors with massacres, enslavement, and the merciless slaughter of women, children, and the elderly. When their victims finally rose in revolt, they returned the cruelty without mercy, wiping the Assyrians from history.

The lesson is clear. Just as the Babylonians and Medes avenged the horrors inflicted upon them, so too will oppressed peoples rise against their conquerors. In Gaza, Israel's Prime Minister Benjamin Netanyahu has shown no mercy in his genocidal war on Palestinians. He mirrors the Assyrian cruelty, massacring women, children, and the defenseless. And as history teaches, such cruelty is never forgotten. The oppressed will one day return the violence visited upon them.

The white settler states, America, Britain, France, Germany, Canada, and Australia, were all built on the same racial logic. Each carried out genocidal campaigns against Indigenous peoples, enslaved Africans, or colonized populations. Each justified this violence as civilization, destiny, or divine mandate. But as Ford reminds us, the empires of oppression always face reckoning. The same nations that once carried the "White Man's Burden" will ultimately feel the pain they inflicted on others—the destruction of families, the deaths of children, and the collapse of their homes and communities.

Decline of America and Israel: The Last Two Racial Apartheid White
Colonial Nations

The State of Israel, like the United States, South Africa, and
Australia, is a direct heir of the British Empire's colonial projects. The
United States itself began as an English colony in 1603, with settlers
immediately embarking on campaigns of extermination against
Indigenous peoples. From 1603 until the massacre at Wounded Knee
in 1890, U.S. armies and militias waged a 300-year war of genocide,
leaving an estimated 150 million Indigenous people dead. Survivors
were forced into concentration-like camps, where today Indigenous
youth struggle with some of the highest rates of suicide and alcoholism
in the world.

South Africa followed a parallel trajectory. Established formally as a
British colony in the early nineteenth century, it attracted white settlers
from England, Holland, and other parts of Europe, including those who
claimed Jewish identity. The land's immense wealth in diamonds, gold,
and other natural resources made it a target for colonial exploitation.
White settlers imposed racial genocide and apartheid on the Black
majority, reducing them to laborers for the enrichment of white elites,
just as their American cousins had done with African slaves.

In 1948, European settlers again enacted this model in Palestine.
Arriving under the sponsorship of Britain and with the support of the
United States, they began a systematic campaign to dispossess and
destroy the Indigenous Palestinian people, who had lived on that land
for thousands of years. For the British and Americans, the goal was clear:
to establish a racially allied outpost in the Middle East, a settler colony
that mirrored their own histories of conquest.

This betrayal was compounded by deceit. In 1917, during World
War I, Britain had promised Palestine to the Arabs in exchange for their
support against the Ottoman Empire. That promise was never honored.
Instead, the British handed Palestine to European settlers under the
Balfour Declaration, affirming their commitment not to justice, but to
white supremacy and the imperial "White Man's Burden."

The colony of Australia was established in 1770 as an English prison
settlement. Britain emptied its jails, shipping thousands of convicts

across the oceans to occupy Indigenous lands. Nevertheless, what began as a penal colony quickly transformed into a campaign of extermination. White settlers, criminals, and colonists alike set about massacring the Aboriginal peoples of Australia, seizing their land, and stripping them of their resources. Aboriginal survivors were often enslaved, forced into servitude just as Africans had been in the Americas. The exploitation mirrored Jamestown, Virginia, where, beginning in 1619, enslaved Africans became the foundation of colonial wealth (Jones, 2018).

This history repeats itself in Palestine. The white settlers who claimed Jewish identity in 1948 cannot expect permanence. As world power realigns, the ground beneath them is shifting. The United States, their greatest patron, is already in decline. Demographic transformation ensures that America will soon be a majority-brown nation; its loyalty to a white settler state in the Middle East will not endure. China, now rising as the central power of the twenty-first century, has no interest in underwriting Israel. Without imperial sponsors, the settler state's survival is impossible.

The reality is already visible in America's Black communities. During the Gaza war of 2024, African Americans overwhelmingly expressed solidarity with Palestinians, recognizing in their oppression a mirror of their own. For them, Gaza is not distant; it is Ferguson, Minneapolis, Selma. The sight of white settlers in Palestine destroying Palestinian homes echoes the sight of white police destroying Black lives in the United States. The moral alignment is clear: Black America stands with Palestine.

The settlers in Israel will therefore face the fate of white settlers in South Africa before 1994. When Nelson Mandela became president, apartheid was dismantled, and the settler minority had to relinquish its absolute rule. In Palestine, after the war in Gaza, the outcome will be harsher. The European settlers who claimed Jewish identity will not be able to remain on stolen land indefinitely. They will be forced to leave, and the world will face the question: where will they go?

The options are bleak. Russia will not welcome them. Germany, Italy, and France, scarred by their own histories, will refuse. The United States, already fractured by its own racial nightmare, cannot absorb another influx of racially exclusive settlers. Canada, a country with a diverse and fragile demographic balance, will not invite them either. The result will be a million stateless people, a population without a homeland, without citizenship, unwanted everywhere.

This is the burden that Prime Minister Benjamin Netanyahu has placed upon his people. His policies of genocide have created an impossible future. Wherever they go, the settlers of Israel will be marked. They will be despised, hunted, and unsafe. Survival, if possible at all, would depend upon the mercy of the very people they have oppressed. Perhaps, if Palestinians chose, they might allow the settlers to live in isolated communities. But mercy is not guaranteed.

The bitter irony is stark: Netanyahu's government has become the mirror of Adolf Hitler's. The very people who claim eternal victimhood for the Holocaust now inflict a holocaust upon Palestinians. In Gaza, Israel has subjected an entire population to destruction, bombing homes, killing children, burying families in rubble. This mirrors precisely the crimes that Jews once suffered in Europe.

Nor is this pattern without precedent. Jewish elites in the nineteenth century, like their white Christian counterparts, were participants in the transatlantic slave system. Judah Philip Benjamin, a Jewish senator from Louisiana, owned hundreds of enslaved Africans and several plantations, making immense profits from cotton harvested by Black laborers (Rosen, 2002). The Monsanto family, Jewish planters in New Orleans, likewise grew rich through the buying and selling of African people. They stood firmly with the Confederacy during the Civil War (1861–1865), not as victims, but as exploiters.

New Orleans itself became one of the largest hubs of slave commerce in the Deep South. The city's auction blocks saw families torn apart, men, women, and children sold as chattel to work the fields of the Cotton Kingdom. But in 1811, enslaved Africans rose in rebellion. Armed with makeshift weapons, they struck back against their oppressors, killing several plantation owners and their families.

The response was swift and brutal. Thomas Jefferson, himself a slave-owning president, deployed the U.S. Army and local slave patrols to crush the revolt. These patrols were authorized by Article II of the Constitution as state militias and were the forerunners of America's modern police system. James Madison, another Virginian slaveholder, wrote the Bill of Rights with specific provisions for these militias. The Second Amendment, often celebrated as the guarantor of liberty, was in truth designed to arm white men against slave uprisings. Guns in the South were not primarily for defense against foreign powers, but for the suppression of enslaved Africans.

The Constitution itself sealed this arrangement. Article IV, Section 2, Clause 3, known as the Fugitive Slave Clause, made the pursuit and capture of runaway slaves a federal mandate. Madison and his fellow slaveholders enshrined in law what they feared most: rebellion. Their wealth was built on human bondage, and the state existed to protect it.

Thus, from America to Australia, from South Africa to Israel, the story is the same. White settler colonies were founded on slavery, genocide, and racial domination. And like the Assyrians, like Rome, their reign will end. History's judgment is inescapable: the oppressed always rise, and empires built on blood always fall.

# Section II:
# Trump, U.S. Political Collapse, Courts, Authoritarianism & White-Nationalist Politics

# The United States Capitol Insurrection January 06, 2021

On January 6, 2021, an insurrection shook the heart of American democracy. A furious mob, angry not just at the outcome of a presidential election but at a changing nation, stormed the Capitol in a desperate attempt to halt the certification of Joseph Biden as the 46th President of the United States. President Biden had won both the popular vote and the electoral college, but for the followers of outgoing President Donald Trump, the truth was unacceptable.

These insurrectionists echoed the rage of a bygone era, the seething fury of 1861, when Southern aristocrats awoke to the news that Abraham Lincoln had won the presidency. Back then, the Civil War was born from the fear of losing power and privilege. In 2021, the rebellion was once again fueled by white Americans, many of whom had long benefited from the empire they now believed was slipping from their grasp. They claimed the election had been stolen, that fraud and illegal votes had robbed their leader of his rightful place. They called it patriotism. But it was a cry of desperation from those watching the myth of their dominance unravel.

Like the dying days of the Roman Empire, when only the elite prospered from conquest and expansion, America had reached a similar breaking point. The working class, once promised the spoils of empire, now found themselves left behind. Their entitlements had vanished. Their comforts diminished. And now, they believed even their vote had been taken. The illusion shattered.

Accusations of a stolen election spread like wildfire. The mob, much like the furious crowd of the French Revolution in 1789, wanted blood. And Donald Trump, their would-be Moses, was more than willing to offer them an enemy to crucify. They marched through the Capitol in search of Speaker Nancy Pelosi and any symbol of the government that dared to contradict their worldview.

They desecrated the halls of American democracy, tearing apart the symbols of a Republic that once stood for democracy, material success, and the grand illusion of freedom. They shattered glass, broke furniture, smeared filth, and waved flags not of unity, but of dominance. These weren't patriots. They were Dreamers of a different sort, those who believed in the mythology of America as a divine project led by white hands.

The truth is darker. The so-called "American Miracle" was not born of democracy or divine favor, but from stolen land and stolen labor. African slaves were dragged into the Empire not as citizens but as tools, forced to harvest the cotton that would power capitalism. The American settlers, landing in Virginia, brought with them a vision fueled by supremacy. They were told they were God's chosen, that their destiny was to rule, to dominate, to dispossess Native peoples by any means necessary.

On January 6, 2021, that delusion returned in full force. The mob had come not only to overturn an election, but to reclaim what they saw as their God-given right to rule over others. To silence, even kill, anyone who stood in the way of their promised land.

Donald Trump, to them, was not a man. He was a prophet. A chosen king. Their Moses to lead them into the new Jerusalem, a land of unearned privilege, wealth, and white dominance. And in response to his call, they came, ready to wage war for their inheritance. Ready to seize their piece of paradise, no matter the cost.

When they realized their chosen God would not reign on Mount Olympus, they sought to burn the mountain down. They destroyed art, furniture, and sacred spaces, not out of political protest, but because they believed their God had been overthrown, and a new order was rising to replace them.

These were not the heirs of 1776. That revolution had been led by wealthy colonists seeking greater wealth, angered by King George III's limitations on their exploitation of the New World. That rebellion, too, was built on the backs of slaves, enslaved Africans working the plantations of George Washington, Thomas Jefferson, James Madison, and Pierce Butler.

In 1772, a British court ruled in *Somersett v. Stewart* that slavery had no basis in English common law. That single ruling terrified the American slaveholding elite. They feared losing their wealth, measured in human lives. And Thomas Jefferson gave them an answer: independence. On July 4, 1776, he declared that "all men are created equal," while knowingly excluding women, the poor, Native Americans, and millions of enslaved Africans.

The mob of 2021 did not desecrate the Capitol to defend democracy; they came to crown a king. In the name of their "God," they defecated on democracy and urinated on the truth. They shattered what they could not control. But as chaos raged through the halls of power, one man, Eugene Goodman, a Black Capitol Police officer and descendant of slaves, stood firm. He redirected the mob, saving countless lives.

It is no small irony that while the insurrectionists claimed to fight for freedom, it was the descendants of America's enslaved who protected democracy from its own children.

This was not just an insurrection. It was a reckoning.

**The Revolution of 1776** was not a revolution of the masses, but a rebellion led by the wealthy elite, landowners, and aristocrats frustrated by King George III's restrictions on their pursuit of greater wealth. This so-called fight for freedom masked a deeper motivation: the preservation and expansion of slavery.

American elites, men like George Washington, Thomas Jefferson, James Madison, and Pierce Butler, built their fortunes on the backs of enslaved Africans. Their plantations thrived on slave labor, and any threat to that institution was a threat to their wealth.

In 1772, the landmark case of *James Somerset v. Stewart* shook the foundations of the colonial slave economy. Lord Chief Justice Mansfield ruled that slavery was unsupported by English common law. The ruling sent shockwaves through the American colonies. If slavery could be outlawed in England, what would stop it from being abolished in the colonies?

Fearing for their wealth and way of life, the colonial elite turned to revolution. Thomas Jefferson, the architect of independence, promised a solution. And so, on July 4, 1776, he penned the Declaration of Independence, boldly stating that "all men are created equal" while denying that truth to women, Indigenous people, enslaved Africans, and poor whites. It was liberty for the few, not the many.

Fast forward to January 6, 2021. A new mob of insurrectionists, overwhelmingly white, stormed the U.S. Capitol, not in the name of justice, but in a desperate attempt to crown their rejected leader, Donald Trump, as a messianic ruler. Fueled by conspiracy theories and blind loyalty, they desecrated the heart of American democracy. They shattered windows, destroyed priceless historical artifacts, urinated and defecated on sacred floors, all in service of a lie.

In a moment of great danger, it was **Eugene Goodman**, a Black Capitol Police officer and descendant of enslaved people, who stood between the mob and members of Congress. His bravery saved lives. Ironically, he protected the very institution that had long profited from the oppression of his ancestors.

These insurrectionists claimed to defend democracy, but in truth, they sought to destroy a republic that had been mythologized as a "shining city on a hill." A nation blessed by God. A new Jerusalem. A white republic where power and privilege were their divine birthrights.

When America's Founding Fathers gathered in 1787 to draft the Constitution, they looked to Ancient Athens as their model, a city built on philosophy, democracy, and slavery. In 80 B.C., Athens had a population of two million, yet only 40,000 were citizens. The rest, enslaved people, peasants, and foreigners, had no voice. America followed suit. The so-called republic was, from the beginning, an exclusive club for the wealthy and white.

Athens embraced **hedonism**, the pursuit of pleasure, and the avoidance of pain. So too does modern America. In its decline, the nation is steeped in consumerism, greed, political corruption, and moral decay. The U.S. government staggers under the weight of addiction epidemics, rampant inequality, and a breakdown of leadership. Society glorifies fame over character, wealth over wisdom.

Meanwhile, people of color continue to suffer. Racial profiling, police brutality, and systemic injustice remain brutal realities. The promise of liberty and justice for all still rings hollow for Black and Brown communities.

The insurrection was not just a riot; it was a reckoning. It laid bare the unresolved contradictions at the heart of the American experiment: freedom built on slavery, democracy limited by race, and equality shadowed by privilege.

Until the nation reckons with its truth, the dream of justice will remain just that, a dream deferred.

The United States, like all ancient empires, is on the path to decline. Both white individuals and people of color are facing challenges in addressing their community issues without resorting to violence. In 2024, America is more racially polarized than it was in 1950. With the ongoing demographic changes, the country may face significant collapse by 2040. The Germanic tribes did not need to attack the walls of ancient Rome; the city had already fallen due to immorality, homosexual behavior, and hedonism.

## President Donald Trump Was Convicted Of Money Fraud In New York District Court

For decades, Donald Trump wielded wealth like a sword and whiteness like a shield. He believed—like so many elites before him— that the American justice system would bend to his power, bow to his privilege, and protect him from consequence. But on May 31, 2024, the unthinkable happened: Trump was convicted on 34 felony counts for concealing illegal payments to a professional sex worker in his

Manhattan case. The man who once occupied the highest office in the United States now faces the possibility of a 20-year prison sentence—not as a political martyr, but as a felon.

Donald J. Trump is the first former president in American history to be convicted of fraud, money laundering, and falsifying business records. Yet even as the verdict reverberated across the nation, many still remembered that this same man once demanded death—not justice—for five innocent boys.

In 1989, a brutal crime shocked New York City. A white woman, jogging alone in Central Park, was raped and left for dead. The crime was horrific. But what followed was more than prosecution—it was persecution. Five teenagers of color—four Black, one Latino—were arrested by the NYPD. Their only "evidence"? Their skin, their poverty, and their presence.

The legal process that followed was not justice. It was a modern-day lynching in the courtroom. These boys—children, really—were interrogated without lawyers. Denied access to their parents. Deprived of food and water. Threatened, intimidated, and coerced. They confessed to crimes they did not commit, not because they were guilty, but because they were terrified. As *the United Nations Commission on Human Rights* would later observe, the American criminal justice system is deeply, structurally racist, particularly toward people of color. The Central Park Five became proof.

And while these boys were being crushed under the weight of lies and systemic bias, Donald Trump inserted himself into the spectacle—not as a defender of truth, but as a champion of vengeance. He purchased full-page ads in four major New York newspapers, calling for the return of the death penalty. He demanded execution for children. He never saw evidence. He never cared about innocence. All he saw were Black and Brown faces—and that was enough.

The media, the prosecutor, the judge, and the jury—each played their part in a performance of white hysteria. The boys were convicted and sent to prison. No physical evidence tied them to the crime. Their confessions were inconsistent and coerced. Yet they were sentenced anyway. Their names were buried beneath the weight of public outrage, while the real rapist remained free.

It would take nearly two decades for justice to speak. In 2002, a man named Matias Reyes—a convicted serial rapist—confessed to the crime. His DNA matched. His story was consistent. He had acted alone. The Central Park Five had been innocent all along. The State of New York released the men and later awarded them over $40 million in restitution. But the time stolen—the youth lost, the trauma inflicted—could never be repaid.

Donald Trump never apologized. Not then. Not now. Not after the confession. Not after the exoneration. Not even after a documentary by Ava DuVernay exposed the full horror of what had been done to those five boys. Trump remained defiant, clinging to a myth of guilt because to admit otherwise would require him to confront the racism within himself.

And yet this same Trump, who once called for the execution of innocent children, now stands convicted—not by rumor or rage, but by fact. The Manhattan District Court, the same judicial body that once wrongfully imprisoned five teenagers, has now turned its gavel toward the architect of birtherism, bigotry, and bombast.

The irony is not lost on history.

As *Dr. Deshay David Ford* writes in *Why Muslim People Hate Donald Trump and America* (2024), this is the true face of the American legal system: one that punishes the powerless with brutal speed, but hesitates for decades before confronting the crimes of the powerful. Justice in America has never been colorblind—it has been color-coded.

The legacy of racial injustice is not confined to the courtroom. During World War II, the United States imprisoned over 120,000 Japanese Americans in internment camps. The justification? National security. The reality? Racism. A federal investigation, authorized by President Jimmy Carter, later concluded that there was no evidence of Japanese disloyalty. The report, *Personal Justice Denied,* named racism as the driving force behind the incarceration. One of the architects of that policy was Karl Bendetsen, a Jewish-American bureaucrat who carried out Roosevelt's Executive Order 9066.

While the U.S. was incarcerating its own citizens, Nazi Germany was rounding up Jews, Roma, and political dissidents and sending them to death camps. Adolf Hitler, deep in his genocidal "Final Solution," oversaw the extermination of millions. Jews were worked to death in concentration camps, just as Africans had been centuries earlier in the sugar fields of the West Indies, the cotton fields of Mississippi, and the rice swamps of Georgia.

The connection is clear, as *Dr. Ford* notes. In both cases—whether it was Black bodies under white capitalism or Jewish bodies under Aryan fascism—human life was reduced to labor, to profit, to nothing. As Ford observes in *Why Muslim People Hate Donald Trump and America*, racism is not simply personal hatred. It is systemic architecture, designed to elevate some and erase others.

That same architecture continues today. It is embedded in the courtrooms that still give longer sentences to Black defendants. In the banks that redline communities of color. In the police departments that treat traffic stops like war zones. In the prisons that are now the new plantations.

Donald Trump is not an outlier.

He is a product of this system. A system that allowed him to rise. A system that shielded him when he lied. That empowered him when he attacked. That cheered when he demanded death for boys whose only crime was existing while Black.

His conviction on 34 felony counts does not cleanse the stain. It merely confirms what so many already knew: that behind the myth of law and order lies the machinery of exploitation.

And for once, that machine turned on one of its own.

Justice came late.

But it came.

And the world is watching.

# Donald Trump, Former United States President, Found Guilty Of Falsifying Business Records In Manhattan Court, In New York

On May 30, 2024, in a historic and unprecedented moment in American history, Donald J. Trump, the 45th President of the United States, was convicted by a jury of his peers in a Manhattan criminal court. Found guilty on all 34 felony counts of falsifying business records, Trump now faces the potential of up to 20 years in New York State Prison. The charges stemmed from a scheme to hide a $138,000 payment made to adult film actress Stormy Daniels, in an effort to silence her from revealing sexual encounters with Trump during and after the 2016 presidential campaign.

The irony was not lost on many Americans, particularly Black and Latino citizens, who remember that this same Manhattan legal system once wrongly convicted five teenage boys of color in 1989. Known as the Central Park Five, these youths were coerced, intimidated, and deprived of legal counsel or parental presence during brutal police interrogations. They were falsely accused of raping a white jogger, and the entire nation, including Donald Trump, demanded their execution. Trump even paid for full-page ads in New York newspapers calling for the death penalty, before any trial had begun. The teens were later exonerated, after years in prison, when the real perpetrator confessed and DNA evidence cleared them.

This legacy of racist double standards in American justice is deeply embedded. For centuries, men of color, especially Black men, have been lynched, imprisoned, or executed merely for being accused of harming white women. From Emmett Till in 1955, who was brutally beaten and murdered after being falsely accused of whistling at a white woman, to the present day, these stories are told in Black families as generational warnings. As a result, many African American parents teach their sons strict codes of conduct for surviving encounters with law enforcement and navigating a society that still criminalizes their existence.

Decline of America and Israel: The Last Two Racial Apartheid White
Colonial Nations

The United Nations, in its 2016 *Report on Racial Disparities in the
U.S. Criminal Justice System*, confirmed that racial profiling and systemic
discrimination against Black and brown men persist in nearly every
American jurisdiction. These disparities extend from street-level
policing to courtroom sentencing.

Despite this deep history of injustice, Donald Trump's conviction
has highlighted the enduring privilege of whiteness and power in the
United States. Unlike typical convicted felons, Trump was not
interviewed in custody. Instead, on June 11, 2024, he met with a
Manhattan probation officer via Zoom from his private residence,
accompanied by his attorney Todd Blanche. The interview was atypical
in both format and content. The probation officer, introduced only as
Stephanie G., reportedly asked Trump invasive questions regarding his
wife and son, including: *"How does your family feel about living with a
convicted felon?"*

When the officer inquired whether Trump would accept
responsibility for falsifying business records and cheating on his wife, his
attorney objected. Stephanie G. then muted her microphone, allegedly
to consult off-camera. She reportedly told Trump that Judge Juan
Merchan was considering probation with electronic ankle monitoring,
rather than prison. Trump reacted angrily, allegedly responding: *"If I
ever wore one, it would be wired with an explosive. Yours too. That way, if
you step past your door, it detonates."* This chilling remark, while not
widely reported, has raised serious questions about Trump's fitness for
public office and the double standards in the treatment of wealthy white
felons.

Yet Trump remains a political juggernaut. In spite of his criminal
conviction, and a separate civil ruling in which a New York jury found
him liable for sexual assault against a woman in a department store, he
is the leading candidate in the 2024 presidential election. His legal
record includes financial fraud, sexual misconduct, and obstruction of
justice. He has paid millions in civil settlements, including for the rape
case, while continuing to deny all allegations.

Trump's name also appeared on Jeffrey Epstein's private flight logs, frequently cited in discussions around the late financier's sex trafficking operation. Although no charges have yet been brought against Trump related to Epstein's Island, the association with Epstein, along with other prominent figures such as Prince Andrew, Alan Dershowitz, and David Copperfield, has cast a long shadow over Trump's personal conduct and the company he keeps.

If Trump is re-elected in November 2024, he will become the first president in U.S. history to serve as a convicted felon, a civilly liable sexual predator, and a figure surrounded by allegations of ties to sex trafficking networks. And yet, within the same country that imprisoned the innocent Central Park Five, Trump continues to receive protection, privilege, and support from white conservative institutions and media outlets that once demanded harsh penalties for young Black boys accused of lesser crimes.

Evident from the record, the man who once demanded the execution of Black teenagers was himself found guilty by the same court system. And the same forces that allowed him to rise to power now seek to normalize his crimes to wash away his corruption in the cleansing language of patriotism, wealth, and whiteness.

But the truth remains. In the face of history, we must ask:

What kind of nation elects a man like this again?

And what does it mean for those who have always suffered under a system that punishes the poor and protects the powerful?

## Republican Convention In Milwaukee – Donald Trump Assured White People That He Was Going To Restore White Racism And Apartheid In America

The Republican National Convention in Milwaukee was not simply a political gathering. It was a celebration. It was a rally for the restoration of the racial order that white nationalists have long dreamed of bringing back. In that convention hall, white Republicans cheered as Donald

Trump, their chosen champion, stood before them and promised to "Make America Great Again." The message, to them, was unmistakable. It was a pledge to return to the so-called "Good Old Days" when white supremacy was law, when apartheid was the unspoken but enforced order, and when Black, Brown, and Indigenous people were kept in their place by the power of the state.

The euphoria in the room echoed with a dangerous familiarity. Eighty years earlier, in 1939, Adolf Hitler had promised the German people that he would "Make Germany Great Again." His vision, like Trump's, was built on exclusion, racial hierarchy, and the suppression of those deemed unworthy of citizenship. For Germany, that promise ended twelve years later in total ruin: the country reduced to rubble, millions dead, and Hitler's empire dissolved in the fires of defeat. The dreams of greatness lay in ashes alongside the man who had promised them.

Today, America's empire stands as a decadent, fractured mirror image of its own myths. It is a mirror shattered into a million pieces, each shard reflecting a different form of decline. The military has faced defeat after defeat: in Vietnam in 1975, in Afghanistan in 2021, with disastrous interventions in Syria and Iraq. Its cities rot in decay, while millions live unhoused in tents and on sidewalks. The mental and physical health of the American people has sunk to historic lows. Young white men, once the backbone of military recruitment, increasingly refuse to wear the uniform. Like ancient Rome in its waning years, the American empire suffers from moral rot, the acceptance of societal decay, and a normalization of the very vices it once claimed to condemn.

The opioid epidemic sweeps across the country, leaving death in its wake. The Sackler family, through Purdue Pharma, engineered and profited from this plague, distributing OxyContin with lies about its addictive nature, destroying hundreds of thousands of lives for the sake of billions in profit. Yet the Sacklers are not an anomaly. Their greed is not exceptional, it is foundational. America itself was built on greed.

Decline of America and Israel: The Last Two Racial Apartheid White
Colonial Nations

The English colony of Jamestown, founded in Virginia in the early 1600s, was established for one reason: profit. In 1603, English settlers began a campaign of racist genocide against the Indigenous people of the region. By 1619, they had initiated the enslavement of Africans, bringing men, women, and children across the Atlantic to labor under the whip. In 1776, when the colonies declared independence from Britain, it was not solely for lofty ideals of liberty. The wealthy elite were protecting their economic interests. The Somerset v. Stewart decision in 1772 had declared slavery unsupported by English common law. If British rule continued, plantation owners like George Washington, Thomas Jefferson, James Madison, James Monroe, and Andrew Jackson, men who collectively held thousands of enslaved Africans, might have to relinquish what they considered property.

Independence was, for these men, a means to preserve their wealth. On July 4, 1776, they severed ties with Britain. After years of war, the Treaty of Paris in 1781 granted them their independence. In 1787, at the Constitutional Convention, they ensured that slavery was enshrined in the nation's founding document. Article IV, Section 2, Clause 3, the Fugitive Slave Clause, guaranteed that enslaved people who escaped to free states could be seized and returned to bondage. In 1857, Chief Justice Roger B. Taney, himself a slaveholder, declared in the Dred Scott decision that Black people had no rights the white man was bound to respect.

From its birth, the United States pursued a policy of racial genocide against Indigenous peoples, waging wars of extermination and driving survivors from their lands. This history is not unique to America. With few exceptions, every white European NATO country—Britain, Canada, Australia, France, Belgium, Holland, and Germany—was built on colonial conquest and the oppression of Black and Brown peoples. These nations expanded their empires through slavery, genocide, and exploitation, enriching themselves at the expense of those they subjugated.

When South Africa brought charges of racial genocide against Israel, it placed the mirror in front of these former colonial powers. The same countries now defending Israel's occupation and oppression had themselves committed centuries of racist atrocities. None of them are innocent.

The Republican convention in Milwaukee was therefore more than a political event—it was an unbroken thread in the tapestry of white supremacy that has shaped America since its inception. Trump's promise to restore greatness is a promise to restore the racial hierarchy, to roll back the clock to a time when power was defined by whiteness and enforced through violence.

It is a promise America has made before. And, as history has shown, such promises always end in ruin.

## America's White Nationalists Celebration Of Selecting Donald Trump As Their Presidential Candidate

The celebration of Donald Trump's nomination was not just a political rally, it was a moral collapse. In Milwaukee, white nationalists erupted in applause, not for a leader of integrity, but for a man whose public record is a litany of criminality. A crook. A felon. A man accused of sexual misconduct, of predatory behavior against children. A man tied by friendship and association to Jeffrey Epstein, the infamous trafficker who preyed on the vulnerable. This was the man they lifted to the altar of the presidency.

By cheering him, the white electorate crossed a point of no return. There can be no restoration of moral credibility for a nation that elevates such a figure to its highest office. The United States forfeited its claim to moral normalcy. The path ahead is one of bloodshed, lawlessness, and destruction.

Donald Trump has shattered what little trust remained in America's judicial system. With him as the symbol of political leadership, the people will no longer believe in the courts. The day is coming when the law itself will be a commodity for sale to the highest bidder. In this new era, greed and organized crime will reign. Police forces, once bound, at least in theory, to constitutional limits, will themselves become criminal organizations, unaccountable to law, answerable only to power and profit.

The streets of America's cities will become unsafe after dark. Citizens will be forced to arm themselves at home, barricading their families against the chaos outside. The racial hatred simmering in urban America will spill out unchecked. Cities will begin to resemble the shattered landscapes of Iraq, Syria, and Afghanistan, armed gangs roaming by day, chaos and violence ruling the night. In such a climate, the U.S. government will declare martial law, seeking to restore control over a country it has already lost.

History offers the warning. In 410 A.D., the armies of Alaric, king of the Visigoths, laid siege to the once-great city of Rome. At that time, Rome's population was drowning in moral decay: depravity, corruption, sexual degeneracy, and indulgence in every vice. The city was so diseased and morally bankrupt that the Visigoth warriors saw no need to rape or pillage; the rot had already consumed its people.

A similar fate awaits the United States. When the Chinese arrive, whether as military victors, economic masters, or inheritors of a fallen empire, they will find America's cities steeped in immorality, corruption, and vice. Like the ancient invaders of Nineveh, they may simply move on, leaving behind the ruins of a city unworthy of conquest.

Nineveh, capital of the Assyrian Empire, fell in 612 B.C. to the combined forces of the Medes, Persians, and Babylonians. The destruction was so complete that no historians from the city survived to record its fall. The only accounts that remain are from the victors, who chronicled how they razed a ruthless enemy as a warning to others. The Assyrians themselves had long used this tactic: when confronted with resistance, they would destroy a city completely to instill fear in all who might dare defy them.

The United States has followed this same pattern in its own military campaigns. In Vietnam, Afghanistan, and Iraq, American forces bombed hospitals, schools, electrical grids, water plants, and other vital infrastructure with the clear intent to break the spirit of the people. Under George W. Bush's war in Iraq, women, children, the elderly, and even infants were killed. No structure that could sustain life was spared.

Today, the State of Israel is committing racial genocide against the Palestinian people in Gaza. Its attacks are deliberate, calculated, and aimed at extermination. The United States, far from being an impartial observer, is complicit in arming Israel, funding its operations, and enabling the destruction of an entire people. The moral stain is shared equally by Washington and Tel Aviv, and by the other allies who lend their silence or support.

Trump's nomination is not an isolated political moment. It is a symptom of imperial decay, of a nation following the same trajectory as every corrupt empire before it. From Rome to Nineveh, from the Assyrian armies to modern war machines, history tells the same story: when a people abandon morality for power, when they trade justice for domination, the end is inevitable.

And in that end, there are no heroes.

Only ruins.

## Donald Trump – America Savior – Promises To Make America Great Again

Donald J. Trump rose to power not as a statesman, nor as a visionary, but as a salesman of nostalgia. To millions of white Americans, he cast himself as their "Great White Savior," a man who promised to banish their fears, erase their insecurities, and restore to them the supremacy they believed was their birthright. His slogan, "Make America Great Again," was never about greatness in the universal sense—it was about whiteness. It was about a return to a racial order in which white men reigned unquestioned and unchallenged.

This was not a new performance. Nearly a century earlier, Adolf Hitler promised the German people that he would restore their pride, their power, and their place in the world. His slogan, too, was a call to "greatness," a vow to undo humiliation and restore racial purity. Millions believed him, and their belief led Germany into catastrophe—twelve years of dictatorship, genocide, and ultimately, the smoldering ruins of a defeated nation.

Trump's rise echoed this dark history. White America, taught for generations that it was inherently superior, had grown accustomed to privilege. They were told, from pulpits and podiums, that they carried a divine destiny to rule. They were told that the world was theirs to shape, and that any shift in the balance of power was an injustice against them. When demographic change and cultural pluralism began to erode this monopoly, they looked for someone to assure them that the past could return. Trump offered himself as that man.

At the heart of this alliance stood white Evangelical Christianity. Robert P. Jones, in *The End of White Christian America* (2010), exposed the central truth: white evangelicals were not merely a voting bloc; they were Trump's foundation. Yet behind their sanctimony, their churches harbored rot. Congregations accused their leaders of concealing sexual predators, protecting men who preyed on children while preaching morality from the pulpit. In Arkansas, at Emanuel Baptist Church, the scandal was not hidden—it was systemic. Victims pleaded for justice. The leaders refused transparency. The cover-up became part of the institution.

These same churches, draped in the language of salvation, became the strongest supporters of Donald J. Trump—a man who himself carried the legal stain of sexual misconduct. In New York, Trump was convicted of sexual abuse. His close associate, Jeffrey Epstein, became infamous for his child trafficking operation, ferrying underage girls to his private island for the pleasure of powerful men. Trump was on the flight logs. So was Prince Andrew. So was lawyer Alan Dershowitz. Epstein's "suicide" in a federal prison cell remains a shadowed scandal, a reminder that wealth and influence can make accountability vanish overnight.

The sickness, however, is not confined to individuals. The United States itself has become one of the global centers of human trafficking. Reports from the United Nations confirm that the trade in bodies, particularly women and children, has grown into one of the most profitable industries in the world—outpacing arms sales and narcotics in its scale and reach. Eastern European girls are shipped into Israel, into the United States, into Europe, consumed by networks of men whose power shields them from exposure. Epstein's island was not an anomaly. It was a symbol.

The trafficking business thrives because it is too profitable to destroy. Too many powerful hands are stained by it. Attempts at regulation, whether through the United Nations or through domestic law enforcement, collapse against the reality of wealth. The system is not broken. It functions precisely as designed: to extract pleasure and profit from the vulnerable, while ensuring the untouchability of the perpetrators.

Donald Trump's America, then, is not a departure from history. It is the continuation of an old empire of exploitation—slavery transformed into trafficking, plantations transformed into prisons, and white supremacy repackaged as patriotism. The promise to "make America great again" is the same promise Hitler made to Germany: that racial supremacy, moral corruption, and authoritarian rule can somehow be called "greatness."

But history tells us where such promises lead. Not to renewal. Not to justice. Not to salvation. They lead to ruin.

## Donald Trump Won The 2024 Presidential Election

On November 5, 2024, the United States revealed once again the moral bankruptcy of its democracy. Donald J. Trump, a man accused of sexual predation, fraud, and corruption, was elected to the presidency for a second time. His victory was not a surprise; it was the logical outcome of a nation whose white majority, fearful of demographic change and the decline of its supremacy, turned once more to a demagogue who promised restoration.

Trump's rise echoes the words and tactics of Adolf Hitler. In 1933, Hitler told the German people that he would make their nation great again, blaming the country's problems on Jews and immigrants. In 2016 and again in 2024, Trump told white America that he would "make America great again" by targeting immigrants, Muslims, Black communities, and anyone who challenged white dominance. Trump did not invent this politics; he borrowed directly from the pages of Hitler's *Mein Kampf*, where fear, racial hatred, and scapegoating became political weapons.

According to historian Howard Zinn (1980), America was never a democracy for all—it was designed as a white man's country. Its wealth was built on genocide and slavery. Native Americans were exterminated for their lands and resources (Brown, 1970). Africans were brought in chains from 1619 onward to labor as slaves (Ford, 2022). Chinese workers were imported in the nineteenth century to build the transcontinental railroad, only to be excluded, lynched, and scapegoated once their labor was no longer needed. Every immigrant population of color has experienced exclusion and violence, while whiteness has remained the standard of citizenship. Trump's election must therefore be understood not as an aberration, but as the latest expression of this racial foundation.

By 2024, white Americans had become deeply anxious about their demographic future. Census projections showed that within a generation they would lose their majority status. Trump's campaign capitalized on this fear, telling white voters that he alone could protect their dominance. His rhetoric was not about economics or policy, but about race. He offered white America what they most desired: a leader who would reflect their prejudices, validate their fears, and promise that they would remain at the top of the racial pyramid.

Trump's personal scandals, crimes, and moral corruption were irrelevant to his supporters. On the contrary, his open defiance of decency only strengthened his appeal. For a declining empire, the elevation of corrupt leaders is not accidental but inevitable. Rome in its final days was ruled by emperors who indulged in debauchery and vice, reflecting the moral collapse of the society itself. Dr. Deshay David Ford (2022) argues that in the final phase of empire, the ruling class sacrifices morality first. Trump's election is the fulfillment of this principle: America's white population chose a man whose very life embodied their degeneration.

Trump's associations underline this point. He was a close friend of Jeffrey Epstein, the billionaire sexual predator who trafficked underage girls to powerful men. Trump was filmed at Epstein's parties and traveled on his infamous "Lolita Express." These were not accidents of association but reflections of a ruling class steeped in sexual exploitation, predation, and abuse of the vulnerable. Trump's cabinet appointments in 2024 reinforced this depravity. He nominated Congressman Matt Gaetz, accused of trafficking minors, as Attorney General. He appointed Pete Hegseth, a Fox News personality dogged by allegations of misconduct, to a senior cabinet position. Linda McMahon, head of World Wrestling Entertainment (WWE), became Secretary of Education, despite her company's record of covering up cases of sexual abuse of young boys by employees. In each case, Trump elevated individuals who mirrored his own corruption, ensuring that the state itself became a haven for predators.

This pattern is not new. In the late Roman Empire, emperors filled their courts with sycophants and degenerates, rewarding loyalty over competence and vice over virtue. America under Trump is the mirror of Rome in decline. The moral rot of its leadership is not a deviation from American history but its culmination.

Dr. Ford's Realignment Theory situates this moment within a larger global shift. The United States, he argues, is the "last white man's empire," now collapsing under the weight of its own corruption, racism, and decay. Trump's re-election in 2024 is therefore not a victory but a death rattle. It reveals a people desperate to cling to power, even at the cost of democracy itself. White America chose Trump because he reflects what they have become: fearful, corrupt, and morally bankrupt.

The 2024 election was not about policy or governance; it was about survival. White America saw in Trump their last chance to preserve supremacy in a world moving toward brown and Black majorities. In electing him, they revealed what history has always taught: when empires die, they do so not with dignity but with debauchery.

Trump's America stands as proof. Like Rome, it is crumbling. Like Hitler's Germany, it has embraced a politics of hate. And like all white empires before it, it will not endure. History's judgment is inevitable.

# The American Presidential Election Of 2024 Between Kamala Harris And Donald Trump Symbolizes The Fall Of America

The existence of Donald Trump has laid bare a truth that some have tried to deny: America's race problem is still alive, and it is thriving. Trump's entire political career has been built on the currency of racism. His attacks on African Americans, Latinos, Asians, and immigrants, most of whom are people of color, are deliberate strategies designed to appeal to a base of white voters who feel threatened by demographic change and cultural transformation.

At seventy-six years of age, I can say with painful honesty that my entire life has been shaped by the persistence of racism in this nation. For more than seven decades, I have witnessed discrimination, violence, and systemic inequality directed at Black people and other communities of color. I have lived through segregation, Jim Crow, civil rights struggles, and the promises of reform that too often ended in disappointment. And through it all, the reality has remained consistent: racism in America is not an exception but the rule.

Are all white Americans racist? No. There are many who stand for justice, equality, and dignity for all people. But the truth is that a majority of white Americans continue to uphold racism—sometimes openly, sometimes through silence or complicity. The millions who support Trump do so because they believe his slogan, *"Make America Great Again,"* is really about making white people dominant again.

History provides a sobering reminder of where such thinking leads. Adolf Hitler promised the German people in the 1930s that he would make Germany great again. Instead, he plunged Europe into a catastrophic war from 1939 to 1945, leaving millions dead and his nation in ruins. Trump, though not Hitler, has followed the same script of scapegoating minorities, demonizing immigrants, and encouraging violence in order to maintain white supremacy.

Yet even in this dark moment, I hold to hope. I pray that America will make wiser choices in the future that citizens will rise above fear, hatred, and division to select leaders who bring the nation together rather than tear it apart. With all of our imperfections, America remains a country of great potential. It has the capacity to be better, to be a place where justice and equality are more than words.

I pray for a day when the American people elect a president who embodies unity, compassion, and integrity, a leader who can make all Americans, regardless of race or background, proud of their country once again. The challenge before us is great, but so is the possibility. Whether we rise to the occasion or sink deeper into division will determine the fate of the American experiment.

# The American Supreme Court, On July 01, 2024, Granted Absolute Power To President Donald Trump

On January 6, 2021, the sitting president of the United States, Donald J. Trump, incited and encouraged a violent assault on the Capitol Building in Washington, D.C. It was not a protest. It was not a demonstration. It was an attempted coup d'état. Trump's objective was singular: to prevent the lawful certification of Joe Biden as the next president of the United States. The outgoing president, having lost the

2020 election by over seven million votes, refused to accept the results of the democratic process. He called the election fraudulent. He called the outcome stolen. And he called his supporters to Washington to overturn the will of the people.

What followed was an act of domestic terrorism broadcast live to the world. His followers, draped in Trump flags and white nationalist symbols, stormed the chambers of Congress, smashing windows, assaulting Capitol police, and erecting gallows outside the building. Elected officials were forced to flee. The vice president was targeted for execution. The democratic process was halted by violence.

The chaos was not spontaneous. It was engineered.

Donald Trump spent weeks spreading lies about voter fraud, pressuring state officials to "find votes" that did not exist, and attempting to manipulate the certification process. In Georgia, he personally called the secretary of state and demanded that election results be altered. He mobilized a legal army to file baseless lawsuits across battleground states. One by one, those lawsuits were rejected. The courts found no evidence of fraud. Independent election monitors confirmed the results. Even Trump's own attorney general, William Barr, acknowledged that there was no evidence of widespread voter fraud that could have changed the outcome.

Still, Trump persisted.

His final hope was the United States Supreme Court. In the final days of his presidency, Trump sought judicial validation for a conspiracy rooted in fantasy. The Court, at that time, unanimously rejected his claims. All nine justices confirmed the integrity of the election and the legitimacy of Joe Biden's victory. The rule of law held firm, for the moment.

But the story did not end there.

Following his departure from office, Donald Trump became the first former U.S. president to face multiple criminal indictments. In Georgia, he was charged under state racketeering laws for attempting to overturn the election results. At the federal level, the Department of Justice brought forth charges related to obstruction of justice, conspiracy to defraud the United States, and the incitement of insurrection.

Trump's defense was unprecedented. He claimed that a president cannot be prosecuted for actions taken while in office. His legal team argued that the office of the presidency is shielded by what they called "absolute immunity." In other words, a sitting or former president, if acting in an official capacity, could not be held criminally responsible for their actions, even if those actions included the violent suppression of democracy.

This was not a legal argument. It was a declaration of imperial privilege.

In early 2024, the case reached the Supreme Court once again. And on July 1, 2024, in a ruling that shattered precedent and signaled the death rattle of American constitutional democracy, the Court sided with Trump.

In a 6–3 decision, the Court's conservative majority, composed entirely of justices appointed by Republican presidents, ruled that presidents are presumptively immune from criminal prosecution for any acts carried out within the "outer perimeter" of their official duties. The language was intentionally vague, deliberately broad, and strategically devastating. The Court held that unless the government can conclusively prove that prosecuting a president for an official act poses absolutely no threat to the functions of the executive branch, that president cannot be charged.

This was not a ruling rooted in constitutional fidelity. It was the formal legalization of autocracy.

The decision did not merely apply to Trump. It applied to all future presidents. The office of the presidency, once constrained by law and subject to checks and balances, had now been placed above the law. A president could, under this ruling, use the power of the office to target political opponents, pressure election officials, or deploy military force domestically, and claim immunity so long as the act fell within the outer boundary of their official role.

The implications were immediate and devastating.

Legal scholars, civil rights organizations, and former federal judges condemned the decision. Historians compared it to the rulings that upheld slavery and racial segregation. The American Civil Liberties Union warned that the ruling effectively dismantled the separation of powers. And yet, the ruling stood.

Trump, now emboldened by legal invincibility, declared the decision a total vindication. His allies in Congress called it a historic victory for presidential authority. His opponents called it the end of American democracy.

In practical terms, the Supreme Court had created a new category of citizen: the president of the United States, who, by virtue of holding office, could no longer be held criminally accountable in the same way as any other citizen. This was monarchy in democratic clothing. A dictatorship in all but name.

The ruling drew immediate comparisons to imperial Rome, where emperors claimed divinity and immunity. It was also likened to the rise of fascist regimes in the 20th century, where legal institutions were manipulated to justify authoritarian control. The German courts in the 1930s, under Hitler, had also issued rulings that enabled the Führer to act without constraint. Now, the American Supreme Court had followed suit.

In dissent, the three liberal justices warned that the majority's decision created "a class of untouchables" immune from accountability. They wrote that the ruling would have allowed Richard Nixon to avoid prosecution for Watergate, that it would have permitted future presidents to orchestrate coups without consequence, and that it opened the door to tyranny cloaked in legality.

But dissent did not matter. The decision was binding. The consequences irreversible.

With one ruling, the Supreme Court had transformed the presidency from a public office into a throne. And Donald Trump, once impeached twice and rejected by the voters, had been granted retroactive immunity for his crimes by the very institution meant to safeguard justice.

The American experiment, forged in revolution against monarchy, had now enshrined the very tyranny it once rebelled against.

And history, again, was watching.

# America In The Process Of Falling As A Result Of Racism, Immorality, Debauchery, Wars, Degeneracy, And Culture Polarization

The American Empire has entered a stage of decline where its institutions, once claimed as pillars of democracy, no longer function for the people they were said to serve. The courts, which were supposed to stand as the last refuge of the oppressed, have become inaccessible fortresses. Justice in the United States is no longer a right, it is a luxury good.

For the poor, the disabled, and the working-class, the very act of seeking legal recourse has been transformed into an economic burden. Filing fees in federal and state courts are set so high that the price of entry alone shuts out millions. In theory, every citizen has the right to present a grievance; in practice, only those with resources can afford to cross the courthouse threshold.

For Black and Brown Americans, the barrier is not only financial but racial. The judiciary, rooted in centuries of legal discrimination, remains a system designed to protect whiteness and punish color. From jury selection to sentencing, from civil rights lawsuits to criminal prosecutions, the pattern is constant: people of color face a harsher standard, a smaller chance of success, and a greater likelihood of being dismissed, ignored, or silenced. The law in America does not simply fail them. It is weaponized against them.

Decline of America and Israel: The Last Two Racial Apartheid White
Colonial Nations

The COVID-19 pandemic in 2020 stripped away the last pretenses. Under the glare of global attention, the United States revealed the truth many had lived for generations: its healthcare system is built on racial hierarchy. Poor Black and Brown Americans died at far higher rates than their white counterparts—not because the virus discriminated, but because the system did. Quality care was rationed by ZIP code, by insurance coverage, by skin color. Hospitals in white suburbs received supplies, ventilators, and vaccines in abundance. Clinics in Black and Latino neighborhoods waited, begged, and buried their dead.

Meanwhile, the streets told their own story. The homeless crisis in America has grown so vast that local governments have all but abandoned any meaningful solution. Entire tent cities line the underpasses of Los Angeles, San Francisco, Seattle, and Philadelphia. People sleep in cars, in doorways, on sidewalks under blankets made from discarded tarps. The scale is now beyond containment, and the official response is no longer to solve the problem, but to move it, shifting the unhoused from block to block in a grotesque game of human displacement.

Poverty and racism have overwhelmed the American political system. Leaders speak in empty platitudes, promising reform while privately acknowledging that no comprehensive plan exists. The reality is grim: they have surrendered. The machinery of government now manages crises rather than preventing them.

America stands like the Titanic after striking the iceberg—its course set, its fate sealed, its leaders incapable of steering away from disaster. The passengers, rich and poor alike, may still be on the same vessel, but they do not occupy the same deck. The wealthy enjoy lifeboats; the poor are left to sink with the ship.

Taxation reflects this imbalance with brutal clarity. The wealth of the nation is extracted from those least able to give. The rich, shielded by loopholes, offshore accounts, and an army of accountants, contribute a fraction of what they owe. The poor and working-class, on the other hand, shoulder a disproportionate share of the tax burden, their meager earnings drained to fund a system that does not protect them.

In America, the rich get richer while the poor sink deeper into generational poverty. The children of the privileged are groomed for leadership, investment, and influence, and they are shielded from the blood price of military service. Wars are fought not by the sons and daughters of the wealthy, but by the children of the dispossessed—poor white youth from rural towns, and Black and Brown youth from urban neighborhoods.

The American military has become a force built on the backs of the racially oppressed. It recruits from the economic desperation of communities starved of opportunity, offering enlistment as one of the few available paths to stability—though that stability often comes at the cost of life, limb, and mental health. For the privileged, military service is a choice. For the oppressed, it is a necessity.

This is the empire America has become: a nation where the courts are closed to the poor, the hospitals serve according to color, the streets overflow with the unhoused, the tax system rewards the wealthy, and the military fights with soldiers drawn from those who have already been sacrificed in peacetime.

Like every empire before it, the United States is discovering that no amount of wealth or weaponry can save a system that has turned against its own people. Decline is not coming. It is here.

## Former President Donald Trump Destroyed The American Empire And Established A Dictatorship

According to Colbert I. King at *The* Washington Post, when Donald Trump was questioned during the January 6, 2021 riot—during what should have been the most solemn defense of American democracy—he casually dismissed responsibility, declaring, *"I had nothing to do with that; they asked me to make a speech"* (Colbert I. King, September 15, 2024). Yet the historical record reveals the opposite. The mob that assaulted approximately 140 police officers, damaged federal property, and looted the very halls of Congress was not spontaneous. It was summoned to Washington by Trump himself. He encouraged them to march upon the U.S. Capitol with the explicit purpose of disrupting the lawful process of affirming the results of the presidential election. Standing before his supporters, Trump told them the election had been stolen. He warned, *"If you do not fight like hell, you are not going to have a country any longer."*

Imagine, then, the man most responsible for inciting the worst assault on the seat of the federal government since the Civil War of 1861–1865, looking the American people in the eye and insisting, "I had nothing to do with that" (Colbert I. King, 2024, Sunday Arkansas Gazette). Trump's claim belongs to the same pattern of lies that has defined his public life. During the presidential debate on September 10, 2024 against Kamala Harris, Trump repeated a cascade of falsehoods, further proof of the deliberate deceit with which he manipulates his followers (King, 2024). To turn quickly from those lies would be to ignore the devastating consequences of the mob he inspired on January 6, 2021. That day, he even attempted to portray Ashli Babbitt—the rioter killed while forcing her way into the House Chamber—as a martyr, while refusing to acknowledge the violence of her actions.

The hypocrisy is staggering. Consider the contrast with Colin Kaepernick, the American football player who, by kneeling peacefully to protest police killings and brutality against Black and Brown people, was subjected to racist hate mail and denied opportunities to play the game he loved (Ford, 2024). Kaepernick's protest was civil, dignified, and deeply patriotic—an act of conscience in the tradition of America's best dissidents. Yet he was punished and blacklisted. By contrast, Trump incited a violent insurrection against the state itself, and white America still elevated him as their leader. This double standard exposes the truth of America's racial order: Black athletes protesting injustice are crushed, while white politicians leading insurrections are celebrated.

History offers more such examples. In the 1968 Olympic Games in Mexico City, Tommie Smith, John Carlos, and Australia's Peter

Norman raised their fists in protest against racial genocide and were subjected to hatred, exclusion, and humiliation (Ford, 2024; Zinn, 1980). Smith and Carlos were expelled from the Olympic Village; Norman was vilified in his own country for standing with them. These men represented the moral conscience of humanity, yet they were treated as enemies. By contrast, America's white majority selected Donald Trump, a man of corruption, debauchery, and deceit, as their fearless leader. He is not an aberration but the living symbol of white America's moral decline.

Trump has even gone so far as to claim that no one was killed during the January 6 insurrection except Ashli Babbitt. This is false. Three Capitol police officers lost their lives as a result of that day's violence. And Trump, instead of expressing remorse, promised that if re-elected he would pardon all of the January 6 insurrectionists. The danger of this promise cannot be overstated. On July 2024, the Trump-controlled Supreme Court handed down a ruling granting the American president absolute immunity for acts committed while in office—including acts of murder, brutality, and persecution. This ruling codified dictatorship into American law.

In the forty-four months since January 6, 2021, the U.S. Attorney for the District of Columbia has charged more than 1,500 defendants with crimes tied to the attack on the Capitol. Yet the white electorate's decision to renominate Donald Trump is not merely a condemnation of American democracy; it is a condemnation of the white American population itself. As Professor Robin DeAngelo argues in *White Fragility*, the majority of white Americans are racist. Their allegiance to Trump is proof of her thesis.

The comparison to Germany in the 1930s is unavoidable. Adolf Hitler rose to power not by accident but because the majority of the German people supported him. They were anti-Semitic, they embraced his racist policies, and they endorsed his genocidal ambitions. Trump's base mirrors this historical reality. As Hitler blamed Jews for Germany's defeat in World War I, Trump blames immigrants, Muslims, and Black

Americans for the supposed decline of the United States. Both men rose on the tide of racial hatred.

The historical record of exploitation and genocide stretches further still. Jewish bankers and traders were deeply involved in the Atlantic slave trade of the seventeenth through nineteenth centuries, profiting from the sale and suffering of African people (Rosen, 2000; Rosen, Robert, *The Jewish Confederates*, University of South Carolina Press). Today, the Sackler family, Jewish owners of Purdue Pharma, stand guilty of unleashing the opioid epidemic on America. By falsely claiming their drug OxyContin was non-addictive, they murdered hundreds of thousands of American citizens between 2008 and 2024 while amassing billions in profit. Though sued by state attorneys general, the Sacklers retained much of their fortune, proving once again how profit shields perpetrators from justice.

Nor is this pattern limited to America. Jewish merchants were involved in the Chinese Opium trade in the nineteenth century, a trade that devastated China between 1839 and 1860 and contributed to what the Chinese call their "Century of Humiliation." The United States and other white colonial powers also profited from this destruction. Chinese laborers were later exploited as near-slaves to build the U.S. Continental Railroad in 1869, their bodies expended as casually as those of African slaves. White imperial powers not only extracted labor but also spread sexual diseases among Chinese women, a degradation only ended after the Communist revolution of 1949 (Ford, 2024).

Thus, Trump's re-election campaign and his promise of pardons for insurrectionists cannot be seen in isolation. They are the latest expression of a centuries-long pattern of white supremacy, exploitation, and genocidal violence. Trump embodies the collapse of American democracy and the moral rot of white America. He has not only destroyed the American empire's legitimacy but also inaugurated its transformation into dictatorship.

# Section III:

# Israel / Palestine — Apartheid, Genocide, Origins & Settler-Colony Collapse

# Terror In The Womb — Israel's Origins In Violence

The modern State of Israel, heralded by its Western benefactors as a beacon of democracy in the Middle East, did not emerge from the fires of moral necessity or international consensus. It was birthed in terror—midwifed not by peace treaties, but by bombs, assassinations, and systematic ethnic cleansing. Long before the Declaration of Independence was read in Tel Aviv in 1948, two paramilitary organizations—*Lehi*, better known as the Stern Gang, and *Irgun Zvai Leumi*—laid the groundwork for what would become the Israeli state. Their methods were not diplomatic; they were terroristic.

These organizations, branded even by the British as terrorist outfits, waged a brutal campaign of violence against British colonial forces in Palestine and against the Indigenous Palestinian population whose existence stood in the way of the Zionist dream.

Lehi, or the Stern Gang, was founded by Avraham Stern, a man consumed not merely by nationalism, but by a vision that equated the land of Palestine with Jewish destiny and treated Palestinians as disposable. Stern was not a freedom fighter. He was a zealot with a gun. Under his leadership, Lehi carried out assassinations, bombings, and acts of terror not just against the British, but against civilians, Arab and Jewish alike, who opposed his doctrine of Zionist supremacy.

Lehi's ideological foundation was clear: ethnic cleansing was not a tragic byproduct of war, but a prerequisite for nationhood. Palestinians, who had lived in the land for millennia, were marked for removal. Their villages were to be emptied, their homes demolished, their names erased.

One of Lehi's most notorious members was Yitzhak Shamir, who would later become Israel's Prime Minister (1983–84, 1986–90). Shamir personally oversaw operations that included political assassinations, sabotage, and the systematic targeting of those deemed enemies of the Zionist cause. His political ascent did not negate his past—it institutionalized it. The terrorist became the statesman, and the bloodshed was recast as patriotism.

Irgun Zvai Leumi, commonly referred to as Irgun, operated under similar principles but with even broader international ambitions. Led at one point by Menachem Begin—who would also become a Prime Minister of Israel—Irgun carried out a string of high-profile bombings and assassinations throughout the 1930s and 1940s. These were not random acts of violence. They were calculated strikes designed to terrorize the British into abandoning their mandate and to ethnically cleanse Palestinians from the land.

Irgun's most infamous act came on July 22, 1946, when they bombed the King David Hotel in Jerusalem, killing 91 people—including British officials, Arab staff, and Jewish civilians. This was not an accident. It was a deliberate attack on a civilian infrastructure target, and it became a blueprint for modern terrorism. Yet, in the halls of Israeli power, those who orchestrated it were hailed as heroes.

The group was not above moral betrayal either. During World War II, as Allied forces fought against the genocidal machinery of Nazi Germany, Irgun engaged in secret talks with representatives of Fascist Italy and Nazi Germany, seeking collaboration for a Jewish state in exchange for support. While Jews were being slaughtered in Europe, these Zionist militants were negotiating with the murderers. That is not resistance, it is opportunism dressed in nationalist rhetoric.

In November 1944, Lehi operatives assassinated Lord Walter Moyne, the British Minister of State for the Middle East, in Cairo. It was an act of political terrorism on foreign soil—an international signal that Zionist militants would stop at nothing. Lord Moyne had been viewed as an obstacle to unlimited Jewish immigration into Palestine. His murder marked a turning point. Even Winston Churchill, a lifelong supporter of Zionism, was appalled. But outrage was fleeting. The machinery of Western support for Israel continued undeterred.

In February 1942, British police tracked down and killed Avraham Stern in his apartment in Tel Aviv. But by then, his ideology had metastasized. Lehi continued its campaign, attacking British airfields,

sabotaging railways, and laying bombs at key strategic sites. These were
not resistance operations—they were blueprints for a violent ethnostate.

Menachem Begin, leader of Irgun and architect of numerous terror
campaigns, would one day accept the Nobel Peace Prize. But his past
cannot be whitewashed. Under his command, Irgun committed the
Deir Yassin massacre in April 1948—a slaughter of over 100 Palestinian
civilians, including women and children. The psychological terror it
induced caused a mass exodus of Palestinians, enabling the demographic
engineering of the new Israeli state.

And yet, this same man became Prime Minister. This same man
shook hands with world leaders. The message was clear: if your terror is
successful enough, it becomes diplomacy.

After the declaration of Israel's independence in 1948, members of
both Lehi and Irgun were absorbed into the Israel Defense Forces
(IDF)—the formal military of the new state. The transformation was
not a cleansing. It was a rebranding. The same men who had placed
bombs in marketplaces now wore uniforms. The same hands that had
assassinated British officers now saluted the Israeli flag. Terrorism was
not punished—it was promoted.

And to this day, the legacy remains.

The tactics pioneered by Lehi and Irgun—collective punishment,
targeted assassinations, home demolitions, and terror disguised as
national security—are standard operating procedures for the modern
IDF. The ghosts of Stern and Begin walk the streets of Gaza and the
alleyways of the West Bank. The Nakba, the catastrophic expulsion of
750,000 Palestinians in 1948, was not an aberration—it was the plan.

To understand Israel today, we must abandon the myth that its
birth was clean, moral, or defensive. The state did not rise from ashes, it
rose from corpses. It was not a refuge; it was a fortress built on
ethnonationalism, funded by imperial allies, and legitimized through
Western silence.

Those who still refer to Israel as the "only democracy in the Middle East" ignore the roots from which it sprung. Democracies are not born in bombs. Republics are not rooted in massacres. Freedom is not built upon expulsion.

The truth is this: the founding of Israel was engineered by terrorists, justified by colonial logic, and sanctified through historical revisionism.

The world did not gain a democracy in 1948. It gained another settler colony. Another apartheid regime. Another empire carved by blood, defended by myth, and whitewashed by history books.

And the world is still paying the price.

# The Destruction Of Warsaw And Gaza:
## TWO CHAPTERS, ONE GENOCIDAL SCRIPT

In the searing summer of 1942, under the tyranny of Adolf Hitler's Third Reich, more than 265,000 Jewish men, women, and children were forcibly deported from the Warsaw Ghetto in Poland to Treblinka, one of the Nazi regime's most ruthless death camps. It was not a deportation. It was a mass extermination in slow motion. Bodies were packed into cattle cars like grain, transported not to a place of refuge, but to a place of mechanized annihilation.

The Jewish youth of Warsaw, faced with extermination and betrayal, refused to go quietly. They formed a resistance movement, the Zydowska Organizacja Bojowa (ZOB)—the Jewish Combat Organization. Led by the brave Mordechai Anielewicz, these young fighters issued proclamations, urging their people not to board the trains of death. They took up arms against a regime that had classified them as subhuman.

Their uprising in January 1943, though tragically outgunned, was not a failure. It was a declaration: *we will not march willingly into the furnace of genocide.* Their resistance was a moral fire, burning through the steel of tanks and the lies of empire.

Fast forward to October 7, 2024.

## Decline of America and Israel: The Last Two Racial Apartheid White Colonial Nations

The land is different. The names have changed. But the story remains.

In Gaza, the world's largest open-air prison, another group of oppressed Indigenous people mounted a desperate resistance. Hamas, like the ZOB before them, arose not as an offensive force but as a response to decades of displacement, ethnic cleansing, siege, and starvation. Gaza is Warsaw in slow motion—its people walled in, bombed from the sky, deprived of clean water, electricity, and dignity. And yet, they fight.

On March 2024, the Republic of South Africa—whose own history is steeped in the blood of apartheid—filed a formal charge of genocide against the State of Israel at the International Court of Justice in The Hague. This was not merely a legal document. It was a mirror held up to the face of white imperial hypocrisy. For just as the Nazis sought to erase European Jews, so too has the Zionist government sought to erase the Palestinian people from their ancestral land.

This charge came from a country that knows genocide intimately. South Africa, once brutalized by white Dutch settlers, once carved into racial zones by colonial cartographers, once reduced to Bantustans and passbooks, recognized the pattern. The architects of apartheid in Tel Aviv and Washington, D.C., are simply applying old blueprints with new bombs.

It is no coincidence that in the era of apartheid, Israel and the United States were the main military suppliers to the white regime in Pretoria. When Nelson Mandela languished in prison for daring to imagine a non-racial South Africa, the U.S. and Israel were arming his jailers. When Black students protested, they were shot with bullets marked "Made in the USA." And now, when Palestinians protest, they are crushed under the treads of American-funded tanks.

Let us call this what it is: a transnational alliance of white colonial violence.

On the day Hamas launched its offensive on October 7, 2024, it did not target civilians out of malice. It struck out against a settler population backed by the full might of Western imperialism. What followed was not retaliation—it was a premeditated campaign of racial extermination. Prime Minister Benjamin Netanyahu, armed with billions of dollars in U.S. military aid, announced what can only be described as Israel's *Final Solution* to the Palestinian Question.

The parallels to Hitler's own plan are more than metaphorical.

Just as the Nazis sought to "cleanse" Europe of Jews, Israel now seeks to depopulate Gaza and the West Bank, to erase the memory, the bodies, and the rights of a people who have lived in the land for more than two millennia.

This is not hyperbole. It is the cold arithmetic of genocide. Bulldozed hospitals. Bombed refugee camps. Mass graves disguised as "counterterrorism." Over 30,000 Palestinians—half of them children— were slaughtered in less than a year. The Israeli Defense Forces (IDF), while proficient in killing women and children, have shown no courage when faced with real resistance, such as the Iranian military. Netanyahu has tried desperately to drag the United States into yet another war, not for freedom, but for fear that without U.S. protection, the apartheid regime would collapse like the Berlin Wall.

Back home in America, President Joseph Biden now finds himself in a moral and political crisis. His blind support for Israeli aggression has alienated the very people he claims to represent. African Americans, Indigenous peoples, and Latinx communities—all of whom know the sting of racial subjugation—see their own struggle reflected in the Palestinian fight for survival.

By 2030, the United States will be a majority-minority nation. The tides are turning. And with that demographic change comes a shift in loyalty. The next generation of American citizens—Black, Brown, Muslim, Indigenous—does not see Israel as a "beacon of democracy." They see it for what it is: the last active white settler colony on earth.

They remember.

They remember the Jewish Confederate slavers like Judah P. Benjamin, who owned hundreds of African people and helped design the legal architecture of the Confederacy. They remember the Monsanto family, Jewish plantation owners who made their fortune in human trafficking. They remember the Sacklers, who introduced OxyContin and fueled an opioid epidemic that destroyed millions of working-class lives. They remember Jeffrey Epstein, a Jewish financier and serial abuser who built a sex trafficking empire for America's most powerful white men.

These crimes are not about ethnicity. They are about power, privilege, and protection. The same systems that protected slavers, that armed apartheid, that excused genocide in Warsaw, now shield the genocidaires in Gaza.

Let us be clear: *to resist oppression is not to hate.* It is to survive.

And survival, for the Palestinian people, means standing against one of the most heavily armed regimes on earth—a regime whose legitimacy is not drawn from history or morality, but from colonial documents, imperial favor, and racial myth.

As the U.S. continues to arm and defend Israel, it, too, stands trial.

Just as the Jewish fighters in the Warsaw Ghetto made a last stand against extermination, so too do the people of Gaza. Their weapons may be crude. Their resistance may be desperate. But it is righteous.

Let history record: the United States and Israel are not defenders of democracy. They are architects of racial apartheid.

And like every empire built on bones, their reckoning is not a matter of *if,* but *when.*

## Israel: The Last White Apartheid Colony In The 21st Century Middle East

The modern State of Israel did not emerge naturally. It was strategically, militarily, and politically installed by two white imperial powers: Great Britain and the United States. The purpose was not liberation or safety for a historically persecuted people, but geopolitical control, specifically over the immense oil wealth of the Middle East. The creation of Israel marked a continuation of white colonial logic: to implant a culturally and racially aligned settler population into an indigenous landscape and secure dominance through dispossession, violence, and apartheid.

The European Jews who migrated to Palestine in the wake of the Balfour Declaration of 1917 did so under the patronage of the British Empire. These were not Semitic peoples indigenous to the land, but rather white Europeans, including Poles, Germans, and Russians, who were granted political legitimacy by Britain and later received military and economic support from the United States. Their settler logic mirrored that of the Afrikaners in South Africa—white Dutch Protestants who laid claim to African land and called themselves native. The architects of apartheid in South Africa were armed, funded, and defended by the same Western powers that built and now sustain Israel.

During the height of South Africa's racist regime, the governments of the United States and Israel worked in tandem to support the apartheid state. Arms flowed. Intelligence was shared. Ideologies aligned. In Palestine, as in South Africa, colonial settlers declared themselves the rightful heirs of land they did not originate from and began systematic campaigns of violence against the native population. These campaigns were not isolated clashes; they were organized acts of ethnic cleansing.

Israel was marketed to the world as a sanctuary for Holocaust survivors. But it has become an instrument of racial genocide against Palestinians, a people whose only crime has been existing in their own homeland. The irony could not be more grotesque. A state born from the ashes of European genocide now enacts, with U.S. weapons and funding, a slow-moving holocaust of its own.

This is not a metaphor. It is history repeating.

The parallel is clear: just as British settlers in Jamestown, Virginia, began the systematic extermination of Native Americans in the 1600s, so too did white European Jews, upon arriving in Palestine in 1948, begin a campaign of displacement and destruction. Like all colonial ventures, Canada, Australia, the United States, Belgium, France, Germany, and Japan, Israel joined the ranks of white-dominated democracies that masked genocide in the language of civilizational progress.

When South Africa filed a case at the International Court of Justice in 2024, charging Israel with racial genocide, it shattered the myth of Israel as a democratic exception. The nations that rose in defense of Israel were the very same powers who had blood on their hands: Britain, France, Germany, Australia, and the United States, each guilty of genocide in their colonial past. Their defense of Israel is not about justice. It is about protecting a system of white settler supremacy.

The Balfour Declaration itself, a 1917 letter from Lord Arthur James Balfour to Baron Rothschild, reveals the imperial design: a pledge that Britain would support a Jewish homeland in Palestine, not out of moral obligation, but as a tactical move to secure Zionist support in World War I. The indigenous population, Arab Palestinians, were never consulted. Their rights were never considered. They were the silent obstacle to be erased.

Following Israel's declaration of statehood in 1948, Zionist militias launched campaigns of terror—massacres in Deir Yassin, expulsions of entire villages, the erasure of Arabic names, and the destruction of olive groves that had stood for centuries. These actions echo the tactics used by European settlers across the Americas: divide, dispossess, and destroy. The Palestinian Nakba (catastrophe) is the Native American Trail of Tears, replayed in real time.

Ancient Rome once relied on the Middle East as its primary source of food. Jerusalem and Palestine provided food and taxes that sustained the empire. Today, it is oil. And the West's method of control remains unchanged: install loyal settlers, remove the natives, and extract the wealth. Israel is Rome in modern form—its generals wear suits, its legions fly drones.

Decline of America and Israel: The Last Two Racial Apartheid White Colonial Nations

Economists and historians alike recognize the project's unsustainability. According to Dr. Richard D. Wolff of the University of Massachusetts, Israel's militarized occupation cannot endure indefinitely. The moral, political, and economic costs are too high. As the United States funnels billions into Israel's military, it hemorrhages credibility across the Arab world. China, Russia, and Iran wait in the wings, building new alliances and shaping a multipolar world that no longer depends on the white Western order.

The war in Gaza, the conflict in Ukraine, and the larger battles for narrative dominance are not isolated. They are theaters in the final act of the Western empire. For over 500 years, Europe and its descendants have ruled through conquest and slavery. But that era is closing. In *The Half Has Never Been Told*, Dr. Edward Baptist documented how capitalism itself was built on the backs of enslaved Africans. Israel is simply the latest installment of that system, a settler colony pretending to be a democracy.

This pattern is older than Israel. In 1953, the CIA orchestrated a coup to remove Iran's democratically elected leader, Mohammad Mossadegh, after he attempted to nationalize the country's oil. The British-owned Anglo-Iranian Oil Company (now BP) had grown wealthy off Iranian resources while the population suffered in poverty. With President Eisenhower's approval and direct action by CIA agent Kermit Roosevelt Jr., Mossadegh was overthrown, and the Shah was installed. Roosevelt was later rewarded with a vice presidency at Gulf Oil.

Israel fits perfectly into this imperial lineage. Its creation and maintenance were never about Jewish safety; they were about Western access to Middle Eastern oil. Britain betrayed its promises to Arab leaders after World War I. The United States betrayed its own constitutional ideals by endorsing apartheid abroad while denying civil rights at home. Both powers viewed European Jews not as exiles, but as racial allies. Palestine was the frontier. Zionists were the new settlers.

The British allowed Jewish immigration under the condition that it would not harm native Palestinians. But like the Jamestown settlers before them, the Zionist movement treated the indigenous population as obstacles. What followed was a campaign of dispossession, state violence, and systematic erasure, continued today under Prime Minister Benjamin Netanyahu and supported, without shame, by President Joe Biden.

America has always followed the same model. After winning its independence from Britain, the United States waged a war of extermination against its Native population, breaking 381 treaties and constructing a reservation system so brutal that Nazi officials studied it as a model for their own concentration camps. According to historian Benjamin Madley, Senator Judah P. Benjamin, a Jewish lawmaker from Louisiana, helped fund California's Indian extermination campaigns with over $800,000 of federal money.

Judah P. Benjamin, a Confederate statesman and plantation owner, later served as Secretary of War under Jefferson Davis. He was deeply entangled in slavery and may have had links to the assassination of President Abraham Lincoln. As Robert Rosen details in *The Jewish Confederates*, many Jewish communities in the South supported the Confederacy, not as outsiders, but as participants in white supremacy.

Genocide is not an anomaly of history; it is its foundation. From settler colonies in the Americas to Zionist settlements in Palestine, from the Transatlantic Slave Trade to drone strikes in Gaza, the logic remains unchanged: take the land, erase the people, rewrite the narrative.

But the world is shifting. The empire is in decline. And history, long silenced, is speaking again.

## South Africa Charges Israel With Genocide

In March 2024, the Republic of South Africa—herself once shackled by the iron grip of apartheid—rose before the International Court of Justice at The Hague to declare what many in the Global South had long known: that the State of Israel, in its relentless military campaign against the Palestinian people, had committed acts constituting genocide. This was not merely a political gesture; it was a moral indictment—a confrontation with history.

This formal accusation came as bombs rained on Gaza, as homes were reduced to rubble, and as Palestinian women, children, the elderly, and the unborn were buried beneath the weight of Western silence. Israel, backed unequivocally by the United States and its NATO allies, pursued its campaign with impunity, cloaking military brutality in the language of self-defense while silencing international outcry through diplomatic threats and media manipulation.

But South Africa's charge cut deeper than current headlines. It peeled back centuries of colonial logic and exposed the transnational architecture of white supremacy.

Those nations who rejected the charge—America, Britain, Canada, Australia, Germany, and France—did so not because the evidence was lacking, but because the mirror was too clear. To indict Israel was to indict themselves. Each had authored their own genocidal scripts— scripts soaked in Indigenous blood, in stolen lands, in broken treaties and enslaved generations.

The United States, which proudly calls itself the leader of the free world, has never reckoned with its own genocidal past. From the genocide of Native nations during the 19th century to the systematic oppression of African-American people through slavery, lynching, Jim Crow, mass incarceration, and structural poverty, America's history is a symphony of erasure—its instruments of terror polished into symbols of national pride.

As I noted in *Why Muslim People Hate Donald Trump and America* (Ford, 2024), the United States is not innocent. Its record is one of persistent and unrepentant racial violence. This includes the calculated campaigns of extermination waged against Native populations in California between 1846 and 1876, where local militias funded by state and federal dollars massacred entire tribes. Historian Benjamin Madley calls it by its name: genocide. (Madley, 2018)

And yet, these crimes are not aberrations—they are precedent.

During the apartheid era, when Nelson Mandela led the fight against the white-minority regime in South Africa, it was the United States and Israel who armed that regime, feeding it weapons, intelligence, and financial aid. The victims were Black South Africans. The allies were white settler nations. The line of solidarity was drawn in race, not in justice. (Ford, 2022)

Just as the United States supported the dismantling of Indigenous sovereignty to fuel settler expansion, Israel was born of a similar betrayal. In 1917, the British Foreign Secretary Lord Balfour issued his infamous declaration promising a "national home for the Jewish people" in Palestine—land already inhabited by an Indigenous population. This promise was not forged from compassion but from political calculation. The European Zionist movement agreed to support Britain's war effort against Imperial Germany in exchange for colonizing Palestine. (Hourani, 1991)

In 1948, that colonial promise matured into the State of Israel. And from the moment of its declaration, a campaign of ethnic cleansing began. Over 700,000 Palestinians were driven from their homes in what is remembered as the *Nakba*, or "catastrophe." Entire villages were razed, communities shattered, and a nation scattered. The colonizer's script was reissued—this time with a different accent, but the same imperial intention.

As Howard Zinn explains, American history is not a progression toward justice but a masterclass in denial. Presidents like Woodrow Wilson, often praised for their diplomacy, were, in truth, devout racists who believed deeply in white superiority and colonial governance over non-white peoples. (Zinn, 1980)

The Sykes-Picot Agreement of 1916, followed by the Balfour Declaration in 1917, codified this imperial ideology. Whiteness, oil, and geopolitical control—not justice—determined who would inherit Palestine. Britain promised the land twice: once to the Arabs who fought alongside them against the Ottomans, and once to the Zionists. But betrayal is the language of empire.

When European Jews, many of them from Russia, Poland, Germany, and England, began settling in Palestine in large numbers, they did not come as neighbors. They came as settlers. Armed with European military training and fueled by a sense of racial-religious entitlement, they sought not coexistence but conquest.

In doing so, they replicated the very genocidal logic once used against them.

Israel today is not merely a state—it is the last surviving white racial settler colony engaged in a live campaign of extermination against its Indigenous population. Its existence as an apartheid regime is affirmed by human rights organizations across the globe, from Amnesty International to Human Rights Watch. Its policies of occupation, forced displacement, military blockades, and apartheid walls are not aberrations—they are standard practice.

In the courtroom of international conscience, South Africa stood alone among former colonial subjects, raising its voice not in vengeance, but in remembrance. For South Africa remembers what it meant to live beneath white boots. It remembers what it means to be told your life is less valuable, your culture irrelevant, your resistance criminal. And it recognizes that in Palestine, that same apartheid system has been perfected with Western support.

In 1956, African-Americans filed a formal petition to the United Nations, accusing the United States of genocide. Their documentation—detailing lynchings, segregation, denial of health care, and economic deprivation—met the same fate as today's charges: denial, dismissal, delay.

History does not forget.

Dr. Ford, in *Decline of America: The Last White Man's Empire and Rise of China: The Brown Empire* (2022), argues that the United States and Israel remain the last bastions of institutional white apartheid. Both nations incarcerate more people than any other on Earth. Both criminalize Black and Brown lives with impunity. Both mask their domestic genocidal practices beneath the language of freedom, democracy, and national security.

But the tide is turning.

The Global South, once colonized and voiceless, is now rising. The same nations that were once footnotes in imperial textbooks are standing on the floor of the world stage, demanding truth. Demanding accountability.

Those who voted in favor of South Africa's charge at The Hague are not merely states—they are survivors. Survivors of British hangings, French napalm, American coups, and Belgian mutilation. They recognize genocide because they have lived it.

The question before us is no longer whether genocide has occurred. It is: *How many times must the victims speak before they are heard?*

Let the record show: what South Africa filed in 2024 was not an accusation against Israel alone. It was a mirror held up to centuries of white colonial violence—American, British, French, German, and now, Israeli.

And in that mirror, the world saw its truth.

## The State Of Israel And The Final Solution For The Palestinian People

The modern State of Israel, formally established in 1948, did not emerge from divine decree or moral necessity. It was the direct byproduct of European imperialism, shaped by British foreign policy, and formalized through a promise never theirs to give. That promise came in 1917, with the Balfour Declaration—an infamous letter in which British Foreign Secretary Lord Arthur James Balfour assured Zionist leaders of British support for a Jewish homeland in Palestine. The land, however, already had a people. It had history. It had memory. That memory was Palestinian.

Decline of America and Israel: The Last Two Racial Apartheid White Colonial Nations

As documented in *Why Muslim People Hate Donald Trump and America* (Ford, 2024), the creation of Israel was less about justice for European Jews than it was about preserving Western hegemony in the oil-rich Middle East. Britain needed strategic allies. The United States needed regional footholds. And both found in Zionism a convenient vehicle for continued colonial influence.

Fast forward to 2024. Under the leadership of Israeli Prime Minister Benjamin Netanyahu—armed with billions in military support from U.S. President Joe Biden—Israel has unleashed what many now describe as its own "Final Solution" for the Palestinian people. With every missile strike, every blockade, and every home demolition, Israel advances a vision not of coexistence but of erasure. The language may differ from that of Adolf Hitler, but the logic remains chillingly familiar: define a people as a threat, and then eliminate the threat.

The Palestinians, the indigenous people of the land, have lived in Palestine for over 2,000 years. Their presence predates the modern state of Israel. Their connection to the land is spiritual, historical, and ancestral. And yet, they are labeled as "terrorists" in their own homes, denied the right to return, denied citizenship, denied dignity.

This settler logic is not new.

In 1603, when English colonists landed at Jamestown, Virginia, they declared that *God had given them the land.* The Native American nations who had lived in North America for over 10,000 years were soon slaughtered, displaced, or forced onto reservations. The justification was always religious. The violence was always racial. The settlers claimed they were "the chosen," and the Indigenous peoples were marked for removal.

This same divine delusion now drives Israel's actions. Zionist settlers—many of them white Jews from Poland, Russia, Germany, and the United States—claim that God promised them Palestine, and that their possession of the land is a fulfillment of Biblical prophecy. But I cannot reconcile this narrative with history. I cannot visualize people

with pale European skin—descendants of cold northern climates—
claiming to be the original Semitic people of Abraham, Isaac, and Jacob.

Let us speak plainly: European Jews, like white Dutch Afrikaners in
apartheid South Africa, or white British settlers in Australia, are foreign
to the land they now dominate. Just as the Boers claimed Africa as theirs,
and the British claimed Australia as a penal colony, European Jews claim
ownership of a land their ancestors neither sowed nor suffered for.

And the land is telling a different story.

The intense sun of Palestine, like the deserts of Africa and the valleys
of the American Southwest, was not made for pale skin. That is not an
insult—it is biology. The human body adapts to its environment. *Skin
color is determined by the climate and the ultraviolet exposure of a region.*
Pale skin is an evolutionary adaptation for survival in places where
sunlight is scarce—places like the forests of Germany or the snow-
capped Alps of Austria.

As a security staff member at the J. Paul Getty Museum, I observed
a simple but profound truth. Italians from the Mediterranean—Sicily,
Naples, Sardinia—were dark-skinned, bronze, and sun-weathered. But
Italians from the Alpine North were pale, freckled, and unable to bear
prolonged exposure to California's sun. Same nationality. Different
climate. Different color.

Modern science confirms what ancient geography already knew: 
*There is no such thing as a "white race."* There are humans with low
melanin, whose bodies adapted to colder regions with minimal sunlight.
And there are humans with high melanin, whose skin protected them
under equatorial suns. Pale skin is not a mark of superiority—it is a mark
of deficiency in ultraviolet protection.

According to studies by the American Institute of Dermatology,
melanin is the skin's natural defense system, a pigment shield forged
through millennia of sunlight. Those we call "white people" are not
white by nature, but by the suppression of the melanin-producing gene.
And that suppression is an evolutionary compromise—one that allowed
survival in dim climates, but left them vulnerable in hot ones.

Decline of America and Israel: The Last Two Racial Apartheid White Colonial Nations

A doctor once told me that many African-American children in California are diagnosed with Vitamin D deficiency. The irony is not in their health, but in their heritage. Their skin, rich with melanin, was designed for the African sun. But in northern latitudes, that melanin blocks the limited UV light needed to synthesize Vitamin D. Their very biology remembers where they are from—even if America has forgotten.

And here is the deeper truth: *people of color can produce children of all skin tones*—from light to dark. But white-skinned people cannot biologically produce color. The gene for melanin exists in them, but it is dormant, suppressed, silenced. This is not a moral failure—it is a scientific fact.

So when white settlers in Israel claim to be "the chosen people," to inherit a sun-drenched land they were never shaped for, we must ask: *Is this God's promise—or man's theft?*

We have heard this theology before. The same theology justified Manifest Destiny. It justified apartheid. It justified slavery. And now it justifies occupation, blockades, airstrikes, and the ethnic cleansing of Gaza and the West Bank.

Let the record show: *Zionism is not Judaism*. It is colonialism in religious disguise. The Torah did not mandate bulldozers and bombs. The prophets of old did not speak of apartheid walls and sniper towers. And no divine covenant authorizes the slaughter of children in refugee camps.

The State of Israel, in its current form, is not a refuge. It is an armed outpost of Western imperialism. And its treatment of Palestinians is not an exception to history—it is the continuation of it.

Like Jamestown. Like Cape Town. Like Sydney. Like Wounded Knee.

Palestine is the next chapter in the long, bloody book of settler-colonialism.

And this time, the world is watching.

## The World Court Has Issued An Arrest Warrant For The Top Hamas And Israel Benjamin Netanyahu

In a move that sent tremors through the corridors of global power, the International Criminal Court (ICC) at The Hague issued arrest warrants for top officials from both Hamas and the Israeli government, including Prime Minister Benjamin Netanyahu. It was a rare act of judicial clarity in a world accustomed to shielding the powerful. For the first time in recent history, the global legal system acknowledged that no leader stands above the law, and that state-sponsored terror, whether carried out by a stateless militant group or a Western-backed democracy, deserves equal scrutiny.

The origins of the World Court trace back to 1905, when Czar Nicholas II of Russia, haunted by the specter of war consuming Europe, proposed a tribunal that could arbitrate disputes before they turned into bloodshed. He envisioned a system that might check the ambitions of empires and preserve peace across continents. It was a noble idea, but nobility has never fared well in the face of empire. Especially the American Empire.

Following World War II, the United States, having emerged as the dominant superpower, chose to withdraw its support from the World Court. It feared not the injustice of others, but the accountability of its own. The architects of the American military-industrial complex knew what they were building: a permanent war machine, armed not just with bombs, but with immunity. To subject American generals, CIA agents, or elected officials to international law would threaten the illusion of moral superiority that undergirded every invasion, occupation, and coup.

That fear was not unfounded.

The World Court has since issued arrest warrants for former U.S. officials, including Henry Kissinger, whose orchestration of violence in Vietnam, Cambodia, and Chile transformed diplomacy into a tool of terror. George W. Bush, along with his Secretary of Defense Donald

Rumsfeld and Vice President Dick Cheney, remain wanted for their crimes during the Iraq War, where deceit was policy and destruction was the outcome. These men do not travel to Europe, not because they lack interest, but because Interpol would be waiting.

Only a handful of Bush's inner circle escaped the net. Colin Powell, who famously presented false evidence of weapons of mass destruction to the United Nations, avoided prosecution, though history has rendered its own judgment. Condoleezza Rice, the Secretary of State, likewise evaded formal charges. But the stain remains.

The crimes of the Bush administration were not abstract. They were etched into human flesh—in prisons, in bomb craters, in bodies never recovered. At Abu Ghraib Prison in Iraq, the United States stripped away its pretense of civility. American soldiers, aided in some cases by Israeli advisors, engaged in acts of torture that recalled the darkest pages of 20th-century history. Detainees were beaten, electrocuted, subjected to waterboarding, and sexually violated. The humiliation was not just physical—it was spiritual. Naked bodies were stacked like cargo. Human beings were made into props of dominance. And the images were not leaked by accident. They were part of a psychology of power, a message sent not only to the Arab world but to any population that dared to resist American hegemony.

When the images surfaced, they did not circulate on CNN or MSNBC first. Al Jazeera, the Arab world's leading news network, broadcast the atrocities to every corner of the Muslim world. The footage was graphic. But the truth often is. Muslims across continents— young and old, devout and secular—watched as the myth of Western democracy disrobed itself. The United States, which for decades had sold itself as the champion of liberty, was revealed in full depravity: naked, violent, and unrepentant.

And America did not act alone.

Israeli forces, with whom the United States shares billions in military aid and joint training operations, were complicit in many of the tactics used in Iraq. The Israeli Defense Forces (IDF), seasoned in the oppression of Palestinians, became informal advisors in interrogation, surveillance, and crowd control. What was tested in Gaza and Hebron was exported to Fallujah and Baghdad.

The Muslim world watched, not with shock, but with confirmation. What America called freedom, they saw as occupation. What America called democracy, they experienced as an invasion. What America hailed as human rights, they saw as rape, torture, and drone strikes.

And then America asked them to believe.

Believe in elections, while their leaders were overthrown. Believe in peace, while their children were blown apart. Believe in justice, while their prisoners were disappeared.

It was not a misunderstanding. It was a design.

The West preached freedom, but never practiced it where brown and Black lives were concerned. The language of democracy was often code for oil, control, and military dominance. And when challenged, the empire did not provide an explanation. It retaliated.

Now, in 2024, the World Court has done what few dared to expect. It has placed Benjamin Netanyahu, the head of the so-called only democracy in the Middle East, on the same legal footing as Hamas militants. It is not an equation of morality, but a recognition of method. Both have killed civilians. Both have bombed schools. Both have used fear as policy.

The charge is not biased. It is overdue.

When Netanyahu ordered the bombing of refugee camps in Rafah, when he blockaded humanitarian aid in Gaza, when he treated the deaths of Palestinian children as acceptable collateral damage, he crossed every threshold of international law.

And the world watched.

Just as they watched when American soldiers tortured prisoners. Just as they watched when drone strikes leveled wedding parties in Yemen. Just as they watched when Black bodies in Ferguson were gunned down with military-grade weapons in what was supposedly a democratic republic.

Let the record show: justice is not vengeance. Justice is the truth spoken aloud, without apology, and enforced without exception.

And let the record also show: those who speak of human rights while funding occupation have no moral ground left to stand on.

The Hague has spoken.

Now, the world must decide whether the law applies only to the defeated or whether even the powerful must answer for their crimes.

And if we are to survive, as a species and as a civilization, the answer must be this:

No one is above justice. Not Netanyahu. Not Bush. Not America. Not Israel.

Not anymore.

## President Joseph Biden's Support Of Israel In Their Brutal Genocide Of Palestinian People In The Israel-Palestinian War Of 2024 China Led China's Domination Of The Middle East

History does not turn on sentiment. It turns on action, arrogance, and blood. As the United States continues to finance and defend the ongoing genocide perpetrated by Israeli Prime Minister Benjamin Netanyahu, one that has already claimed the lives of over 40,000 Palestinian children, women, elderly, and noncombatants, the ground beneath the Western empire begins to crack. The foundations of American dominance in the Middle East, long fortified by oil wealth and military occupation, are beginning to collapse. And into the vacuum steps a new power: China.

Unlike the United States, China does not carry the legacy of racial genocide across three continents. It did not enslave Africa. It did not annihilate Native nations. It did not incinerate cities under the false banners of democracy and defense. And because of that, China approaches the Global South not as a colonizer, but as a rival to the colonizers.

The unraveling of Western influence in the Middle East is not an accident. It is a consequence. A consequence of American complicity. A consequence of decades of double-dealing, racialized warfare, and imperial arrogance dressed in diplomatic language. And now, after generations of propping up dictators, undermining democracy, and funding apartheid regimes, the West is being expelled from the very region it once claimed to control.

The United States and Great Britain, the twin architects of modern imperial policy, were the principal forces behind the birth of the settler-colonial State of Israel in 1948. After the devastation of two world wars, they sought to secure permanent access to the Middle East's oil fields by placing a friendly white outpost, armed and loyal, on Palestinian land. The Jewish state, carved by bullets and bolstered by Western arms, became the forward operating base of empire. Not a homeland for the oppressed, but a fortress for the oppressors.

This was not about Jewish survival. It was about Western supremacy.

In 1953, when Iran's democratically elected Prime Minister Mohammad Mossadegh dared to nationalize Iranian oil and redirect its profits to the Iranian people, the U.S. and Britain responded with fury. They conspired to remove him. The Central Intelligence Agency, working in tandem with British intelligence, launched **Operation Ajax**, a coup masquerading as a liberation. It was orchestrated by CIA station chief Kermit "Kim" Roosevelt, grandson of Theodore Roosevelt. For his service to Western oil interests, he was rewarded not with condemnation but with corporate appointments, particularly in Gulf Oil, the very entity that had eyed Iran's natural resources like a starving beast.

This was the true face of American foreign policy: democracy when convenient, dictatorship when profitable.

## Decline of America and Israel: The Last Two Racial Apartheid White Colonial Nations

The establishment of Israel was not simply a political favor to Zionist ideology, it was a military calculus. A geographic strategy. Britain and America needed an anchor in the Middle East, the same way Britain served as the staging ground for Allied forces in World War II. Israel was designed to be that island, a white colony in a sea of brown resistance. It would be armed to the teeth, subsidized by billions in U.S. aid, and shielded by vetoes at the United Nations.

It would be the new fort on the imperial frontier.

The model was not new. During the Indian Wars in North America, the U.S. military built forts across Indigenous lands. These forts were not symbols of defense. They were the machinery of extermination. Soldiers emerged by day to raid, burn, and massacre. By night, they returned behind the safety of walls. This strategy of racial warfare of fortress and fire led to the near-erasure of Indigenous nations. That same blueprint, exported to the Middle East, became the operational doctrine of Israel's occupation: destroy by day, retreat by night, repeat until nothing remains but rubble and ruins.

This was not policy. It was genocide by design.

And those who now rally to Israel's defense, especially President Joe Biden, are not neutral brokers. Biden, like many American politicians, is shackled to the interests of the pro-Israel lobby. Billionaires and lobbyists aligned with the Zionist agenda helped bankroll his campaigns, his coalitions, and his silence. When Gaza burned, Biden did not speak of ceasefires. He sent bombs. When Palestinian children were pulled from the wreckage, Biden offered condolences to Israel.

This is not diplomacy. It is complicity.

So when South Africa, a nation that endured white apartheid, rose before the International Court of Justice and charged Israel with genocide, the response from the so-called "civilized" West was predictable. Every colonial power that had once practiced genocide—Britain in Kenya, France in Algeria, Germany in Namibia, Canada against Indigenous children, Australia against Aboriginals, Spain across Latin America, and, of course, the United States itself rallied behind

Israel. They could not afford for this charge to stick, because it would implicate them all.

A conviction of Israel is a conviction of colonialism itself.

The West is not defending Israel out of alliance. It is defending itself from the mirror.

But that mirror has already cracked. The world is watching. The Global South is rising. And China, unburdened by the crimes of white colonialism, is moving in, not as an invader, but as a partner. Across Africa, Asia, and now the Middle East, China offers infrastructure instead of invasions, investment instead of regime change. It is not innocent, but it is not colonial.

The United States is bleeding out, not from foreign attacks, but from the moral hemorrhage of its hypocrisy. Its empire is dying in real time, not with a bang, but with a whimper—broadcast from Rafah, from Tehran, from Johannesburg, from Beijing.

The 21st century will not belong to the West.

It will belong to the survivors of its crimes.

And the fall of American influence in the Middle East is not just geopolitical. It is poetic.

For those who have lived under its bombs, buried their children under its rubble, watched their democracies strangled by its sanctions, and wept in the shadows of its embassies.

This is not the end of history.

This is justice, long delayed, finally arriving.

## Final Solution To The Jew-Palestinian Problem

**January 20, 1942, The Nazis Met at Wannsee for the Final Solution of the Jews' Problem.**

**On October 7, 2023, Benjamin Had His Final Solution to the Palestinians' Problem.**

Decline of America and Israel: The Last Two Racial Apartheid White
Colonial Nations

On January 20, 1942, high-ranking members of the Nazi regime
gathered at a villa in Wannsee, outside Berlin, to formalize what they
called the "Final Solution to the Jewish Question"—a systematic plan
for the racial extermination of all European Jews under Nazi control.
That conference, chaired by Reinhard Heydrich and authorized by
Adolf Hitler, marked a dark inflection point in modern history: the
moment genocide became government policy, carried out with chilling
bureaucracy and mechanized murder.

Eighty-one years later, on October 7, 2023, the State of Israel under
Prime Minister Benjamin Netanyahu convened his war cabinet in the
aftermath of the Hamas attack. What followed was not just a military
response—it was a calculated campaign of collective punishment against
the entire Palestinian population of Gaza, the West Bank, and Rafah.
Just as the Nazis used an act of resistance as a justification for mass
killing, Netanyahu's administration seized on a moment of violence to
initiate what many now describe as a modern-day Final Solution. This
time, not against Jews, but against Palestinians.

Netanyahu's war cabinet unleashed 2,000-pound U.S.-made bombs
on densely populated civilian areas. Apartment complexes, schools,
hospitals, churches, and refugee shelters were obliterated. Entire families
were buried under rubble, and survivors were denied food, water, and
medical aid. The United Nations discovered mass graves in Gaza, one
trench held the bodies of over 300 Palestinian men, hands bound,
executed in clear violation of international law. The pattern was
unmistakable. This was not counterterrorism. It was extermination.

The ideological parallels are undeniable. Netanyahu, like the Nazis
at Wannsee, sat with his ministers not to discuss peace, but to strategize
eradication. His weapons were supplied by the United States, and his
propaganda was reinforced by Western media. Like Heydrich,
Himmler, and Eichmann, who methodically drafted the Nazi blueprint
for genocide, Netanyahu and his inner circle operated with impunity,
believing the world would look away—or worse, approve.

## Decline of America and Israel: The Last Two Racial Apartheid White Colonial Nations

As Dr. Robert Fantano observed in *Empire, Racism, and Genocide* (2013), the United States has long supported white settler regimes engaged in racial conquest. From South Africa's apartheid government to the occupation of Palestine, U.S. policy has consistently sided with colonial powers rather than the colonized. During the Cold War, the U.S. labeled Nelson Mandela a terrorist while arming South Africa's white regime. Israel was among its strongest allies, sharing intelligence, weapons, and methods of suppression.

Even in Mandela's most desperate years, the United States and Israel provided arms, training, and funding to the apartheid military that massacred Black South Africans. Meanwhile, it was the Soviet Union that provided support to Mandela and the African National Congress, exposing the hypocrisy of American foreign policy. The United States has never supported an armed struggle of a non-white population fighting for liberation from a white colonial regime. Whether in Cuba, Vietnam, Iran, Chile, Guatemala, or Palestine, the U.S. sided with the colonizers every time—funding repression, training torturers, and silencing dissent.

On October 7, 2023, Netanyahu's final solution did not begin, but it intensified. The Gaza Strip, already under a 16-year blockade, became a free-fire zone. Civilians were ordered to flee south, only to be bombed there. The U.S. Biden administration, while calling for "restraint," authorized billions in emergency military aid to Israel, including bunker busters, missile systems, and ammunition. The bombs that fell on Palestinian hospitals were made in Tucson, Arizona, and shipped with bipartisan approval.

And just as Nazi propaganda dehumanized Jews with films, caricatures, and false accusations, Zionist propaganda today paints Palestinians as inherently violent—terrorists, animals, human shields. The same rhetorical devices once used to justify genocide in Europe are now employed to rationalize genocide in the Middle East. Israel's media, with global syndication, echoes Hollywood's historic racism, where Black and brown bodies are always threats, never victims, never human.

Decline of America and Israel: The Last Two Racial Apartheid White Colonial Nations

The ideology of Zionism, declared by the United Nations in 1975 to be "a form of racism and racial discrimination," is built on the premise that Jewish sovereignty in historic Palestine necessitates the removal, or rather, extinction, of its Indigenous Palestinian inhabitants. And like the Nazi ideology of racial purity, Zionism in its most radicalized political form refuses coexistence. It requires domination, erasure, and myth-making.

Let it be known that what Netanyahu's government pursued in October 2023 was not defense, it was a campaign of racial genocide. And it was not possible without the weapons, the financing, and the political cover of the United States of America.

In 1942, the Nazis enacted their industrial campaign of racial extermination using Zyklon B, a toxic gas originally developed as an insecticide. With this chemical, they murdered millions in concentration camps across Europe, primarily Jews, but also Roma, Slavs, communists, and others they deemed unworthy of life. Today, the tools are different, but the intent is no less lethal. In Gaza, Rafah, the West Bank, and East Jerusalem, the Israeli state, under Prime Minister Benjamin Netanyahu, has executed its own campaign of racial genocide, this time using F-16 fighter jets, bunker-busting bombs, and drone-guided missiles provided by the United States government.

Where the Nazis passed the Nuremberg Laws to legalize Jewish exclusion, modern Israel enforces laws rooted in religious apartheid, denying citizenship, voting rights, and legal protection to Palestinians and non-Jewish individuals. Israeli rabbinical codes prohibit marriage between Jews and non-Jews, echoing the Nazi laws that banned Aryans from marrying so-called "racial inferiors." The parallel is not merely rhetorical, it is legal, cultural, and violent.

And just as the United States once had anti-miscegenation laws, outlawing interracial marriage until the 1967 Loving v. Virginia Supreme Court ruling, it too operated as a white apartheid state, particularly before the Civil Rights Movement. According to Dr. Nikole Hannah-Jones in *The 1619 Project* (Jones, 2018), America's legal structure, culture, and politics were constructed explicitly to uphold white supremacy. In 1936, Black American Olympic athletes could stay in German hotels and eat in German restaurants—but back home, they were banned from white establishments. It was not until African Americans demanded full rights, through sacrifice and protest, that the United States began to move toward true democracy.

Yet the project remains incomplete.

America still echoes the colonial logic of racial hierarchy. Like Nazi Germany and colonial Britain, the U.S. engaged in the genocide of Indigenous peoples, the enslavement of Africans, and the continued suppression of Black and brown populations. In *Death in a Promised Land*, historian Scott Ellsworth (1982) documents the 1921 Tulsa Race Massacre, where white mobs, supported by law enforcement, murdered over 300 Black residents of Greenwood, Oklahoma. No one was ever prosecuted. The violence was buried—both literally and historically.

In modern Israel, the violence against Palestinians is not buried. It is broadcast. On March 22, 2022, the United Nations Special Rapporteur for Human Rights in the Occupied Palestinian Territory declared Israel to be a racist apartheid state. In 2023 and 2024, South African jurists and human rights organizations brought charges of genocide against Israel before the International Court of Justice, naming Netanyahu as the architect of what they described as a campaign of racial extermination. The evidence: bombed hospitals, mass graves, starvation, and the destruction of schools was televised to the world.

This campaign did not take place in secret. It unfolded live, with the complicity of the American government, which continued to fund, arm, and diplomatically shield Israel as thousands of civilians were killed. Netanyahu's war cabinet, much like the Nazi officials at Wannsee, coordinated logistics for ethnic cleansing. And the United States, led by President Joe Biden, enabled the machinery of genocide.

Biden now faces a reckoning.

His re-election campaign for November 2, 2024, is clouded by anger within the Black community, a community historically aligned with peace, human rights, and anti-colonial struggle. Many African Americans, rooted in the moral clarity of Dr. Martin Luther King Jr., who opposed the Vietnam War, now reject the administration's blind support for Israel's war on Gaza. Unlike the white American majority, who were seduced by propaganda during wars in Iraq, Afghanistan, and Vietnam, the Black community has consistently stood for justice over empire.

African Americans have always understood the nature of racial war.

They saw it in South Africa, where Israel and the U.S. supplied arms to the white apartheid regime. And they saw it in Palestine, where that same formula is being replayed: white settlers, backed by Western powers, subjugating Indigenous people in the name of security.

In contrast, Cuba, under Fidel Castro, provided critical support to South Africa's liberation. The Cuban military victory at Cuito Cuanavale in Angola (1987–1988) marked the beginning of the end for apartheid. Cuban soldiers, Black and brown, defeated the white supremacist South African army on African soil, turning the tide of history and making it possible for Nelson Mandela to walk free after 27 years of imprisonment. The United States and Israel, by contrast, supported the apartheid government until the very end.

Mandela's release was not a gift from the West—it was a victory won by anti-colonial resistance and global Black solidarity.

And now, that solidarity has turned toward Palestine.

As in South Africa, this is not merely a territorial conflict, it is a racial and colonial war. The Palestinians are Indigenous people. The Israeli settlers are predominantly white Europeans—Germans, Russians, Poles, Americans, and Britons, who arrived after 1948, following the United Nations' partition plan, with military backing from the United States and Britain. Since then, Israel has become the military extension of Western imperialism in the Middle East.

On October 27, 2024, Netanyahu's government launched a new phase of genocide, bombing Gaza and the West Bank, displacing families, seizing land, and continuing a project that began not with security, but with settler colonialism. The goal is not peace. The goal is control of land, water, gas, and oil, the natural resources of the region.

And once again, the West has chosen whiteness over justice.

## The Fall Of Israel Is The Last Stand Of Western Civilization In The Middle East

The fall of Israel, as it begins to unfold in the geopolitical and moral court of world opinion, represents far more than the decline of a single state. It signals the last stand of Western imperial domination in the Middle East. From the moment of its inception, Israel has functioned not only as a national homeland for displaced Jews of Europe but also as a Western outpost of colonial power, constructed atop the dispossession and erasure of an Indigenous population. Its fate, then, is inextricably linked to the legacy of empire, and its potential collapse marks the beginning of the end for Western dominance in the region.

The roots of modern Israel were planted not in 1948, but in 1917, when British Foreign Secretary Arthur James Balfour issued a letter to Lord Rothschild, pledging British support for the establishment of a "national home for the Jewish people" in Palestine. This promise, known as the Balfour Declaration, was made during World War I in exchange for Zionist political and financial support in undermining the German war effort. At the Paris Peace Conference of 1919, the British and French redrew borders and distributed colonial possessions, betraying both Arab nationalists, who had been promised independence for aiding in the defeat of the Ottoman Empire, and the Indigenous Palestinian people who had lived on the land for centuries.

The British and their American allies had no intention of absorbing the large number of displaced European Jews into their own borders. Instead, they sought to export the "Jewish problem" to Palestine. President Woodrow Wilson, an ordained Presbyterian minister and outspoken white supremacist, backed the British colonial vision. The Zionist project in Palestine was not born of humanitarian concern—it was engineered from the same ideological material that fueled British colonialism, American Manifest Destiny, and the racial hierarchies that upheld slavery and segregation.

When the modern state of Israel was declared in 1948, its foundation echoed the beginning of another settler-colonial experiment: the British colony of Jamestown, Virginia, in 1607. Just as the English settlers seized Indigenous American lands, slaughtered their inhabitants, and confined survivors to reservations, the Jewish settlers, largely European, immediately launched a campaign to remove Palestinians through massacres, forced displacement, and military conquest. The war of 1948 did not create a homeland, it initiated a Nakba, or catastrophe, that persists to this day.

And just as the United States was built upon genocide of Native Americans and enslavement of Africans, Israel, too, was founded upon the displacement of Indigenous Palestinians and militarized racial exclusion. As Dr. Deshay David Ford (2022) writes in *Decline of America: The Last White Man's Empire*, these twin settler colonies—America and Israel—mirror each other not just in structure, but in purpose: the creation of racial hierarchies for economic and political dominance.

The South African government, in 2024, filed formal charges at the International Court of Justice, accusing Israel of committing genocide against Palestinians. And predictably, every Western power that voted against this charge, the United States, the United Kingdom, Germany, France, the Netherlands, Belgium, and Canada, had itself been built upon the bones of Indigenous peoples in Africa, Asia, or the Americas. To indict Israel would be to indict themselves.

As historian Dee Brown documented in *Bury My Heart at Wounded Knee* (1970), the United States' own genocidal campaign against Native Americans spanned over 300 years and continues today through systemic poverty, reservation ghettoization, and erasure. Meanwhile, Palestinians endure the same structures of land theft, military occupation, and cultural elimination.

And the echoes of empire do not end there.

Many of the financiers and architects of modern American capitalism, particularly families like the Monsantos of New Orleans, profited first from the transatlantic slave trade, then transitioned into chemical and agricultural empires. As Dr. Ford notes, the Monsanto family, originally involved in the slave shipping business, later founded the chemical giant Monsanto Corporation, infamous for manufacturing Agent Orange, a defoliant that caused cancer, birth defects, and environmental devastation during the Vietnam War.

Similarly, the Sackler family, Jewish-American owners of Purdue Pharma, knowingly marketed OxyContin, an opioid that has killed hundreds of thousands of Americans. In pursuit of profit, they ignited one of the worst drug epidemics in U.S. history, leading to mass addiction, broken families, and rural economic ruin. Despite massive lawsuits, the Sacklers managed to protect over $1 billion in personal wealth, further demonstrating that in America, power rarely faces consequence, especially when cloaked in whiteness or wealth.

These economic empires, whether in plantation slavery, toxic pharmaceuticals, or military-industrial weapons sales, interlock with Zionism's economic ambitions. Natural gas off the coast of Gaza, pipelines, arms contracts, and surveillance technologies are not incidental to the war, they are central to it.

The State of Israel, under Prime Minister Benjamin Netanyahu, continues to receive unconditional military, financial, and diplomatic support from the United States, even as evidence of ethnic cleansing in Gaza, Rafah, and the West Bank mounts. Netanyahu's government has leveled hospitals, refugee camps, and UN shelters, often with U.S.-made weapons—killing tens of thousands, many of them women and children.

The world has watched this real-time genocide, streamed live on phones and televisions, as Palestinians are slaughtered, starved, and silenced. And yet, Western governments invoke the language of "security," just as Adolf Hitler's Nazi regime once invoked the need for security in its "Final Solution."

What Israel is doing in Palestine is not different in substance from what Nazi Germany did to Jews, Roma, and others in Europe. It is genocide; a racialized, systematized extermination of a people, made possible by the same logic of supremacy, settler conquest, and mythologized victimhood.

When American politicians speak of human rights, they do so with the same duplicity as Nazi propaganda minister Joseph Goebbels, who cloaked atrocity in the language of patriotism and purity. The United States has no moral authority to denounce genocide, it has committed it, funded it, and continues to enable it.

The tragic irony is that many American Jews, historically victims of the Holocaust, now live in a nation whose policies support another people's holocaust, and that some leaders in Israel cite Jewish suffering as justification for perpetrating new suffering. But genocide is never justified, not by memory, not by trauma, and certainly not by faith.

Let us remember that the descendants of enslaved Africans, the descendants of colonized Native Americans, and the descendants of Holocaust victims all live in this world today. But only some are allowed to claim innocence while they repeat the sins of history.

The United States and Israel share not only weapons and ideology—they share a common destiny as settler empires built on blood. As one falls, so too does the other. And the world, long silent, is beginning to rise.

# The Oslo Accords Of 1995, An Agreement Between Israel And The Palestinian People

Benjamin Netanyahu, the white racist leader of Israel, presides over an apartheid state that continues to perpetrate genocide against the Palestinian people. This genocide is not an accident of war or a tragic misunderstanding of politics. It is deliberate, systematic, and tied directly to the natural resources that lie off the coast of Gaza. Beneath the waters of the Mediterranean rest vast reserves of oil and natural gas, resources whose value runs into the trillions. It is for these resources that Israel, with the backing of the United States and Europe, wages war upon an already displaced and suffering people.

The Oslo Accord of 1995, signed between Israel and the Palestinian Liberation Organization (PLO), formally granted the Palestinian National Authority the rights to control the natural gas and oil resources off Gaza's coast. That agreement, fragile and limited as it was, recognized Palestinian ownership of these resources. And it is precisely this recognition that Netanyahu and Israel's far-right coalition cannot accept. Their goal is to erase the Palestinian people in order to seize these resources for themselves. Netanyahu and his allies—the Israeli equivalent of Nazi racists—mask their objectives in the language of security, but the truth is plainer: they want the oil and gas that belongs to Palestine.

The United States is deeply complicit. Like Israel, America is a racist, apartheid nation whose elites see Gaza's resources not as Palestinian wealth but as fuel for the survival of the American empire. Just as white settlers in South Africa once declared themselves "Afrikaners" and imposed apartheid upon Black South Africans, so too do white settlers in Israel declare themselves Jews while building an apartheid state upon Palestinian land. Their claim is not rooted in Indigenous identity but in European colonialism.

The parallels are undeniable. During Nelson Mandela's struggle against the white settler regime in South Africa, both the United States and Israel supplied weapons to the apartheid government. Those weapons were used to kill and murder Indigenous Black South Africans who demanded freedom and dignity. Today, the same powers repeat the same crime: the United States arms Israel's settlers to kill and murder Indigenous Palestinians. The weapons may be newer, the language more modern, but the logic is the same—white power armed against brown life.

Decline of America and Israel: The Last Two Racial Apartheid White Colonial Nations

Most white Americans support this transfer of arms. Their solidarity lies not with the oppressed but with the oppressors. By contrast, African Americans have long recognized the struggle of the Palestinian people as their own. Black people in the United States know from lived experience the machinery of racism, genocide, and dispossession. In 1951, a delegation of Black activists, including Paul Robeson, submitted a petition to the United Nations charging the U.S. government with genocide against its Black citizens. Their case documented lynchings, state-sanctioned violence, and systemic oppression, placing America in violation of the Genocide Convention.

This charge was no exaggeration. As historian Dee Brown shows in *Bury My Heart at Wounded Knee* (Brown, 1970), the United States committed a racist holocaust against its Indigenous peoples, seizing their lands and natural resources through war, massacre, and forced removals from 1781 to the present. By 2024, Indigenous communities in America still survive in inhumane conditions, confined to reservations that function as concentration camps.

The Oslo Accord, then, was not simply a piece of diplomacy. It was a recognition of Palestinian rights to their own wealth, rights now under direct assault by Netanyahu's Israel and its Western allies. The genocide in Gaza is not only about politics; it is about resources. The Palestinians are being erased because their land and waters hold what empire desires most.

# Section IV:
# U.S. Wars, Torture, Covert Programs &
# Imperial Atrocities

# Abu Ghraib Torturing And Prison Abuse Iraq

During the U.S.-led invasion of Iraq in March 2003, the American empire once again revealed its imperial logic through blood and cruelty. At the Abu Ghraib prison, once a symbol of Saddam Hussein's brutality, the U.S. military and intelligence services, aided by Israeli operatives and private contractors, created a theater of horror. Men, women, and even children were subjected to a program of systemic torture: beatings, electrocution, rape, forced nudity, sodomy, psychological torment, and murder.

This was not the isolated conduct of a few rogue soldiers. It was institutionally sanctioned sadism, carried out with strategic intent. Photographs later leaked to the public—images of hooded men, human pyramids, and leashed prisoners—revealed not only the depravity but the pride with which these war crimes were committed. One of the figures central to this horror was Sergeant Charles Graner, a former corrections officer from Virginia's prison system with a history of documented brutality. At Abu Ghraib, Graner did not deviate from his past, he simply brought the tactics of the American carceral state to foreign soil under the banner of freedom.

The American president at the time, George W. Bush, justified the invasion with the rhetoric of democracy and anti-terrorism. But like all empires, his true motive was oil. Iraq, with its vast reserves, was never merely a geopolitical adversary—it was a target for its resources. Bush's campaign echoed Adolf Hitler's 1941 invasion of the Soviet Union: both sought control over oil as a means to global dominance. The attacks of September 11, 2001, gave Bush the perfect alibi. Behind the smokescreen of national security, the U.S. embarked on a war long in the making, fueled by greed, orchestrated through lies, and executed through genocide.

Since the close of the Second World War, the United States has anchored itself in the Middle East, not as a liberator, but as a colonial force. Whoever controls the region's oil controls the empire's future. But

Bush failed. His campaign to seize Iraq's oil wealth, destabilize the region, and impose American hegemony collapsed under its own contradictions. Instead, the tides shifted eastward.

China, with patience and precision, began investing diplomatically and economically in the very region the U.S. sought to dominate by force. Beijing secured agreements with the Saudi crown, deepened partnerships with Gulf states, and expanded its naval capacity. The Chinese navy now eclipses America's in size, with warships steadily deployed and built, not through conquest, but through strategic alignment. While the U.S. bleeds from endless wars and internal division, China builds. The era of the white empire is coming to a close. The Chinese century is not something from the future. It's already here.

But America has not retreated quietly. Its unwavering alliance with Israel remains a central pillar of its imperial identity. In supporting the Israeli occupation and genocide in Palestine, the U.S. has tied its legacy to one of the most visible and brutal settler colonial projects of the modern era. Since 1948, Israel has worked not for coexistence, but for the erasure of an entire people, the Palestinians. Through bombardment, military checkpoints, land seizures, and apartheid walls, Israel has enacted what legal scholars and human rights experts have now named explicitly: genocide.

The Israeli Defense Forces, with full financial and military backing from the United States, have targeted schools, hospitals, mosques, and refugee camps. The goal is not just to acquire territorial control, but cultural and racial extermination. This settler violence mirrors the historical pattern of other white colonial regimes, most notably apartheid South Africa.

In South Africa, white settlers claimed Afrikaner identity while dispossessing native populations under racial laws. Nelson Mandela's African National Congress (ANC) rose to resist, only to be labeled terrorists by Western governments, including the United States. During the Angolan conflict of the 1980s, it was not the U.S. or NATO that stood for African liberation; it was the Cuban army under Fidel Castro that decisively turned the tide against white South African forces. The same U.S. government that armed Israel also armed apartheid South Africa. The parallels are not accidental. They are structural. They are imperial.

When the post-apartheid government of South Africa filed charges of genocide against Israel at the United Nations, it reignited a deep historical memory. The same white powers: Britain, France, the U.S., Canada, Australia, Germany, and Belgium, who once colonized the Global South and perpetrated unspeakable genocides, now stood once again on the side of racial violence. These nations not only enabled the colonization of Palestine; they armed it.

Michael Lynk, former UN Special Rapporteur on Human Rights in the Occupied Palestinian Territories, concluded in his reports that Israel's fifty-five-year military occupation constitutes a system of apartheid. This was not speculation. It was a legal fact, supported by evidence, survivor testimony, and historical documentation.

The United States, long the loudest voice of moral superiority, has become the silent partner to genocide. Its presidents shake hands with war criminals. It's Congress that funds bombs that fall on refugee camps. It has chosen a side—the side of racial violence, settler colonialism, and permanent war. All the while, it proclaims itself a beacon of democracy.

But the truth is written in the ruins: Gaza, Fallujah, Kandahar, My Lai, and Hiroshima. The United States was never merely a nation; it was an empire built by enslaved labor, sustained by violence, and addicted to dominance.

Even before it became a formal state, the colonial settlers in Jamestown, Virginia, engaged in genocidal campaigns against the Indigenous nations of North America. Between 1603 and 1890, the U.S. government, through forced removals, massacres, and broken treaties, committed what international law would today recognize as genocide.

And yet, America teaches its children about freedom. It tells them it was born of liberty, not slavery. It says nothing of the fact that it remains the only modern industrial power whose infrastructure was literally constructed by enslaved Black bodies.

An empire built on bones cannot endure. And history remembers, even when nations forget.

# United States' Airforce Pilots Massacred Thousands Of Iraq's Citizens On Road Of Death

In the waning days of the Gulf War in February 1991, as ceasefire terms had already been negotiated and hostilities formally declared over, one of the most gruesome and morally indefensible war crimes of modern American military history was committed; buried beneath the rhetoric of victory, sanitized by Pentagon press releases, and erased from the annals of "just war." It occurred on a six-lane highway stretching from Kuwait to Basra, now known across the Arab world as the **Highway of Death**.

As thousands of Iraqi soldiers, many of them young conscripts forced into battle, retreated northward alongside civilians attempting to flee the devastation, U.S. Air Force and Navy pilots rained hell upon them. These were not armed combatants in an active war zone; these were retreating, defeated men, many of whom were surrendering, some were wounded, and others were simply hoping to return to their families. Alongside them were women and children, packed into cars, buses, and military trucks. The attack, executed with cluster bombs, missiles, and heavy machine-gun fire, turned the highway into a corridor of charred flesh and twisted metal.

More than 2,000 human beings were incinerated, their bodies left to rot in the desert sun. Tanks and buses became funeral pyres. The official justification was simple: military necessity. But the truth, stripped of its patriotic veneer, is far more sinister. The United States Air Force did not engage an enemy; it exterminated a retreating population.

Even some within the military's own command structure saw the horror for what it was. General Colin Powell, then Chairman of the

Joint Chiefs of Staff, was reportedly informed of the scale and nature of
the massacre and ordered an immediate halt. But by then, the damage
had been done. Thousands lay dead, slaughtered after the guns were
supposed to be silent.

This grotesque display of racialized militarism mirrored the darkest
atrocities of the 20th century. Heinrich Himmler, architect of Hitler's
Final Solution, once lamented that the act of constant killing eroded the
psyche of German soldiers. And yet, for the white American pilots
tasked with raining death upon Arabs fleeing across the sand, there
seemed to be no such anguish. According to firsthand accounts and later
journalistic investigations, they took pleasure in it. They laughed. They
posed for photos. They watched bodies scatter beneath the firepower of
the world's most advanced killing machines.

This is not a defense. This is not security. This is imperial carnage
disguised as "precision warfare." And like every colonial massacre before
it—be it My Lai in Vietnam or Sand Creek in Colorado-it was
committed not against an equal foe, but against a people designated
inferior, expendable, non-white.

Race continues to be central to American militarism. The soldiers
on that road were brown, while the civilians were Muslim, situated in
Arab land. In the sky, the pilots, symbolizing the overwhelming force of
Western military dominance, were predominantly white men raised in
a culture that perceives Arab lives as mere afterthoughts in the quest for
empire.

This event, conveniently buried in history books and omitted from
most mainstream curricula, remains a glaring example of American
hypocrisy. The very nation that claims to uphold international law
violated it in broad daylight. The very military that boasts of its "moral
clarity" burned human beings alive after declaring peace.

**It was a war crime. And it was racialized.**

The Pentagon never stood trial. The pilots were never charged.
There was no tribunal, no reckoning, no reparations; just silence and
smoldering wreckage stretching for miles across the desert. The global

media, subservient to American narratives of triumph, referred to it as a "victory." But those with eyes to see understood it for what it was: a massacre, engineered by imperial arrogance and executed with chilling efficiency.

# United States Engaged In Terrorist Assassinations And Murdering In Vietnam In The Phoenix Project 1965-1975

The mythology of American war-making often paints its violence as virtue, its bullets as the price of freedom, its interventions as noble crusades against tyranny. But the truth, buried beneath a thousand medals and a million lies, is that the United States has long mastered the art of terror. Nowhere is this more grotesquely evident than in the Central Intelligence Agency's covert operation known as The Phoenix Program, conducted in South Vietnam between 1965 and 1975.

This was not a war against communism. It was a campaign of state-sponsored assassination, torture, and psychological warfare—waged not on enemy soldiers in open combat, but on civilians, elders, teachers, students, and entire villages suspected of mere sympathy toward the North Vietnamese.

The Phoenix Program was conceived under the guise of "neutralizing the Viet Cong infrastructure." In reality, it was a blueprint for systematic elimination. Its architects, sitting safely in Langley and Saigon, drew up blacklists of suspected communist sympathizers, often without evidence, due process, or trial. Once named, these individuals were marked for interrogation, disappearance, or execution.

At the center of this machinery of death stood the CIA, which operated through shadowy detention centers scattered across the countryside. These were not intelligence stations. They were torture chambers. Under CIA training and oversight, South Vietnamese operatives were taught not just how to extract information, but how to break the human spirit through electric shocks, waterboarding, mutilation, sexual violence, and staged executions.

The scale of violence was staggering. According to the CIA's own records, over 20,000 people were *assassinated* during the Phoenix Program—many of them civilians. Others place the number far higher. And the goal was never rehabilitation or justice. It was liquidation.

In his seminal work *Decent Interval* (1978), CIA analyst Frank Snepp, stationed in Saigon, chronicled the inner workings of the program. What he revealed was not an operation gone wrong—it was one functioning exactly as designed. Torture was not a tool of last resort. It was standard operating procedure. Detainees, including women and children, were routinely subjected to brutal physical and psychological abuse.

Snepp described how American personnel, unburdened by conscience or oversight, would oversee interrogations with voyeuristic fascination. Vietnamese women prisoners were especially vulnerable— treated not as enemy combatants but as objects for humiliation and sport. After the screams stopped, after the bruises had set, the same men would retreat to Saigon's brothels, drowning their depravity in whiskey and sex.

There was no moral conflict. There was only routine.

Overseeing this nightmare from the shadows was William Colby, the CIA station chief in Vietnam and later Director of Central Intelligence. Colby defended the Phoenix Program as a necessary evil, a "counterinsurgency tactic" designed to win hearts and minds. But hearts were stopped, not won. Minds were broken, not persuaded.

Colby claimed that Phoenix made Vietnam safer for democracy. But what it created was a wasteland of suspicion, betrayal, and terror. Families were turned against each other. Children watched their parents dragged away. Villages vanished overnight. And all of it was funded, equipped, and authorized by the U.S. government.

To speak of war crimes in Vietnam is to speak of the entire American presence there. But Phoenix stands out as a model of mechanized terror—one that would later inspire counterinsurgency tactics in Latin America, Iraq, and Afghanistan. What began in the jungles of Southeast Asia would become a transnational doctrine of suppression, exported under the banner of freedom.

The program trained over 85,000 South Vietnamese agents in methods of psychological and physical warfare. These were not soldiers. They were executioners with clipboards. Targets were identified, dossiers prepared, and "neutralization" orders signed without trial or testimony. A knock on the door at midnight often meant the end of a life and the disappearance of a truth.

To this day, the Phoenix Program remains one of the least-discussed atrocities of the Vietnam War. It is not taught in American classrooms. It is not enshrined in monuments. There are no national apologies, no trials at The Hague, no Truth and Reconciliation commissions. Instead, its architects were promoted, its files sealed, and its lessons studied for future use.

The same tactics that defined Phoenix—black site torture, indefinite detention, extrajudicial killings—would reemerge decades later in Abu Ghraib, Guantánamo Bay, and the drone warfare programs of the War on Terror. The names changed. The victims changed. But the logic remained: eliminate resistance by eliminating people.

This is not history; it is policy.

The Phoenix Program was not a rogue operation. It was not a deviation from American values. It was the manifestation of those values warped by empire, sharpened by fear, and deployed with impunity.

The United States, in its imperial quest to crush communism in Vietnam, became what it claimed to fight. It murdered civilians. It tortured women. It silenced the truth. And it built an empire of terror on the ruins of another nation's sovereignty.

Let the record show: the CIA's Phoenix Program was not counterterrorism.

It was terrorism.

By design. By doctrine. By deliberate, bureaucratic choice.

And the blood it spilled is still drying in the soil of Vietnam.

# The United States Placed Nelson Mandela On Their List Of Terrorists For 1990

History has a strange habit of labeling the oppressed as aggressors and the liberators as terrorists—especially when those liberators threaten the interests of white colonial regimes. So it was with Nelson Mandela, the face of African liberation and the moral titan of South Africa's anti-apartheid movement, whom the United States officially branded a terrorist.

Yes, the man who would one day become a global symbol of justice and reconciliation—who would be awarded the Nobel Peace Prize and welcomed as a hero at the White House—remained on the United States terrorism watchlist until 2008. Not during his days as a young revolutionary, but *well after* his release from prison in 1990, even as he stood as the first democratically elected Black president of South Africa.

This wasn't a clerical error.

This was policy.

A deliberate attempt to criminalize the struggle for Black freedom because that struggle challenged the white colonial order that America, Israel, and their Western allies were deeply invested in maintaining.

Before its democratic transformation in 1994, South Africa was not a state—it was a settler fortress. A European enclave forged through blood, forged through theft, and maintained through institutionalized racism. Apartheid was not an aberration. It was the system. And America supported it. And Israel armed it.

The apartheid regime of South Africa—white, European, and fiercely nationalist—found its ideological twin in the State of Israel, particularly under the rule of Prime Minister Benjamin Netanyahu, whose ongoing campaigns in Gaza, Rafah, and the West Bank mirror South Africa's tactics of racial segregation, containment, and extermination.

Decline of America and Israel: The Last Two Racial Apartheid White
Colonial Nations

Where apartheid South Africa built townships and imposed
passbooks, modern Israel builds walls, imposes blockades, and drops
bombs. The goal remains the same: to remove and erase the Indigenous
population.

In Nazi Germany, Adolf Hitler tried to conceal his crimes. The
trains ran at night. The camps were hidden in the forests. The
Holocaust, monstrous and methodical, was carried out in the shadows.
But Benjamin Netanyahu has no such fear of the world's gaze. His war
on the Palestinian people is broadcast in high definition.

Since October 2023, and again in 2024, the world has witnessed in
real time what South Africans once endured behind prison walls and
razor wire: a campaign of collective punishment, mass displacement, and
ethnic cleansing. Whole neighborhoods in Gaza have been reduced to
rubble. Families buried beneath concrete. Hospitals turned into mass
graves.

It is apartheid unmasked. Genocide digitized.

As South Africa once stood isolated in the international community
for its racial crimes, so now does Israel, with the crucial difference being
that Israel is protected, not punished, by the United States. The same
United States that once called Nelson Mandela a terrorist now sends
billions in military aid to the architects of mass death in Gaza.

America, a nation that claims to revere Mandela, spent decades
branding him an enemy. Why? Because Mandela dared to challenge a
system that resembled America's own legacy of racial apartheid.

The apartheid regime of South Africa was not isolated. It was
propped up by the West. American and Israeli weapons flowed freely
into Pretoria. Intelligence-sharing was routine. Economic sanctions
were resisted for years. The message was clear: white power, no matter
how brutal, was preferable to Black liberation.

Even as images of Mandela languishing in a Robben Island prison
cell stirred global conscience, the United States kept him on the
watchlist. Even as South Africans marched, died, and voted for freedom,

the U.S. State Department maintained its position: Mandela was dangerous. Mandela was subversive. Mandela was a terrorist.

But who defines terror?

Tulsa 1921: America's Mandela Moment

To understand how the United States could support apartheid abroad, one needs only to look inward, at Tulsa, Oklahoma, 1921. On June 1, a white mob, armed and sanctioned by silence, obliterated the thriving Black community of Greenwood, known as Black Wall Street. Over 300 Black Americans were slaughtered. Thousands were left homeless. And for decades, the massacre was scrubbed from textbooks, censored from libraries, and omitted from the public record.

The white power structure didn't just erase lives—it erased the evidence.

Just like Hitler.

Just like Netanyahu.

The pattern is consistent: genocide hidden by propaganda, terror sanitized through national myth.

The Final Solution, Then and Now

In 1941, Adolf Hitler launched the "Final Solution"—the calculated extermination of European Jews. Six million lives extinguished. The world said, "Never again."

And yet, on October 20, 2024, Benjamin Netanyahu began what can only be described as his own final solution—a campaign to "solve" the Palestinian question by eliminating its people. In Gaza, in Rafah, in the West Bank, Palestinians were bombed, starved, caged, and buried.

Unlike Hitler, Netanyahu did not hide his actions. He invited the world to witness—armed with American bombs, emboldened by Western silence. He counted on complicity. And he was right.

America, the same nation that outlawed Mandela while arming apartheid, now defends Israel's right to self-defense, while offering no such defense to Palestinians being vaporized in their homes.

Decline of America and Israel: The Last Two Racial Apartheid White
Colonial Nations

Nelson Mandela was not a terrorist, he was a freedom fighter. He was imprisoned for resisting a white colonial regime funded and defended by the same Western powers that now applaud his memory while perpetuating his enemies' methods.

Benjamin Netanyahu is not a liberator.

He is a modern-day pharaoh, unleashing plagues on the people of Palestine. He bombs civilians, destroys hospitals, imprisons children, and calls it security.

And the United States, once again, stands on the wrong side of history.

They did it in Tulsa. They did it in Vietnam. They did it in South Africa.

And they are doing it in Gaza.

The world cannot afford amnesia.

We must remember not only Mandela's smile but his rage—his commitment to armed resistance when peaceful protest was met with bullets. We must remember that America called him a terrorist not because he was violent, but because he was Black, defiant, and unwilling to bow to whiteness.

And we must remember that justice delayed—especially when filtered through white hands—is justice denied.

Nelson Mandela once said:

"It is always the oppressor, not the oppressed, who dictates the form of the struggle."

Let the record show—when freedom becomes terrorism, and genocide becomes defense, it is time to rewrite the definitions.

It is time to remember what the powerful want us to forget.

And it is time to say, clearly and without compromise:

Nelson Mandela was never a terrorist.

America was.

# George Herbert Walker Bush's War Against Saddam Hussein 1990-1991

In 1990, George Herbert Walker Bush launched what would come to be known as the Gulf War. The justification presented to the American public and the world was the Iraqi invasion of Kuwait, a small oil-rich nation strategically vital to the West. But beneath the surface of that conflict were deeper motivations—motivations tied to oil, to empire, to race, and to the unspoken theology of American domination.

Iraq's president, Saddam Hussein, had indeed invaded Kuwait, claiming historical territorial disputes and accusing the Kuwaiti regime of economic sabotage through oil overproduction. But once Iraqi troops crossed the border, the reaction from Washington was swift and absolute. President Bush refused all offers from Hussein to withdraw, refused to engage in negotiation, and refused any attempt to prevent war. This was not because peace was impossible. It was because war was already chosen.

The Gulf War was not just about oil. It was a spectacle of supremacy. A message from the United States to the Global South that no nation of color, no Arab leader, no military in the Middle East could ever challenge the authority of white Western empire.

Bush did not speak of racial conquest in those terms, but his actions were saturated with it. He referred to Saddam Hussein as a tyrant, a madman, a beast, evoking the same racialized dehumanization that Western leaders have long used to justify violence against Black and Brown nations. Beneath the language of freedom and democracy was the logic of punishment. Bush wanted to teach Hussein a lesson. Not for invading Kuwait, but for daring to stand up to the United States.

And to do so, Bush sought divine permission.

Before launching the attack, George H. W. Bush reportedly consulted with Reverend Billy Graham, the most prominent spiritual figure in white American evangelicalism. Graham told Bush that war was necessary. That violence, in this case, was justified. That bombing Iraq was not only politically sound, but spiritually endorsed.

This was not the first time Billy Graham had aligned Christianity with American warfare. He had long been the spiritual counselor of presidents, a voice that sanctified state violence as divine duty. During the Vietnam War, he publicly supported U.S. military intervention and used his influence to shield his son, Franklin Graham, from the military draft. When thousands of young African American men were being shipped to Southeast Asia to fight and die for a country that denied them civil rights at home, Billy Graham remained silent on the injustice. Worse, he personally urged Dr. Martin Luther King Jr. to convince Black youth to register for military service.

King refused. He saw through the hypocrisy.

Graham, however, remained steadfast in his alliance with the war machine. During the Nixon Administration, he regularly visited the White House and advised on military policy. In one chilling conversation, recorded by Nixon's Oval Office surveillance system, Billy Graham suggested that the United States bomb a Vietnamese dam in order to drown the population. Nixon, no stranger to brutality, responded that such an act would constitute a war crime under international law. But the very fact that the idea was proposed by the so-called spiritual leader of America is an indictment not only of Graham, but of the entire political-religious alliance that undergirds U.S. imperialism.

Graham's title as "America's Pastor" must be reconsidered. He was not a prophet of peace. He was a court preacher for empire. He was the theological wing of the Pentagon. His prayers floated upward on smoke from burning villages. His sermons were written in the language of missiles.

There has never been a U.S. war that Billy Graham did not support. Korea. Vietnam. Grenada. Panama. Iraq. Afghanistan. Every conflict waged by the American military was blessed by Billy Graham, as though Jesus himself had given the order.

In this context, his role in the Gulf War should surprise no one. Bush invoked Graham not merely for comfort, but for cover. The bombing of Baghdad and Basra would not be seen as an act of imperial aggression, but as a holy mission. A sacred duty. A war wrapped in prayer.

But history sees through the charade.

The Gulf War devastated Iraq's infrastructure. Civilian casualties mounted. Bridges, water plants, hospitals, and schools were reduced to rubble. The sanctions that followed led to the deaths of hundreds of thousands of Iraqi children due to starvation and disease. The destruction was not surgical. It was systemic.

And yet, in American media, it was celebrated. Television anchors cheered the precision of air strikes. Military officers held press conferences with bomb footage. The war became a video game. A demonstration of what the United States could do to any nation that disobeyed its orders.

It was not justice. It was dominance.

George Herbert Walker Bush did not end that war because peace had been achieved. He ended it because the message had been sent. The lesson had been taught. The Arab world had been reminded of its place in the racial hierarchy of global power.

And Billy Graham smiled. He always did.

Let us not forget that the cost of this war was not just military. It was moral. It revealed that American wars are not fought solely with weapons, but with preachers. Not just with tanks, but with theology. The cross and the sword remain allies. And until that alliance is broken, the blood will continue to flow.

The Gulf War was not a war for democracy. It was a war for discipline.

It was a declaration.

You will submit.

You will obey.

And if you resist, we will pray while we bomb your children.

Let history be evident that the first Gulf War was not a victory.

It was a prophecy.

One that led directly to the second Gulf War.

One that paved the road for occupation, for torture, for Guantanamo, for Abu Ghraib.

And one that began with a prayer.

## African-American Communities Have Historically Opposed America's Wars Of Imperialism

From the earliest days of American empire, African American communities have consistently stood in moral opposition to the violent expansionism of the United States. While white America marched behind the banners of Manifest Destiny and military conquest, Black Americans saw clearly the racism, greed, and bloodshed masked beneath patriotic rhetoric. For centuries, they have refused to be complicit in a system built on the subjugation of non-white peoples across the globe.

In 1899, when President William McKinley oversaw the illegal annexation of Hawaii, African Americans opposed the seizure. The Hawaiian people were stripped of their sovereignty, and their islands were converted into an American military and corporate outpost. This invasion was not about democracy—it was about domination. The Dole Pineapple Company, spearheaded by Sanford B. Dole, initiated the economic colonization of the Hawaiian Islands, using corporate interests as justification for imperial rule. Native Hawaiians became slaves in their own homeland, victims of a settler-colonial project no different from the one that had already devastated the Indigenous nations of North America.

One of the loudest proponents of this imperial agenda was Theodore Roosevelt. In 1897, as Secretary of the Navy, Roosevelt gave a lecture at the United States War College declaring that Anglo-Saxons were chosen by God to rule the "lesser breeds" of the world: Black, brown, and yellow people alike. His beliefs were not fringe. They were echoed by academics, clergy, and statesmen. John W. Burgess, then dean at Columbia University, wrote in 1890 that white nations had the right, even the obligation, to impose civilization by force. Protestant minister Josiah Strong went further, claiming that America had a divine mission to "regenerate" the world with its supposed superior Christianity.

Such ideology laid the groundwork for the brutal conquest of the Philippines from 1899 to 1901. McKinley's administration ordered the invasion of the islands under the guise of liberation. In truth, it was another chapter in America's imperial expansion. U.S. troops massacred entire Filipino villages. In 1901 alone, American soldiers slaughtered between 2,000 and 3,000 civilians in a single assault. That same year, U.S. forces introduced the infamous "Water Cure," a torture technique in which victims were forced to ingest massive quantities of water before being beaten—an early version of what would later become known as waterboarding. The CIA would revive the method in Iraq between 2003 and 2008, under the orders of George W. Bush. The same brutality, repackaged for modern times.

African American voices opposed these atrocities then and continue to oppose them now. Black communities were among the first to denounce the Vietnam War, long before white America turned against it. From 1965 to 1975, over three million Vietnamese civilians were killed. The real motive, as many Black leaders understood, was profit. The U.S. military-industrial complex, fueled by arms manufacturers and defense contractors, made billions while Vietnamese villages were napalmed and American youth were sent home in body bags. The CIA's Phoenix Program tortured over 40,000 Vietnamese citizens, as confirmed by former CIA operative Frank Snepp.

Fifty-eight thousand American soldiers died in that war. Most of them were poor. Many were Black. They died not for freedom but for empire.

The same pattern repeated itself in Iraq. Between 2002 and 2007, George W. Bush launched a war based on lies. The Bush administration claimed Iraq possessed weapons of mass destruction, but no such weapons were ever found. African American communities did not fall for the deception. They saw through the false pretense and understood that the war was about oil, not security. Over one million Iraqis were killed. Women, children, and elders, slaughtered in their homes, marketplaces, and places of worship. Yet Bush was never held accountable. He violated international law, including the United Nations Charter, which prohibits unprovoked military invasions. Still, there was no trial. No justice. No remorse.

African Americans also remember the wars waged not just abroad but at home. During the Indian Wars of the 19th century, the U.S. military killed over 150 million Indigenous people, according to historical estimates rooted in land loss, starvation, and biological warfare. As Dee Brown chronicles in *Bury My Heart at Wounded Knee* (1970), these were not battles, they were acts of extermination. Native Americans were forced onto concentration camps called reservations, stripped of their languages, cultures, and futures.

Black communities understood these atrocities not as distant history but as parallel struggle. They lived their own genocide in places like Tulsa, Oklahoma. On June 1, 1921, the thriving Black community of Greenwood was destroyed by a white mob. Three hundred people were murdered. Homes and businesses were burned to the ground. It was a racial cleansing on American soil. There were no trials. No reparations. No justice.

From the Philippines to Fallujah, from Little Rock to Gaza, African Americans have consistently recognized the pattern. Empire does not protect, it exploits. It does not liberate, it enslaves. And whenever the United States has declared war in the name of peace, it has done so at the expense of people of color, both abroad and at home.

The flag-waving of empire has never fooled African Americans. They have been its victims. And they have stood in opposition, not only because of shared suffering, but because of a moral clarity born of survival.

# Section V:
# Geopolitical Realignment, Civilizational Decline, and Rise of China

# Dr. Alfred Mccoy, Professor University Of Wisconsin, The G-7, Wrote In His Book That The U.S. And Israel Will Fall In 2030

The myth of invincibility has long cloaked the United States and Israel, two settler-colonial states built on stolen land and sustained by overwhelming military force. But history is not kind to empires that mistake firepower for endurance. The U.S. support for Israel in its war against Hamas is not a display of strength, it is the final act in a theatre of defeat.

Israel, despite its sophisticated weaponry and billions in U.S. military aid, failed to defeat Hezbollah in 2006, a fact confirmed even by European military analysts. That defeat is not an anomaly. It is a harbinger. Just as America could not conquer Vietnam or pacify Afghanistan, Israel cannot break the will of a people fighting for their survival.

Technological superiority means nothing when you lack moral legitimacy.

The Israeli Defense Forces (IDF) are capable of obliterating apartment blocks, hospitals, and refugee camps, but they have no answer for resistance rooted in memory, in trauma, in justice. They are well-trained in the language of domination, but illiterate in the grammar of liberation.

And the United States knows this story too well.

From the jungles of Vietnam to the mountains of Afghanistan, U.S. forces have repeatedly found themselves outfought not in arms, but in will. American soldiers were backed by aircraft carriers and satellites, and routed by guerrilla fighters in sandals. The lesson was always there: no empire, no matter how mighty, can extinguish the fire of the oppressed.

Like Israel, the United States wields the most advanced tools of war—drones, tanks, surveillance networks. But these tools are blunt when faced with adversaries who know the land, who are willing to die for it, who carry history like a weapon.

Adolf Hitler's Wehrmacht learned this lesson at Stalingrad in 1943. Despite overwhelming firepower and a blitzkrieg strategy that had crushed much of Europe, the Nazis could not conquer the Soviet will to resist. The Russian people, battered and starving, held their ground. Field Marshal Friedrich von Paulus, once triumphant, was forced to surrender his 6th Army. The myth of German invincibility crumbled in the snow.

Napoleon's Grand Army met the same fate in 1812. Armed with discipline, strategy, and imperial ambition, they marched into Russia. Few marched out. It wasn't just winter that killed them—it was resistance. Relentless, national, moral.

Israel's military may win battles, but it will never win Gaza. Just as the French could not defeat Algerian independence, just as apartheid could not crush South African freedom, the IDF cannot exterminate Palestinian resistance. Bombs will bury bodies, not history.

The consequences will not be limited to Gaza. The United States, in tying its fate so tightly to Israel's genocidal campaign, has signed a political death warrant in the region. The era of American dominance in the Middle East is ending, not with diplomacy, but with disgrace. China and Russia, unburdened by the need to mask imperialism as democracy, are moving in to fill the vacuum. They will claim not only influence, but access to the region's most coveted prize: oil.

Make no mistake—this is not geopolitics. This is racism.

The United States supports Israel not because of shared values, but shared origins. Both are settler states forged by white Europeans—Polish, German, Russian, British—who displaced Indigenous populations through terror. Both claim the mantle of civilization while waging war on civilians.

In 1953, the U.S. orchestrated a coup in Iran to overthrow the democratically elected Mohammad Mossadegh. In 1954, it ousted

Guatemala's President Jacobo Árbenz, installing a brutal dictatorship. In 1973, it supported the bloody overthrow of Chile's Salvador Allende, replacing him with General Augusto Pinochet, a torturer, murderer, and darling of the CIA.

This is not the spread of freedom. It is the spread of fascism in a suit.

Under George W. Bush, America lied its way into Iraq, unleashing a war that killed over a million people. The myth of weapons of mass destruction was a smokescreen for empire. Abu Ghraib, with its torture chambers and sexual humiliation, was a standard procedure, not a mistake. And where was Israel? Advising. Training. Participating.

During the apartheid era in South Africa, as Nelson Mandela and the African National Congress fought for liberation, the United States and Israel armed the racist regime. They supported white power while branding Black resistance as terrorism. The same pattern repeats today in Gaza, as the world watches in real time the slaughter of brown bodies, justified by American bombs and Israeli propaganda.

Benjamin Netanyahu, who has ordered the deaths of over 30,000 Palestinians, most of them women and children, is still embraced by U.S. leaders. Meanwhile, Vladimir Putin is labeled a war criminal for attacking white Ukrainians. The hypocrisy is as grotesque as it is predictable. To America, the crime is not murder. The crime is *who* is murdered.

Black and brown bodies do not matter. Never have. Never will under white supremacist empires disguised as democracies.

The United States, with the highest incarceration rate in the world, treats its own Black and Indigenous populations with contempt and cruelty. It holds more prisoners than Russia, Iran, North Korea, or China. Its police murders Black men in the streets with impunity. Its schools teach lies. Its prisons are like plantations, complete with surveillance cameras.

This is not freedom. It is apartheid.

And Israel is not the exception,  it is the mirror.

Together, the United States and Israel represent the final bastions of white supremacy on Earth. Their constitutions enshrined racism. Their economies were built by enslaved Africans and exploited labor. Their foreign policies are rooted in conquest. And their rhetoric of "security" is merely a cover for extermination.

The world sees it.

The Global South sees it.

History sees it.

And history is turning.

Russia and China did not enslave Africans. They did not exterminate Indigenous nations. They did not build empires on racial genocide. The same cannot be said for the United States or Israel. Every inch of land they occupy is soaked in blood.

The American Constitution itself was crafted not to liberate, but to preserve white power. Article IV, Section 2 guaranteed the return of fugitive slaves. The Founding Fathers weren't revolutionaries—they were slavers protecting their wealth.

Even the so-called defenders of freedom in the Jewish community are not exempt. According to *The Jewish Confederates* by Robert Rosen, many Jewish elites in the American South profited from slavery, just as modern Zionists profit from occupation.

Let the record show:

- The United States funded genocide.

- Israel carried it out.

- And the people of the world are no longer deceived.

The defeat of Israel will not merely be military. It will be moral, ideological, and civilizational. It will mark the collapse of a myth—the myth that bombs build democracies, that colonizers can be victims, that brown life is expendable.

In Gaza, the resistance does not fight with tanks or fighter jets. They fight with memory. With purpose. With the unshakable truth that no empire, no matter how white, can crush a people determined to live.

History has spoken.

Empires fall.

And Israel, like America, is no exception.

## China, North Korea, Iran, And Russia Are Countries That Were Not Built By Slave Laborers

The United States of America was not founded in freedom. It was founded in chains. Beneath the marble of its monuments and the parchment of its constitution lies a truth rarely spoken aloud: this nation was built by enslaved Africans, not just in labor but in structure, wealth, and ideology.

Long before the United States declared independence from Britain in 1776, African bodies were forced onto American soil in 1619. They were not settlers. They were not immigrants. They were cargo bound in iron, sold like livestock, and worked to death in fields that fed an economy built on blood. As *The 1619 Project* by Dr. Nikole Hannah-Jones affirms, the true origin of America as a nation begins not with liberty, but with bondage. And that bondage did not end with the Civil War. It evolved.

According to Douglas Blackmon's groundbreaking work *Slavery by Another Name* (2006), emancipation was not freedom. It was a rebranding. After the Civil War (1861–1865), Black Americans were re-enslaved through sharecropping, convict leasing, vagrancy laws, and state-sponsored terror. Plantations became prisons. Chains became laws. The lash was replaced by the badge. The cotton still had to be picked, but now it was done under the illusion of legality.

The myth that Lincoln freed the slaves is as hollow as the parchment it was written on. What he did was shift the method, not the mission.

Capital still demanded free labor, and the South, along with the North, delivered. Slavery was never abolished. It was redesigned.

Dr. Deshay David Ford, in *The Decline of America: The Last White Man's Empire and the Rise of China, the Brown Empire* (2022), bears witness to this reality in lived experience. He recounts how his family in Arkansas could only send their children to school when the weather stopped them from harvesting cotton. The state refused to fund Black education because to educate a Black child was to interrupt the machinery of profit. In this nation, Black life was not seen as sacred. It was seen as seasonal.

This was not an exception. It was policy.

While China was erecting the Great Wall under its first emperor in 210 BCE to protect its sovereignty from foreign invasion, America was being erected to serve the opposite purpose: to invade, extract, enslave, and profit. China, for all its internal flaws, was not built on the backs of stolen Africans. It did not colonize foreign continents to harvest their oil or enslave their children. The Great Wall was a defense. The American frontier was a conquest.

The United States—like its white imperial ancestors in Britain, France, Belgium, and Germany—was founded on racial capitalism. The original American dream was not opportunity. It was ownership of land, of bodies, of wealth ripped from the earth and ripped from the wombs of Black women who were bred like cattle to replenish a labor force they could not replace.

As historian Dee Brown documented in *Bury My Heart at Wounded Knee* (1970), this same nation, forged through slavery, turned its guns on Indigenous people with genocidal precision. It signed over 380 treaties with Native nations—and broke every single one. Behind each broken promise was a trail of blood, a seizure of land, and a gold rush of greed. Racial cleansing was not a byproduct of expansion. It *was* the expansion.

White supremacy was not a shadow on the American project, it *was* the blueprint.

## Decline of America and Israel: The Last Two Racial Apartheid White Colonial Nations

Great Britain laid its colonial roots in Jamestown, Virginia in 1607, driven not by liberty but by commercial charter. The French, meanwhile, began their colonization of Canada with traders and soldiers. The war between France and England over North America, known as the French and Indian War (1754–1763), was not fought for freedom. It was fought for land, slaves, and profit. When the English won, they taxed their American colonies to pay for it. The so-called American Revolution was not a rebellion against tyranny. It was a rebellion against taxation and the threat to slaveholding wealth.

The truth is even darker.

According to Dr. Ford and legal historians, one of the unspoken catalysts for the American Revolution was slavery itself. In 1772, the British royal court ruled in *Somersett v. Stewart* that slavery was unsupported by English common law. Had this precedent reached across the Atlantic, slaveholders like George Washington, Thomas Jefferson, James Madison, and Pierce Butler would have been forced to free the people they legally defined as property. Their wealth was entirely dependent on human bondage and would have crumbled.

So they chose revolution.

Not for freedom, but for the freedom to enslave.

When Thomas Jefferson penned the Declaration of Independence in 1776, he did not mean *all* men. He meant white men. And when the Founding Fathers met in Philadelphia in 1787 to write the U.S. Constitution, they made sure to protect their property, not their citizens. Article IV, Section 2, Clause 3 enshrined slavery into the very soul of the republic. Any enslaved person who escaped to a free state was to be returned to their "owner." The Constitution was more of a contract of bondage than a document of liberty.

These weren't patriots.

They were plantation owners protecting their profits.

They were slavers masquerading as philosophers.

They were empire builders hiding behind powdered wigs and parchment lies.

The lie of American exceptionalism begins here in a nation that has never fully reckoned with the fact that its economic empire was built by enslaved Africans, expanded through Indigenous genocide, and maintained through racial apartheid that endures to this day.

And while the West still celebrates the myth of its moral superiority, China stands in contrast, not as a utopia, but as a civilization that did not enslave continents to build its power. Its people built their own nation, brick by brick, wall by wall. They did not traffic Africans across oceans. They did not colonize North America. They did not plant flags on foreign graves and call it freedom.

We must acknowledge that America was built on the backs of enslaved Black people. Its revolution was driven by the fear of abolition, not the thirst for liberty. Its Constitution was written to preserve white wealth, not human rights. And its founders were not liberators. They were slavers.

This is not rhetoric.

This is history.

And until that truth is taught, shouted, remembered, and burned into the collective conscience of the world, the myth of American democracy will remain just that—a myth.

A lie dressed in red, white, and blue.

And the world, at last, is no longer buying it.

## Dr. Deshay D. Ford's Book: Decline Of America, The Last White Man's Empire, And The Rise Of Chinese Empire

In *Decline of America: The Last White Man's Empire*, Dr. Deshay David Ford delivers a sweeping and unapologetic critique of America's historical arc, tracing the roots of its imperial rise to racism, colonialism, and structural violence. Ford's analysis dismantles the American mythos, exposing how the United States accumulated global dominance not through democracy or innovation, but through enslavement, extermination, and exploitation (Ford, 2022). From its inception, the U.S. relied on the unpaid, tortured labor of enslaved Africans, who fueled its booming economy in agriculture, cotton, and industry. The wealth of America, as Ford asserts, was built on the backs of those it dehumanized, and its legacy remains stained by that original sin.

The enslavement of Black people was not just an economic system—it was a racial caste that permeated every aspect of society. Slavery shaped the American legal code, informed cultural norms, and determined who could access the rights of citizenship. Racism was not incidental. It was foundational. And even after Emancipation, that racial structure mutated into new forms: convict leasing, Jim Crow segregation, redlining, police brutality, and mass incarceration. The violence didn't end, it evolved.

Dr. Ford (2022) contextualizes this domestic racism within a global imperial framework, revealing how the same ideologies that justified slavery at home were deployed abroad. As the U.S. expanded its influence, it invaded and colonized territories like Hawaii, the Philippines, Guam, Puerto Rico, and Cuba, exploiting non-white populations under the guise of freedom. The empire grew not by liberating nations, but by subjugating people of color, just as it had always done domestically.

America's racial legacy continues into the 21st century. In 2024, Black voters across southern states are once again facing systemic voter suppression, with discriminatory laws, gerrymandering, and purges from voter rolls. The same tactics used to block Black participation in Reconstruction have returned in modern form, reinforced by a Supreme Court that has rolled back key provisions of the 1965 Voting Rights Act, especially under Chief Justice John Roberts.

Despite this, the resilience of African Americans remains unparalleled. As Douglas Blackmon argues in *Slavery by Another Name* (Blackmon, 2006), no race of people has endured 450 years of oppression and contributed so profoundly to the cultural, political, and economic life of a nation. African Americans have pioneered music, literature, art, sports, and global popular culture. Jazz, the quintessential American art form, was created by Black musicians and has since evolved into a global academic discipline, spanning from Moscow to Paris, Beijing to New York.

Even genres falsely credited to white performers, such as country and western music, have their roots in the spirituals and rhythms of enslaved Africans. Hollywood, which once distorted and demeaned Black life, eventually became a conduit through which Black creativity, resistance, and excellence reshaped American identity, despite the industry's systemic racism.

Ford also underscores that African Americans have consistently been moral leaders in the global fight for justice. They opposed the Vietnam War, the Gulf War, and the invasions of Iraq, Syria, and Afghanistan. Today, Black activists are at the forefront of supporting Palestinian liberation, condemning U.S. arms sales to Israel, and calling out the racist genocide in Gaza. As President Bill Clinton once admitted, *"If you want to know what's really happening in America, don't ask white people. Ask Black people."*

While the United States continues to unravel under the weight of its contradictions, China is emerging as a dominant world power. The Chinese navy is now the largest on Earth, and Beijing is rapidly expanding its global presence, especially in South America, where countries like Brazil are offering port access to Chinese warships. These developments are not merely logistical; they are symbolic rejections of U.S. imperialism, particularly from nations long brutalized by American interventions.

Ford reminds us that the U.S. has a violent legacy in Latin America. In 1954, the CIA overthrew the democratically elected government of Guatemala, replacing it with a U.S.-backed dictator. In 1973, under Richard Nixon and Henry Kissinger, the CIA helped depose President Salvador Allende of Chile, installing Augusto Pinochet, who unleashed an era of torture, mass imprisonment, and state-sanctioned terror (Rosen, 2019; Zinn, 1980). This pattern repeated across the hemisphere, from Nicaragua to Haiti, where the U.S. armed right-wing death squads and trained dictators at the infamous School of the Americas.

The truth is undeniable: American foreign policy has long relied on covert operations, regime change, and violence to protect corporate interests and maintain racialized global hierarchies.

That pattern extends even further back. The Mexican-American War of 1846–1848, initiated by President James K. Polk, was a deliberate campaign to steal territory from Mexico—lands that would become Texas, Arizona, California, Utah, and Colorado. As General Ulysses S. Grant later admitted, the war was "one of the most unjust ever waged by a stronger against a weaker nation." Polk, a slave-owning southerner, saw expansion not just as nationalism—but as a path to expand cotton plantations and slavery.

The Spanish-American War of 1898 further solidified the U.S. as an empire. After blaming Spain for the explosion of the U.S.S. Maine, the U.S. seized Cuba, Puerto Rico, Guam, and the Philippines. In the Philippine-American War (1898–1902), U.S. troops used waterboarding torture, referred to as the "water cure," and waged a campaign of massacres, village burnings, and racial violence (Zinn, 1980; Fantano, 2013). Soldiers wrote home describing their victims as "niggers"—a clear indication that racial hatred underpinned America's imperialism.

The doctrine of U.S. expansionism was codified even earlier in the Monroe Doctrine of 1823, a policy designed to keep European powers out of Latin America—so that the United States could dominate the region without competition. Countries like Cuba became wholly dependent on the U.S., with corporations owning nearly all of Cuba's natural resources and laboring its people in near-feudal conditions.

Even in the modern era, Henry Kissinger's secret bombing campaigns in Cambodia, Laos, and Vietnam during the early 1970s resulted in the deaths of millions of civilians. According to Ford and supported by Howard Zinn and Robert Fantano, the U.S. military bombed schools, hospitals, and churches, unleashing carnage under the banner of anti-communism.

And then, on August 6, 1945, the United States did what no other nation has ever done: it dropped an atomic bomb on civilians. Hiroshima was instantly incinerated, killing 80,000 people. By year's end, radiation would claim tens of thousands more. Three days later, Nagasaki met the same fate. These acts were not strategic necessities; they were expressions of racist vengeance, fueled by the dehumanization of Asian people. As Ford notes, the U.S. ignored diplomatic surrender signals from Japan and dropped the bombs without warning, choosing annihilation over negotiation (Fantano, 2013).

Let the record show: the United States became an empire not by moral superiority, but by blood, fire, and lies.

And today, as that empire declines, the world begins to turn toward new powers, new alliances, and new possibilities.

Not because China is perfect. But because America is no longer believable.

## America – An Empire Built To Fail

The American Empire, which began with English colonization at Jamestown in 1603, is now entering its final phase. What started as a corporate venture backed by the Virginia Company, protected by royal charter from King James I, expanded into the largest global empire of the modern age, but not without consequence. In 2024, the foundations that once appeared indestructible are fractured. The empire, built on slavery, conquest, and extraction, is collapsing under the weight of its own contradictions.

In 1898, the United States went to war with a dying Spanish Empire. Political figures like Theodore Roosevelt and Henry Cabot Lodge demanded the conflict, not for defense but for expansion. The Spanish-American War allowed the U.S. to seize territories including

Puerto Rico, Guam, and the Philippines. It also marked America's formal entrance into overseas empire. According to Robert Fantano, the war was not an end, but a beginning of racial domination and imperial violence exported abroad under the banner of American exceptionalism.

The brutality that followed in the Philippines from 1899 to 1901 exposed the true nature of U.S. foreign policy. American soldiers committed widespread atrocities. They carried out massacres in villages and used a torture method known as the "Water Cure," forcing detainees to ingest large amounts of water before beating it out of them. The technique would be renamed "waterboarding" and resurrected during George W. Bush's invasions of Iraq and Afghanistan in the early 2000s. These were not isolated incidents. They were part of a long tradition of cruelty dressed up as patriotism.

In Vietnam, the military doctrine of "Search and Destroy" led to the mass murder of civilians, including the My Lai massacre, where over 500 Vietnamese villagers, mostly women, children, and the elderly, were executed in a ditch. The incident, exposed by journalist Seymour Hersh in 1968, was not an aberration. According to Nick Turse's *Kill Anything That Moves* (2010), such atrocities were standard operating procedure. General William Westmoreland, commander of U.S. forces in Vietnam, repeatedly lied to President Lyndon Johnson about the progress of the war. While the government assured the American public of victory, it was losing on the ground. Johnson eventually removed Westmoreland, but the damage was irreversible. By 1975, the United States had lost the war and its myth of invincibility.

The defeat in Vietnam signaled the beginning of imperial decline. That decline accelerated with George W. Bush's catastrophic wars in Iraq, Afghanistan, and Syria. None of these wars produced security or democracy. Instead, they produced death, debt, and geopolitical instability. Bush launched the invasion of Iraq based on a lie, claiming Saddam Hussein possessed weapons of mass destruction. Over a million Iraqis were killed. Thousands of American troops died. And no weapons were ever found.

Decline of America and Israel: The Last Two Racial Apartheid White
Colonial Nations

Donald Trump's election in 2016 symbolized a moral and political collapse. His rise was not an anomaly. It was the inevitable result of decades of imperial decay, racial resentment, and institutional corruption. According to Dr. Deshay David Ford, Trump's election marked the final nail in the coffin of American supremacy. In the same way that Spain's empire crumbled in 1898, the United States entered its final chapter in 2016; not with dignity, but with disgrace.

Empires fall for many reasons: economic overreach, military exhaustion, moral rot. The British Empire began its decline after World War I. The loss of young men in combat, combined with mounting debt, forced Britain to relinquish its colonies. Despite Winston Churchill's efforts to preserve it, history moved on. The United States rose from the ashes of European empires and willingly accepted the mantle of global dominance. But it also inherited their burden: the white supremacist belief that non-white people existed to be governed, exploited, and controlled.

After World War II, the United States embraced its role as the last great white empire. It positioned itself as the defender of capitalism and the enemy of communism. Under George Kennan's doctrine of containment, the U.S. began a global campaign to suppress any nation that defied its authority. It intervened not to spread freedom, but to secure access to resources. Democratically elected governments in Iran, Guatemala, Chile, and the Congo were overthrown. In their place, the CIA installed dictators who murdered and tortured their own citizens, so long as they protected American business interests.

In 1953, the CIA overthrew Iranian Prime Minister Mohammad Mossadegh after he attempted to nationalize his country's oil. Mossadegh was democratically elected, but he stood in the way of British and American petroleum companies. The coup was organized by CIA station chief Kermit Roosevelt, who was later rewarded with a top position at Gulf Oil. Iran would live under brutal dictatorship for decades as a result.

The U.S. did the same in Chile in 1973. President Salvador Allende was assassinated during a coup orchestrated by the Nixon administration, with the help of Henry Kissinger and CIA Director Richard Helms. The democratically elected socialist was replaced by General Augusto Pinochet, whose regime carried out mass executions and torture with full U.S. backing.

Everywhere the United States projected its power, it left behind corpses, prisons, and puppet governments. From Latin America to the Middle East to Africa, American imperialism brought dictatorship, surveillance, and death, not democracy.

The Reagan administration, along with the State of Israel, supported South Africa's apartheid regime. Reagan provided weapons and political cover for a government that legally oppressed its Black majority. Nelson Mandela was labeled a terrorist, and his imprisonment was encouraged by Reagan's advisors. Israel supplied arms and tactical training to the South African military, creating a pipeline of oppression between the two settler-colonial states. Both claimed to be democracies. Both functioned as racist oligarchies.

The United States and Israel, as twin pillars of white supremacy, formed a strategic alliance built on racial domination. They defended each other's crimes. They shared intelligence, weapons, and surveillance systems. They operated not as defenders of peace but as enforcers of apartheid, both at home and abroad.

The American Empire is not collapsing because of foreign enemies. It is collapsing because it was never sustainable. Built on conquest, racism, and greed, it carries the rot of its origins. And history, as always, is watching.

## China Seeking To Access Middle East Oil Resources

History does not repeat itself, but it rhymes. In the third century BCE, two powers clashed for control of the Mediterranean world: Carthage, an African empire built on maritime trade and commercial dominance, and Rome, a landlocked newcomer hungering for conquest.

Decline of America and Israel: The Last Two Racial Apartheid White
Colonial Nations

The three Punic Wars between 264 and 146 BCE were not merely military campaigns. They were struggles for supremacy, for control of trade routes, natural wealth, and strategic geography.

Carthage, based in what is today Tunisia, was the older, wealthier, and more established empire. It controlled major port cities and merchant networks stretching across the Mediterranean. Its navy was unmatched. Rome, by contrast, was a rising force: young, landbound, ambitious, and militarized. But history is not kind to the stagnant. In 146 BCE, after decades of war, Rome laid siege to Carthage, burned the city to the ground, massacred the inhabitants, and sold the survivors into slavery. With that, a new empire was born. Rome rose. Carthage disappeared.

Today, the global battlefield has shifted. But the stakes remain the same.

The United States of America, like Carthage in its twilight years, is a declining empire—stretched thin by military overreach, bloated by consumption, and deluded by myths of eternal dominance. Its economy is deeply reliant on the control of global energy markets, especially the vast oil reserves of the Middle East. And its power is now being challenged by a rising empire, China, the twenty-first-century Rome.

China, the world's most populous nation and second-largest economy, is no longer content to play second fiddle to the Atlantic powers. With its Belt and Road Initiative, massive infrastructure investments, and military modernization, it is laying the foundations of a post-Western global order. And at the center of this contest lies the one commodity that has driven war, revolution, and empire for over a century: oil.

The battle is not fought with legions, but with pipelines. Not with catapults, but with sanctions. Not in open combat, but in diplomatic arenas, energy corridors, and proxy conflicts.

And just like Rome once crushed Carthage, China is now poised to overtake the United States economically, strategically, and ideologically.

## Decline of America and Israel: The Last Two Racial Apartheid White Colonial Nations

The United States' quest for empire began long before oil became its addiction. In 1898, it went to war with a crumbling Spanish Empire, not for liberation, but for acquisition. Through that war, the U.S. gained control of Puerto Rico, the Philippines, and Guam. That same year, under the banner of racial superiority and economic greed, the United States annexed Hawaii, deposed its last monarch, Queen Liliʻuokalani, and enslaved the native Hawaiian population on their own land.

This was not democracy. It was imperial conquest.

Earlier, in 1839–1842, the U.S. partnered with Britain in the Opium War against China, helping force open Chinese markets for the sale of narcotics. The Western powers humiliated the Qing Dynasty, imposed unequal treaties, seized Hong Kong, and flooded Chinese cities with addiction, disease, and degradation.

The British, French, and Americans turned China into an occupied drug den, enriching themselves at the expense of millions of ruined lives. Chinese women were infected with venereal diseases introduced by European soldiers. Epidemics swept through the cities, while Western merchants reaped profit. The devastation was not accidental, it was engineered. And it is etched deeply into Chinese memory.

This era is known in Chinese textbooks as the Century of Humiliation, a period of subjugation, racism, and exploitation at the hands of Western powers. Today, it serves as the fuel for China's geopolitical revival.

The Chinese have not forgotten. And they have not forgiven.

Among the profiteers of China's colonial devastation were the Sassoon and Kadoorie families, Baghdadi Jewish dynasties who trafficked opium across Asia. As Jonathan Kaufman documents in *The Last Kings of Shanghai*, these families built commercial empires in India and China through narcotic imperialism. They collaborated with the British Crown to maintain the drug trade, ignored Chinese efforts to ban opium, and dismissed the destruction as the cost of doing business.

Their profits came not from industry, but from addiction.

The same pattern played out across the Atlantic. In *The Jewish Confederates*, Robert Rosen documents how Jewish families, including the Monsanto family, were heavily involved in the transatlantic slave trade. Operating plantations in North and South America, the Monsantos worked enslaved Africans to death across the 17th, 18th, and 19th centuries. Like the opium traffickers in China, these merchants of human flesh enriched themselves by dehumanizing others.

The historical irony is bitter: those who had once suffered persecution in Europe became perpetrators of exploitation in Asia, Africa, and the Americas when handed the tools of empire.

In the 20th century, Adolf Hitler's Nazi regime implemented the Final Solution, a systematic plan to exterminate the Jews of Europe. Six million were murdered in concentration camps like Auschwitz and Treblinka. Jews were worked to death, gassed, and burned, their identities erased by the machinery of fascist hatred.

And yet, in the 21st century, the Israeli state, founded by white European Jews, has unleashed its own Final Solution upon the indigenous people of Palestine.

From October 27, 2023, through 2024, under Prime Minister Benjamin Netanyahu, Israel launched a full-scale military campaign against the civilian population of Gaza. Using U.S.-supplied bombs, Israeli forces flattened schools, hospitals, mosques, and refugee camps. Thousands of children were killed. Bodies were found mutilated and bound in mass graves. Entire neighborhoods were turned into rubble.

This was not war. It was genocide.

And the world knew it.

In March 2024, the Republic of South Africa filed charges of genocide against Israel at the International Court of Justice, citing overwhelming evidence of racial extermination. Once again, the United States stood on the wrong side of history, not as a neutral party, but as a weapons supplier, financier, and political shield for crimes against humanity.

## Decline of America and Israel: The Last Two Racial Apartheid White Colonial Nations

For decades, Zionist narratives have claimed a monopoly on historical suffering, suggesting that Jewish genocide under the Nazis is unparalleled and unrepeatable. But genocide is not a singular event—it is a pattern. And other peoples have endured it.

The Native Americans suffered systematic extermination beginning in 1603, when English settlers landed in Jamestown. Over centuries, millions were killed, their lands stolen, their cultures erased. The United States has never fully acknowledged, apologized for, or ended this campaign. It continues today in the form of land dispossession, water contamination, poverty, and mass incarceration.

The Tulsa Massacre of 1921—a racial pogrom against Black Americans in Greenwood, Oklahoma—was yet another chapter. Over 300 Black men, women, and children were murdered by white mobs. Entire blocks of Black-owned businesses were destroyed. The city tried to erase the memory from public record. It was only a century later, in 2023, that President Joe Biden formally commemorated the massacre. But no reparations were given. No justice followed.

America's legacy of genocide spans continents.

And Jewish involvement in that legacy, as slave traders, colonial profiteers, and modern enablers of apartheid, must also be recognized. From the Monsanto family in the Atlantic slave trade to the Sacklers in the modern opioid epidemic, from David Sassoon in Shanghai to Benjamin Netanyahu in Gaza, the pursuit of profit has often overridden any commitment to morality.

As Deshay David Ford writes in *Decline of America: The Last White Man's Empire and Rise of China, the Brown Empire, the crimes of the white empire were not committed by Christians alone,* but by anyone who aligned themselves with its logic of domination.

The End of White Empire, The Rise of the Brown World Order

Today, China is not merely seeking oil. It is seeking justice.

It is building an empire not of invasion, but of influence, rooted in economic partnerships, energy alliances, and infrastructure

development. It is investing in Iraq, Iran, Saudi Arabia, and beyond, not
to plunder, but to position itself as the new center of global power. And
as the U.S. falters, embroiled in debt, racism, and permanent war, China
rises disciplined, strategic, and relentless.

The age of white empire is ending.

And in its place, a Brown World Order is being born.

One where memory is power. One where the colonized become the
architects of their own future.

## The Chinese Have Replaced The United States As The Influencial Economic And Military Power In The Middle East

The Middle East, long treated as the chessboard of Western
empires, is now being redrawn by forces outside the grasp of
Washington. The war in Gaza after October 7, 2023, did not only reveal
Israel's brutal campaign of extermination against Palestinians; it also
exposed America's waning influence. For decades, the United States
wielded its dominance through its military bases, its oil companies, and
its uncritical support of Israel. But as Israel unleashed devastation,
killing tens of thousands of Palestinians—women, children, doctors,
teachers, entire families buried under rubble—the world took notice.
America did not restrain Israel; it armed it. Washington called Vladimir
Putin a "killer" and a "mobster," yet refused to apply the same language
to Benjamin Netanyahu as bombs rained on Gaza's hospitals, schools,
and mosques.

The death toll is staggering. By the winter of 2024, over 45,000
Palestinians had been slaughtered. The exact numbers cannot be known
because Israel's blockade has crushed hospitals and erased the systems of
counting. Corpses are buried hastily under debris, entire neighborhoods
wiped out. The moral hypocrisy is plain: white lives in Ukraine are
mourned with urgency, while brown lives in Gaza are dismissed as
collateral damage.

Decline of America and Israel: The Last Two Racial Apartheid White
Colonial Nations

South Africa, a nation forged in the fires of its own struggle against apartheid, recognized the crime for what it was. In December 2023, the South African government brought formal charges of genocide against Israel before the International Court of Justice. To Pretoria, the parallels were undeniable. Just as Black South Africans had endured racial domination, land theft, and state violence under white minority rule, so too do Palestinians endure an apartheid system designed to crush them under Jewish supremacist law. The reaction from Washington was swift—not condemnation of genocide, but condemnation of South Africa. The United States, once again, aligned itself with the oppressor, not the oppressed.

This alignment is not new. During the Cold War, the United States and Britain armed the apartheid regime in South Africa, supplying weapons, intelligence, and diplomatic cover to sustain white supremacy. Nelson Mandela and the African National Congress were labeled "terrorists" by Washington even as they fought for freedom. History repeats. Hamas is now branded as a terrorist organization by the same powers that once criminalized Mandela, yet to millions across the Global South, Hamas represents not terrorism but resistance—a desperate fight for survival against a settler-colonial state.

The deeper truth is this: Western powers created Israel not solely out of guilt for the Holocaust, but out of cold calculation. The Balfour Declaration of November 2, 1917, signed by British Foreign Secretary Arthur Balfour, promised a Jewish homeland in Palestine. It was not charity—it was strategy. Britain sought to plant a loyal outpost in the Middle East to secure its access to oil. The United States inherited this project after World War II, ensuring that Israel would serve as the Western watchdog in a region whose resources fueled the engines of empire.

But the imperial equation is shifting. As America and its European allies double down on supporting Israel's brutality, they are losing legitimacy in the eyes of the world. Into that vacuum has stepped China.

# Decline of America and Israel: The Last Two Racial Apartheid White Colonial Nations

Beijing does not posture as the savior of democracy. It does not wrap its ambitions in the language of human rights. Instead, it offers what the Middle East's rulers desire most: trade, investment, and protection from Western hegemony. Saudi Arabia has already opened its ports to Chinese naval vessels, signaling a historic break from the exclusive military grip of the United States. Oil transactions once priced exclusively in U.S. dollars are increasingly being conducted in Chinese yuan. This shift strikes at the heart of American power, for the dollar's supremacy has long rested on the global oil trade.

China's reach is not symbolic. Its companies now operate Iraq's oil fields. Its warships secure maritime routes once patrolled only by the U.S. Navy. Its diplomats broker regional agreements once thought impossible—between Saudi Arabia and Iran, between rivals that Washington could never reconcile. The message is clear: where America brings war, China brings commerce. Where America insists on domination, China offers partnership, however transactional.

Meanwhile, the American military machine falters. Recruitment numbers plunge year after year. Young white men, once the backbone of U.S. imperial wars, no longer fill the ranks. They turn away from service, unwilling to die for causes they no longer believe in. Increasingly, the burden falls on young men and women of color—Latino, Black, and immigrant youth—children of communities still denied full rights at home, yet sent abroad to fight America's battles. This, too, is empire's logic: the oppressed fight and die to preserve the privileges of the oppressor.

The Chinese leadership watches this decline with patience. They do not need to outfight America directly. They need only outlast it. And in the Middle East—the crucible of oil, faith, and power—they are doing precisely that.

The COVID-19 pandemic of 2020 stripped away illusions that had long cloaked American society. Beneath the rhetoric of equality and progress, the virus revealed the raw truth of race relations in the United States: they were not improving, they were collapsing. By 2024, America stood more racially segregated than it had in the 1950s, the supposed era of Jim Crow. Decades of civil rights victories, diversity initiatives, and symbolic reforms had not produced an integrated, equitable society. Instead, the country had retreated into hardened divisions, a nation unwilling to reconcile its own contradictions.

The clearest evidence of this regression could be found in the presidential campaigns. The success of Donald J. Trump—twice the Republican candidate, and twice a lightning rod for white grievance—proved the point. Trump's message was not cloaked in subtlety. To white men, particularly those fearful of demographic change, he promised salvation. He told them he would "Make America Great Again," which meant, in practice, returning them to a position of unquestioned dominance. Like Adolf Hitler in the 1930s, Trump identified scapegoats: immigrants, people of color, liberals, and the press. He offered them a simple story—your suffering is not your fault; it is theirs.

Yet history shows a harsher truth. The decline of the American empire was not caused by immigrants or by communities of color. It was engineered, encouraged, and perpetuated by white elites themselves. It was they who built the structures of exploitation, they who launched the wars of conquest, and they who siphoned wealth into the hands of the few.

America's overseas wars are a ledger of imperial overreach. From Vietnam (1964–1975), to the Gulf War in Kuwait (1990–1991), to George W. Bush's war in Iraq (2003–2008), and the disastrous occupation of Afghanistan, the pattern has been constant: trillions of dollars spent, thousands of lives lost, and little gained beyond chaos. The comparison to ancient Rome is unavoidable. Rome expanded across continents, feeding its legions with conquest until it could no longer sustain the cost. Recruitment faltered. Soldiers had to be drawn from the very "barbarian" tribes Rome once despised. This was the sign of decline—the dominant group no longer willing to fight for its empire.

Decline of America and Israel: The Last Two Racial Apartheid White Colonial Nations

The United States now finds itself in that same predicament. White youth, especially from privileged backgrounds, refuse to enlist. Recruitment quotas fall short. The burden of service is increasingly carried by Black, Latino, and immigrant communities—the racially oppressed populations whose lives are devalued at home yet exploited for imperial ambitions abroad. History teaches that once an empire can no longer recruit from its dominant caste, its decline is irreversible.

Scholars have warned of this trajectory. Alfred McCoy, professor at the University of Wisconsin–Madison, wrote in *Foreign Policy* that the American empire will collapse by 2030. His warning is not prophecy but analysis: empires built on war, plunder, and racial hierarchy eventually burn out. The clock is running, and time is nearly gone.

The pattern is consistent across history. In 1953, the CIA, under the Eisenhower administration, overthrew the democratically elected government of Mohammad Mossadegh in Iran. His crime was daring to nationalize Iran's oil. In his place, the Shah was installed, and Iran's resources were divided between American and British companies. In 1954, the CIA again intervened, this time in Guatemala, toppling President Jacobo Árbenz and handing power to a U.S.-backed dictator. The Dulles brothers—Allen, Director of the CIA, and John Foster, Secretary of State—profited directly through their connections to the United Fruit Company. Ninety-eight percent of Guatemala's arable land was seized, and Indigenous workers were driven into conditions indistinguishable from slavery.

The pattern repeated in Chile. On September 11, 1973, with the blessing of President Richard Nixon and Secretary of State Henry Kissinger, the CIA orchestrated the overthrow of Salvador Allende, Chile's democratically elected socialist president. American corporations quickly seized Chile's copper wealth, forcing Chilean workers into mines where their labor enriched foreign shareholders.

When the British Empire crumbled after World War II, the United States stepped in as the new global enforcer of white supremacy. America assumed what Rudyard Kipling once called the "White Man's

Burden"—to police, dominate, and exploit nations of color across
Africa, Asia, and Latin America. The rhetoric was always the same:
freedom, democracy, and human rights. The reality was exploitation,
dictatorship, and extraction.

At home, the hypocrisy was no less glaring. America's founding
presidents—George Washington, Thomas Jefferson, James Madison,
James Monroe, Andrew Jackson—were not champions of liberty. They
were slaveholders, men who built their wealth on the stolen lives and
labor of Africans. At the Constitutional Convention of 1787, they
enshrined slavery in the new republic. Article IV, Section 2, Clause 3,
the Fugitive Slave Clause, guaranteed that enslaved people who escaped
could be hunted down and returned like livestock. Freedom, equality,
and democracy were never intended for people of color.

Dr. Martin Luther King Jr. recognized this contradiction with
piercing clarity. He described America's definition of freedom and
democracy as mythological concepts, promises spoken but never
delivered to its Black citizens. Hannah-Jones, in *The 1619 Project*, makes
the same argument: African Americans, not white Americans, have
fought for centuries to make those ideals real. Four hundred and fifty
years of struggle against slavery, segregation, and systemic racism stand
as proof. White Americans declared the dream; African Americans bled
for it.

Meanwhile, Indigenous nations endured genocide. Dee Brown's
*Bury My Heart at Wounded Knee* (1970) records how America's
westward expansion was nothing less than racial extermination, the
systematic destruction of Native cultures, communities, and lands.

By the dawn of the twenty-first century, the United States remained
what it had always been: a racially segregated nation. The forms had
changed—Jim Crow signs replaced by redlined neighborhoods,
segregated schools replaced by underfunded "minority districts," open
disenfranchisement replaced by voter suppression laws, but the
substance remained. Systemic racism and institutional racism still

defined the American experience. For people of color, the American Dream remained, as it always had been, a dream deferred.

# In 2030, Germany Will Become The Dominant Power In Europe

Before the First World War (1914–1918), Germany stood as one of the most advanced nations in the world. In science, technology, philosophy, and industry, it led Europe. German universities produced discoveries that transformed modern chemistry, physics, and engineering. Its military was considered the strongest in Europe, its army disciplined, modernized, and feared. Contrary to the myths propagated at the Paris Peace Conference of 1919, Germany was not the singular cause of the war. Yet, history was written by the victors, and Germany was forced to bear the blame.

The assassination of Archduke Franz Ferdinand of Austria and his wife Sophie in Sarajevo by a Serbian nationalist in June 1914 set the chain of events into motion. Austria-Hungary, demanding justice, sought to send investigators into Serbia. When Serbia refused, Austria declared war. Russia, bound by treaty to Serbia, mobilized its forces. Germany, allied with Austria, declared war on Russia. France and Britain, bound to Russia, declared war on Germany. Thus, what began as a regional conflict spiraled into a world war. It was not Germany that lit the match, but Russia's defense of Serbia that dragged Europe into the abyss.

The war devastated Europe. France lost a generation of young men. Britain bled its empire dry to fight the conflict. And though Germany fought valiantly, it was defeated and humiliated at the Paris Peace Conference in 1919. Economically strangled, militarily crippled, and forced to pay impossible reparations, Germany was cast as the scapegoat.

During the war, another betrayal unfolded: the infamous Balfour Declaration of November 2, 1917. Britain's Foreign Secretary, Lord Arthur Balfour, wrote to Baron Rothschild, a leader of the Zionist movement, promising Palestine to European Jews in exchange for their assistance in undermining Germany and rallying American support. It was a colonial bargain, not a moral pledge. The British saw Zionist support as a weapon of war, and Palestine was the prize.

When Russia fell to the Communists in 1917, they exposed the secret agreements of the Allies, including the Balfour Declaration. Copies reached Adolf Hitler, who drew his own conclusions. To him, this confirmed that Jews were responsible for Germany's betrayal and defeat. By the time of the Wannsee Conference in January 1942, Hitler and his inner circle had committed themselves fully to the "Final Solution"—the genocide of Europe's Jews.

History is filled with bitter ironies. Jews were among the financiers and traders who participated in the Atlantic slave trade of the 17th, 18th, and 19th centuries. They profited from the buying and selling of African men, women, and children, commodifying Black bodies for European wealth. In America, Jewish elites like Judah P. Benjamin of Louisiana owned plantations and enslaved Africans, supporting the Confederacy during the Civil War. As historian Benjamin Madley (2016) and others note, Jewish and Christian elites alike were complicit in slavery and Indigenous genocide. Thus, the cycle of oppression was not limited to one people. Hitler's genocide of Jews was political, born of war and scapegoating, while Jewish participation in slavery was economic, born of profit. Both were genocidal in effect.

Germany lost the Second World War (1939–1945) and lay in ruins, its cities flattened by Allied bombing, its people devastated by hunger and loss. Yet, out of the ashes, Germany rebuilt. Today, it stands as the most powerful economy in Europe, an industrial giant whose exports dominate global markets.

According to Dr. Deshay David Ford (2022), Germany will emerge in the twenty-first century as the leading European power, eclipsing the United States as the primary Western state. The U.S., burdened by debt, decline, and internal division, will become a third-rate power, while Germany will assume responsibility for the defense of Europe. As America fades, Germany rises.

But the twenty-first century is not a European century. It is the Chinese century. As Martin Jacques (2018) argues, China's resurgence marks the return of an ancient power. Unlike European empires, which invaded and colonized nations for resources—gold, silver, oil, and enslaved Africans—China historically built empires of influence, not conquest. It defended itself against invaders like the Mongols in 1274 but did not scour the world for slaves. Europe's wealth was built on genocide and slavery; China's endurance rests on continuity and civilization.

The American empire has mirrored the worst of Assyria, the ancient power that terrorized its neighbors until its fall in 612 B.C. Like the Assyrians, America has waged endless wars, from Hiroshima and Nagasaki to Korea, Vietnam, Iraq, and Afghanistan. Like Assyria, America has slaughtered the vulnerable—women, children, and the poor—for empire and profit. And like Assyria, it will fall, and the world will celebrate its demise.

This book closes on a truth that history repeats without mercy: empires built on slavery and genocide cannot endure. The American empire was built on the extermination of Indigenous peoples, the enslavement of Africans, the exploitation of Asians and Latinos, and the domination of brown nations across the globe. It murdered millions for profit and called it democracy.

Its end will be greeted not with mourning, but with relief. Just as the ancient world rejoiced at the fall of Assyria, so too will the modern world celebrate the death of America's white empire.

Farewell to an empire built on slavery, genocide, and profit.

# Section VI:
# Corporate Profiteering, Opioids & Historical Profiteers

# Jewish Complicity In Slavery And Opioid Profiteering:

History, when told fully, does not flatter. It does not sanitize. It does not excuse participation in systems of oppression based on identity. History, if it is to be a tool of justice, must hold every actor accountable—regardless of religion, race, or nationality. And so we must confront an often overlooked but deeply consequential truth: the role of Jewish families and individuals in systems of racialized capitalism, particularly in the American South and in modern pharmaceutical empires.

According to historian Robert Rosen in his seminal work *The Jewish Confederates* (2006), Jewish Americans were not merely passive observers during the American Civil War—they were participants, profiteers, and in some cases, architects of the Confederate cause. In cities like New Orleans, Jewish families held prominent social and economic positions and owned plantations powered by the labor of enslaved Africans.

One of the most prominent Jewish figures in the Confederacy was Judah P. Benjamin, a former U.S. Senator from Louisiana who became Secretary of War and Secretary of State under Confederate President Jefferson Davis. Benjamin was not simply a politician—he was a wealthy plantation owner who personally enslaved dozens of African men, women, and children. He built his fortune, like many of his white counterparts, on the systematic dehumanization of Black life.

New Orleans, a major hub for the transatlantic slave trade, was home to a thriving Jewish merchant class, many of whom had immigrated from Prussia and other parts of Central Europe. They were white by classification and by privilege—and many exercised that privilege by investing in the slave economy. The port of New Orleans became a marketplace where human beings were bought, sold, and traded alongside cotton, tobacco, and sugar.

Among the most infamous of these families was the Monsanto family, originally of Portuguese-Jewish descent. According to Dr.

## Decline of America and Israel: The Last Two Racial Apartheid White Colonial Nations

Deshay David Ford (2022), the Monsanto dynasty amassed extraordinary wealth through the trafficking of enslaved Africans. They owned sprawling plantations across the American South and the Caribbean and operated slave ships that sailed from Africa to the Americas. These ships did not carry spices, textiles, or goods—they carried chained Black bodies, ripped from their homelands, destined for lives of forced labor and generational trauma.

The Monsantos' legacy is not one of moral courage or humanitarian leadership. It is one of calculated economic exploitation. They trafficked in flesh, profited from torture, and treated human life as cargo. They tore apart families for profit and reinforced the machinery of slavery that underpinned the American economy. Their wealth was not accidental—it was intentional. It was born from the ashes of African civilizations.

Yet, this chapter of Jewish-American history remains largely unspoken. Why? Because it disrupts a popular narrative that frames Jewish communities exclusively as victims of persecution. While it is true that Jews have faced horrific oppression—most notably under Adolf Hitler's genocidal regime during World War II—it is also true that some Jewish families, when afforded whiteness and opportunity, became complicit in the very systems they had once escaped.

Consider the bitter irony: Adolf Hitler, in launching his genocidal campaign against the Jews of Europe, accused them of betrayal during World War I, citing events like the Balfour Declaration of 1917 as evidence. That infamous letter from Lord Arthur Balfour to Baron Rothschild promised British support for a Jewish homeland in Palestine—fueling anti-Semitic conspiracies that Jews had conspired against the German Empire. Hitler's campaign was driven by politics, racism, and paranoia—not profit.

In contrast, the Monsanto family's involvement in the slave trade was not rooted in religious ideology or nationalist revenge. It was driven by pure economic greed. They were not scapegoated—they were empowered. They were not hunted—they were honored in business circles. And the people they destroyed were not Germans—they were

Africans, whose stories were buried in the ledgers of slave ships and the silence of history books.

But the tale of racial capitalism does not end in the 19th century. In the modern era, the Sackler family, another powerful Jewish-American dynasty, built a pharmaceutical empire that devastated millions of American lives. Originally from Poland, the Sacklers founded Purdue Pharma, the company responsible for manufacturing and aggressively marketing the opioid OxyContin.

What began as a "painkiller revolution" soon spiraled into the worst drug epidemic in modern American history. The Sacklers denied OxyContin's addictive potential while promoting it as a safe solution for chronic pain. Doctors were paid, research was falsified, and regulatory agencies were bypassed. As the pills flowed, so did the profits.

While Americans—especially in working-class and rural communities—succumbed to addiction, overdose, and death, the Sackler family accumulated billions of dollars in personal wealth. By the time lawsuits began to mount, the damage had already been done. The Sacklers entered into legal settlements with dozens of states, agreeing to fund addiction treatment programs. But they retained their fortune. They walked away with impunity.

The cost? *Hundreds of thousands of lives lost.* Families destroyed. Children orphaned. Entire communities hollowed out by a pill that had been marketed with the same ruthless efficiency as cotton had been centuries earlier.

As documented by the U.S. Department of Health and Human Services (2022), the opioid epidemic remains one of the greatest public health disasters in American history. And like the slave trade, it was fueled by the pursuit of profit over people.

Whether in the antebellum South or 21st-century boardrooms, the logic of exploitation is the same: *dehumanize, profit, deny.*

This is not an indictment of Judaism as a religion. It is not a condemnation of all Jewish people. It is a reckoning with the truth that no group, however persecuted, is immune from becoming a perpetrator when power and profit are within reach. Identity does not equal innocence. And trauma does not excuse participation in systems of oppression.

To build a more just world, we must stop pretending that some histories are too sacred to interrogate. The suffering of African slaves and the opioid victims of modern America are not footnotes—they are testimonies. They demand acknowledgment, accountability, and an end to selective memory.

As we uncover these truths, we must ask ourselves: *Who benefits from silence? And who pays the price for forgetting?*

Let the record show—the chains of exploitation have simply changed form. Where once it was whips and auctions, now it is prescriptions and profits. But the logic remains.

And so must our resistance.

# Iraq's Jews Participation In China's Opioid Epidemic 1839-1842

Empires do not rise by accident. They are built through blood, trade, and addiction. And sometimes, the merchants of that addiction are cloaked not in uniforms of conquest but in tailored suits, ancient prayers, and ledgers lined in gold. During the 19th century, as the British Empire waged its wars for dominance over Asia, two powerful Jewish merchant families, the Sassoons and the Kadoories, originally from Baghdad, Iraq emerged as key profiteers of one of the most catastrophic drug epidemics in human history: the Opium Wars in China (1839–1842).

According to Pulitzer Prize-winning journalist Jonathan Kaufman in *The Last Kings of Shanghai* (Kaufman, 2020), these families did not merely participate in the economic landscape of colonial Asia, they helped shape it. The Sassoons, often called the "Rothschilds of the East," and later the Kadoories, both of Baghdadi Jewish descent, established vast commercial empires across India and China, fueled in no small part by the trafficking of opium, a narcotic that would enslave millions and hollow out the heart of Chinese civilization.

What makes their role particularly disturbing is not merely the scale of profit but the conscious and unapologetic pursuit of it. Kaufman documents how these families leveraged their deep connections with the British colonial apparatus to oppose all Chinese attempts to outlaw the sale of opium. At every turn, they resisted bans, lobbied against regulation, and viewed Chinese addiction not as a moral crisis, but as a business opportunity.

The Sassoons, arriving in Shanghai as early as the 1830s, did not stumble into the drug trade. They sought it. Opium, trafficked from British-controlled India and imported into Chinese ports by military force, became their golden calf. The Kadoories followed closely, expanding the empire further and embedding themselves in colonial financial institutions. Together, these Iraqi Jewish families were not simply traders. They were architects of empire, a narcotic empire that ruined millions of lives.

As Chinese society collapsed under the weight of mass addiction, British gunboats secured trade routes and British diplomats imposed humiliating treaties. After the First Opium War (1839–1842), Britain forced the Qing Dynasty to sign the Treaty of Nanking, opening Chinese ports to foreign drug merchants and ceding Hong Kong—a decision the Chinese still refer to as the beginning of the "Century of Humiliation." The Sassoons and Kadoories profited enormously from this degradation. Their mansions rose as Chinese families starved. Their fortunes swelled while Chinese workers were dismissed and fired for succumbing to the very addiction the Sassoons had imported.

When asked in later years if they regretted their role in fueling an epidemic that destroyed a civilization, their response was chilling in its candor: "We were just making money."

That money came not only from the suffering of the Chinese people but from the moral conviction that Chinese lives were simply...different. Disposable. Inferior. As Kaufman records, both the Sassoon and Kadoorie families shared in the widespread colonial belief that the

Chinese were culturally and racially "other." Thus, flooding Chinese cities with opium was not immoral, it was business. The same logic that had once justified slavery in the American South now justified drug trafficking in Shanghai.

The Sassoons and Kadoories were not alone. American elites, including the Roosevelt family, whose fortune laid the foundation for two U.S. presidencies, also made vast sums off the Chinese opium trade. Together with British, French, and German colonial powers, they weaponized addiction as a tool of empire. And just as European colonizers enslaved Africans and subjugated Indians, so too did they reduce the Chinese to addicts, laborers, and subjects in their own land.

This is not a story of isolated businessmen. It is a story of global racial capitalism of Jewish merchant families from ancient Babylon (modern-day Iraq) enriching themselves through human degradation, standing shoulder to shoulder with white colonial empires in their contempt for non-white bodies. Kaufman writes that the Sassoons dismissed hundreds of Chinese employees for being "unfit" due to addiction, even as they continued to profit from selling them the very substance that enslaved them.

To understand this moment in history is to confront a wider truth: that empire corrupts not only the conquered, but the conquerors. And that even historically persecuted groups, when handed the reins of colonial power, can become agents of oppression themselves.

The Sassoon and Kadoorie families, hailed in some circles for their philanthropy and contributions to modern China, must also be remembered for their complicity in catastrophe. The opium trade was not a footnote, it was the engine of their wealth. Kaufman is clear: these dynasties helped build modern Shanghai on the corpses of addicted men, the ashes of broken families, and the wreckage of Chinese sovereignty.

Their complicity aligns with a broader pattern. As documented in *The Jewish Confederates* (Rosen, 2006), some Jewish families also played roles in the Atlantic slave trade, profiting from the buying and selling of African human beings in both North and South America. Later, others like the Monsanto family, originally tied to slave labor in Louisiana, transitioned into industrial agriculture and toxic chemical production, such as the herbicide Roundup, which has been linked to cancer in millions of Americans.

This same pursuit of profit over people re-emerged in the late 20th century in the United States, where the Jewish-American Sackler family, through Purdue Pharma, marketed OxyContin to the masses; an opioid epidemic echoing the devastation of 19th-century China.

History, then, is not simply a ledger of facts. It is a mirror of morality. And in that mirror, the Sassoons and Kadoories must be seen clearly, not merely as businessmen, but as profiteers of empire, dealers of addiction, and willing agents in the collapse of one of the world's greatest civilizations.

The Chinese people, remembering this devastation, refer to that era as the *Hundred Years of Humiliation*. And rightly so. For what was done to them through war, drugs, and racism was not just a crime. It was a model. A template for colonial conquest dressed in the garments of commerce.

And in that model, the Sassoons and Kadoories were pioneers.

## The Monsanto Family In New Orleans Made Their Wealth In The African Slave Trade

The Monsanto name did not begin in the soil of American agriculture or the laboratories of chemical manufacturing. Its roots reached across the Atlantic, planted first in Portugal, where Jewish merchants, fleeing the Inquisition's grip, learned how to survive under Catholic monarchies by trading whatever would bring coin. After the American Revolutionary War ended in 1781, members of the Monsanto family crossed the ocean and anchored themselves in New Orleans, Louisiana—a city that was then one of the beating hearts of the transatlantic slave trade.

New Orleans was not simply a port. It was a human marketplace. Ships docked there carrying chained African men, women, and children, dragged from their homelands and branded as property. The Monsanto family did not stand on the docks in protest. They owned the ships. They trafficked the bodies. They turned the misery of an entire continent into their personal fortune.

Robert Rosen, in his book *The Jewish Confederates*, recorded the uncomfortable truth: the Monsantos were not alone. Other Jewish merchant families in the Gulf region participated in the transatlantic slave trade, proving that the brutality of human commerce was not confined to one religion or ethnicity—it was a business model that seduced anyone willing to trade morality for profit. The slave trade did not just enrich a few merchants. It built empires, both personal and national. It poured wealth into the banks of New Orleans and Charleston, into the pockets of planters from Virginia to Mississippi, and into the vaults of European investors who never once set foot on a plantation.

The Monsanto family's wealth was soaked in blood. They dealt in ships that ferried thousands of Africans into the United States, where they were sold into a lifetime of forced labor on cotton, rice, and sugar plantations. These plantations were engines of profit for white masters and merchants, but graveyards for the enslaved. The system was designed to work them to death. Children were born into slavery, not as members of a family, but as assets on a ledger.

Judah P. Benjamin, another Jewish figure in New Orleans, became one of the most powerful politicians in the Confederacy. Serving as the Confederate Secretary of War and later as Secretary of State, Benjamin himself owned a plantation and hundreds of enslaved Africans. His legal brilliance and political cunning made him indispensable to Jefferson Davis, but his wealth—like the Monsanto fortune—was rooted in the sale and ownership of human beings. Benjamin's biography contained its own scandal: expelled from Yale for homosexual conduct, he nonetheless rose to become one of the most influential men in the South, proof that personal disgrace meant little when one's hands were valuable to the machinery of oppression.

Decline of America and Israel: The Last Two Racial Apartheid White Colonial Nations

The transatlantic slave trade, in which the Monsantos played their part, was not a minor historical footnote. It was the largest forced migration in human history. Historians estimate that more than 27 million African lives were stolen, destroyed, or permanently altered through this trade. It was, in every sense, genocide—systematic, deliberate, and profitable. European and American merchants saw African lives not as human souls but as raw material to be harvested.

The violence did not end at the auction block. Enslaved Africans were whipped, mutilated, raped, and murdered with impunity. Disease swept through slave ships and plantations alike, and starvation was used as a tool of control. Resistance was met with torture. For the Monsanto family and their peers, these horrors were not tragedies—they were expenses, calculated and absorbed into the cost of doing business.

When the United States split in 1861, the Confederacy fought to preserve this economy of flesh. The North fought to destroy it in name, but not entirely in practice. Slavery's formal abolition in 1865 did not erase the racial caste system—it merely changed its shape.

A century later, the world would learn of another genocide, the Holocaust, when Adolf Hitler and the Nazi regime sought to eradicate European Jews. At the Wannsee Conference of January 20, 1942, German officials openly discussed the mechanics of mass extermination. Unlike the transatlantic slave trade, which enriched its participants, the Holocaust was not designed for economic profit. It was fueled by ideology and vengeance, with Hitler accusing Jews of betraying Germany during World War I. The Nazis sought annihilation, not labor.

But the parallel remains: both the Holocaust and the African slave trade were industrialized systems of dehumanization. One destroyed six million Jews in less than a decade. The other destroyed tens of millions of Africans over the course of centuries.

The difference lies in motive. The Monsanto family and the Confederate elite destroyed African families for money. It was capitalism without conscience. The Nazis destroyed Jewish families for ideological

purity. Both crimes shattered civilizations. Both crimes left wounds that
still bleed.

The story of the Monsanto family in New Orleans is not simply an
anecdote in a dusty history book. It is a reminder that wealth in America,
from the plantation era to the corporate boardroom, often rests upon
the bones of the exploited. The cargo holds of slave ships were the
foundation stones of fortunes that would later buy mansions, fund
political campaigns, and establish "respectable" family legacies.

It is also a reminder that the narrative of innocence—whether
wrapped in religious identity, national pride, or corporate branding—
cannot erase the truth. The Monsantos were not merely merchants.
They were traffickers in human life. And their wealth was not earned. It
was stolen.

# Richard Sackler Created The American Opioid Epidemic

## How Purdue Pharma Engineered a Crisis for Profit

In the late 20th century, a new epidemic began to spread across the
United States, not from the streets, but from the boardrooms of
corporate pharmaceutical companies. And at the center of this man-
made disaster stood Richard Sackler, heir to the Sackler family fortune
and executive of Purdue Pharma. With the release of OxyContin in
1996, the Sackler dynasty unleashed one of the deadliest public health
crises in American history.

Richard Sackler was not a physician in any meaningful moral sense.
He was a businessman. His mission was not healing but expansion.
Under his leadership, Purdue Pharma developed and aggressively
marketed OxyContin, a time-release formulation of the powerful opioid
oxycodone. The drug was originally intended for severe pain, such as
that experienced by cancer patients, but Purdue, under Sackler's
guidance, pushed for it to be prescribed for far more common ailments,
back pain, arthritis, and post-operative discomfort.

To convince doctors and regulators that OxyContin was safe, Purdue launched a calculated misinformation campaign. They claimed that the drug was not addictive, citing manipulated data, cherry-picked studies, and marketing slogans rather than medical science. Sales representatives were trained to reassure physicians that the risk of addiction was "less than one percent." This was a lie.

That lie became policy.

Between 1999 and 2020, nearly half a million Americans died from opioid overdoses, and OxyContin played a central role in that toll. What began as a pharmaceutical rollout became a mass death event. The Sackler family's profits surged, and as the bodies piled up, Purdue Pharma expanded its reach across the country. According to internal documents later revealed in court, Richard Sackler encouraged higher doses and broader marketing, even as evidence of addiction and abuse poured in.

One internal email from Sackler, uncovered during litigation, stated plainly: "We have to hammer on the abusers in every way possible." In other words, blame the victims. Deny responsibility. Protect the brand.

Purdue Pharma's tactics were both predatory and deceptive. The company targeted poor communities, rural towns, and injured workers. It flooded markets already vulnerable to economic despair and trauma. The very people most at risk were the ones most aggressively pursued.

And the consequence was catastrophic.

Entire towns in Appalachia were decimated. Counties in Ohio, West Virginia, Kentucky, and Tennessee became epicenters of overdose deaths. Foster care systems collapsed under the weight of children orphaned by addiction. Emergency rooms were overwhelmed. Funeral homes filled.

The opioid epidemic was not a public health failure. It was a corporate war crime.

In time, the truth could no longer be buried under settlements and spin. Multiple state attorneys general brought lawsuits against Purdue Pharma, accusing the company of misleading doctors, patients, and regulators. Purdue eventually declared bankruptcy and agreed to pay billions in damages.

But the story did not end there.

The Sackler family, despite agreeing to the financial settlement, retained much of their wealth. Protected by legal maneuvering and bankruptcy court shields, they walked away with billions of dollars untouched. According to investigative reports, the Sacklers transferred more than $10 billion out of Purdue before its bankruptcy to offshore trusts and private accounts. Their name, once proudly displayed on museum wings and university libraries, became synonymous with greed and death.

And yet, to this day, no member of the Sackler family has served a single day in prison.

They did not need to smuggle drugs through back alleys. They simply printed labels.

They did not use street dealers. They used licensed physicians.

They did not flee from the law. They rewrote it.

Richard Sackler and Purdue Pharma transformed the pharmaceutical industry into a death engine. They made addiction a business model. They made suffering a source of revenue. And they made sure that no matter how many Americans died, they would remain untouchable.

Richard Sackler was an architect who designed the whole strategy behind the opioid epidemic and made it look like an accident.

The story of Purdue Pharma is not just about a pill. It is about the rot at the heart of American capitalism. It is about what happens when profit becomes more important than people. It is about a legal system that protects the wealthy while burying the poor.

The Sackler family may one day be remembered not as philanthropists, but as profiteers of mass death. They did not just create a drug. They created a legacy of devastation.

205

# Section VII:
# Race, Policing, Criminal Justice & UN Findings

# California Rodney's King's Race Riot 1991

I moved to California from Arkansas in 1984 with hope in my chest and illusions in my luggage. Back in the South, racism wore no disguise. It came wrapped in Confederate flags, whispered through job rejections, and screamed from courthouse steps. California, on the other hand, wore makeup. It smiled in diversity brochures, paraded its beaches and rainbows, and declared itself the land of progress. But what I found beneath the golden sun was a state no more tolerant than the backwoods towns of Dixie, just better at pretending.

The myth of California as a racial oasis is one of America's most dangerous lies. It suggests that the Pacific Ocean washes away the sins of empire. But I quickly discovered that behind every palm tree was a police badge, and behind every badge, a system that saw my skin as threat, not citizenry.

By 1991, that mask was torn off for the world to see.

The world watched, stunned and horrified, as a Black man named Rodney Glen King was pulled from his car and brutally beaten by officers of the Los Angeles Police Department. The scene unfolded not in secret, not in a dark alley or behind closed jail doors, but on a public street under the indifferent glow of California streetlights. George Holliday, a white man with a camcorder, captured the assault from his apartment balcony. His video became global evidence of a system we, as Black people, had been screaming about for decades: that in the United States of America, and in California especially, the police are often not peacekeepers but predators.

Rodney King did not resist arrest. He did not carry a weapon. He was Black, poor, and out of place in the eyes of men who saw power not as a public trust but as a license to terrorize. They beat him with batons like he was a runaway slave, fifty-six blows in total. Kicks to the head. Tasers. A lynching with a modern soundtrack: the static hum of a police radio and the cracking sound of fiberglass on flesh.

When the trial came, it was moved to Simi Valley, a white suburb filled with LAPD families and friends. There, a jury of nine white people, one Latino, and one Asian decided that the officers were not guilty. Not of excessive force. Not of battery. Not of anything.

Los Angeles exploded.

For six days in April and May 1992, the city burned. Stores looted. Streets blocked. Flames swallowed entire blocks. Over 60 people were killed. Thousands were injured. Billions in property damage. The National Guard was called in. The United States Marines deployed. It was not just a riot, it was a rebellion. It was the inevitable rupture of a city built on segregation, brutality, and lies.

The media called it the "Rodney King Riot," as if it were about one man. It wasn't. Rodney King was the match. The fire had been smoldering since Watts in 1965, when another instance of police violence sparked a similar uprising. Watts was a warning. 1992 was the reckoning.

In 1984, when I first arrived in Los Angeles, I saw the racial lines etched into the concrete: South Central for the poor and Black, East LA for the Brown and forgotten, West LA for the rich and white. The freeway system itself was a racial map architected to bypass Black neighborhoods and funnel wealth to white ones. You could stand on Crenshaw Boulevard and feel like you were in another country entirely. No jobs. No parks. No justice.

The LAPD, under Chief Daryl Gates, was a domestic army. Black boys were prey. Brown men were suspects. And white men were the law. If you were a person of color, especially young and male, every trip outside your house came with a warning: don't run, don't reach, don't speak, don't breathe wrong. Or else.

That was 40 years ago. It hasn't changed.

From the Watts Rebellion in 1965, to the Rodney King Uprising in 1992, to the killing of Oscar Grant in Oakland in 2009, to the murder of George Floyd in Minneapolis in 2020—America has rehearsed this horror so many times it can't pretend to be shocked. Each generation is handed the same script: Black pain, white acquittal, and media gaslighting.

In 2020, during the COVID-19 pandemic, the racial divide was laid bare again. Black and Brown communities died at disproportionate rates, not because of biology, but because of poverty, policy, and systemic neglect. Essential workers were mostly people of color, deemed essential only to capitalism, not to survival. Hospitals turned away our sick. Police killed our children. Billionaires got richer. And we buried our dead.

In 2024, racism remains. The names change. The headlines blur. But the facts do not lie.

America is not a land of equality. It is a racialized empire. Los Angeles is not a multicultural utopia. It is a segregated metropolis built on broken promises and burning neighborhoods. The Rodney King rebellion was not a glitch in the system. It was the system baring its teeth.

I have lived in California for four decades. I have seen its sunshine and its shadows. And I testify, as a man who has endured both, that the racism here is not softer than in the South—it is just slicker. More insidious. It hides behind Hollywood smiles and Silicon Valley diversity pledges. But it kills just the same.

Rodney King once asked, "Can we all get along?" He meant it as a plea, yet America took it as a punchline.

And we are still waiting for an answer.

## Ventura, California – A Racist Court System That Discriminates Against People Of Color

I arrived in the city of Oxnard, California, on May 8, 1984. I came from Scott, Arkansas, a place where racial hatred never wore a mask. It was open. It was proud. It flew its flags high. But when I reached Ventura County, I discovered a different beast entirely. Here, racism wore a badge and a black robe. It passed itself off as law. It cloaked its crimes behind court orders and clerical smiles.

I was not surprised.

Oxnard had, and still has, a large Latino population, a working-class community built on labor, struggle, and survival. Yet, despite being the heart that pumped Ventura County's agricultural and service economy, these Latino families were treated not as citizens but as a labor force to be controlled, surveilled, cited, and drained of dignity.

Ventura County operates like a modern-day Southern plantation, dressed in California sunlight. Two powerful farming families, the Maulhardts and the McGraths, have long held economic dominance in the region. They do not farm only crops, they farm people. They have planted themselves deep into the soil of local politics, law enforcement, and judicial influence. Their fields are irrigated by poverty, and their profits fertilized by injustice.

The structure is familiar. It mirrors the racist plantation model I knew from the South. But instead of chains, they use citations. Instead of overseers, they use officers. Instead of whips, they use court fees.

As documented by Dr. David García in his groundbreaking book *Strategies of Segregation*, Ventura's power structure, composed of white landowners, politicians, and school boards, collaborated with agricultural elites to deliberately sabotage Latino education. The goal was clear: keep Latino students from graduating, thereby ensuring a steady supply of undereducated, cheap, and desperate labor for the fields. García's research confirmed what many of us already knew from lived experience: that the oppression of a people is not accidental. It is strategic. It is policy.

I had seen it before. In Arkansas, the white power elite used every tool possible—segregation, underfunded schools, intimidation—to deny Black children access to education. Not because they feared our ignorance, but because they feared what we might become if we ever broke free from it.

Decline of America and Israel: The Last Two Racial Apartheid White
Colonial Nations

In Ventura, I witnessed this same philosophy embedded in the so-
called justice system. I once attended a courtroom session on traffic
violations—a space supposedly neutral, a place where fairness was to be
decided. What I saw instead was the machinery of racial punishment at
work.

Every case I watched involved a Latino defendant and a white police
officer. The defendants came dressed in humility: construction boots,
work shirts, Spanish-speaking mothers clutching citation slips. The
officers entered with uniforms, confidence, and the assurance of victory.
Each time, the white judge gave both sides a chance to speak, but it was
theater. A ritual. A charade.

The verdict was always the same: the officer was right. The Latino
defendant was wrong.

In one rare case, the roles were reversed. A Latino police officer had
written a traffic citation for a young blonde white woman. Same process.
Same courtroom. But a very different outcome. The white judge, calmly
and without shame, declared that the Latino officer was likely
"confused." That the young white woman must have been wrongly
accused. The officer's testimony was dismissed. Her word was gospel.

The racism was not subtle. It was institutionalized.

But the injustice didn't end there. Once the gavel dropped, the real
exploitation began. Latino defendants were ushered into a system called
the "Pay Plan." The judge would break down the fines into
"manageable" payments, often framing it as a kindness—installments,
interest, court fees, traffic school, late penalties, and administrative costs.
What started as a $150 citation could balloon into over $700 in total
charges. The plan wasn't mercy. It was debt bondage.

These "Pay Plans" functioned like legalized extortion schemes. The
courthouse was not just a place of law—it was a business. And poor
Latino families were its primary customers.

The money extracted through these plans didn't just disappear into
the air. It funded the salaries of courthouse staff. It paid for jail

operations. It covered meals for inmates, utilities, and the overtime of deputies. Every dime squeezed from the working poor flowed into the bloodstream of a justice system designed to profit off pain.

The courtroom became a plantation. The judge was the overseer. The citation was the whip.

White officers were not only encouraged to issue citations to Latino drivers, they were rewarded. Quotas were whispered, if not spoken. Promotions were tied to enforcement records. And enforcement meant targeting the poor, the undocumented, the laborers with brown skin.

It was capitalism with a Southern drawl, wearing a Ventura badge.

There was no Miranda warning for this kind of injustice. No jury of peers. No cameras to go viral. The courtroom didn't need guns to extract obedience. It had bureaucracy. It had bailiffs. It had the law.

In essence, the Ventura County Court System ran like a modern American slave economy. But instead of shackles, it used signatures. Instead of cotton, it harvested compliance. And most disturbingly, the victims paid for their own incarceration.

This is not hyperbole. This is California. This is America.

And Ventura County is its mirror, polished by palm trees and powered by punishment.

# Driving While Latino Or Brown

In the United States, race is not just a category. It is a criminal record, pre-written and pre-policed.

Nowhere was this truth more apparent than in Ventura County, California, where "driving while Latino", or simply being brown in public space, was treated as a de facto crime. The phrase "driving while Black" is well-documented in American legal literature and media coverage, but in Ventura, it was joined by a local corollary: "driving while brown." This phrase wasn't born in jest. It was born in courtrooms and cemeteries.

Ventura County law enforcement, like their counterparts in Arizona and other borderland jurisdictions, systematically profiled and policed Latino and Black drivers at rates far higher than their white counterparts. Stop-and-frisk? That was more culture than policy. Racial profiling wasn't hidden. It was operationalized. It was standard procedure.

The data, when examined, reveals the rot. A 2019 report by the *Public Policy Institute of California* confirmed what communities of color have long testified: Latino and Black Californians are more likely to be searched, cited, detained, and arrested in vehicle stops, despite being less likely to possess contraband than white drivers.

The United Nations has also taken notice. In a 2023 report from the U.N. Working Group of Experts on People of African Descent, U.S. police departments were condemned for their entrenched racial biases in policing practices. The report concluded that Black and Latino individuals are disproportionately targeted in traffic stops, arrests, and use of force, particularly in affluent or majority-white neighborhoods.

Let the record show: the United States, while branding itself as the beacon of democracy, imprisons more people than China, Russia, North Korea, or Israel. With roughly 4% of the world's population, the U.S. holds over 20% of the world's incarcerated, and the overwhelming majority of those behind bars are Black and Brown. The prison system is not separate from racial profiling. It is its final destination.

I, myself, witnessed this architecture of oppression firsthand when I served on the Ventura County Grand Jury from 1996 to 1997. During that year, I saw a judicial process that did not merely mirror racism, it was engineered by it.

One of the cases we reviewed involved a Latino sheriff's deputy who responded to a disturbance call. When he knocked on the door of a white man named Richard Johnson, he was met with immediate gunfire. The deputy was shot on sight. As he lay wounded on the ground, Johnson approached and executed him with a shot to the head.

The District Attorney, a white man named Michael Bradbury, demanded justice. He requested the death penalty, not just because the victim was law enforcement, but because this was a cold-blooded killing. My fellow jurors were given clear direction: this was a capital case. Indict accordingly.

But what followed was a display of racial loyalty, not legal reasoning.

Of the nineteen grand jurors, only three of us voted for the death penalty: I, the only other Black juror, and a white woman from Ventura. The others, all white, most from Simi Valley, a suburb known nationwide as the jury pool that acquitted the officers who beat Rodney King, refused to indict a white man for killing a Latino deputy.

Let me be clear: the man had executed an officer in cold blood. But whiteness, in this country, is a form of immunity.

District Attorney Bradbury later approached me outside the courthouse. With visible disappointment and restrained rage, he hugged me and thanked me for standing on the side of justice. But the wound had already been inflicted. The legal system in Ventura County had failed its own officer, because he wore brown skin beneath the badge.

But the next case, far worse, shattered any illusion that justice in Ventura County was blind.

We were given another death penalty case. This time, the accused was a Japanese-American man, charged with the alleged murder of his white wife. Before we saw a single shred of evidence, before any witness was called, before the accused was even allowed to speak, the Grand Jury indicted him.

The decision was made two days before the accused had his opportunity to address us. He arrived expecting justice, but what he received was a legal lynching in the guise of due process.

When he finally stood before us, trembling and hopeful, pleading for an impartial hearing, I watched the truth collapse in front of me. We had already condemned him. His attorney suspected as much. Later, his legal team contacted me directly. And I, bound not by silence but by conscience, confirmed their fears.

We had indicted a man without hearing his story, without vetting the evidence, without examining the truth.

His only crime? He was a man of color.

His wife? A white woman.

The attorneys filed for a change of venue to Santa Barbara, seeking the bare minimum: a fair trial.

Justice Clarence Thomas once told a journalist that the Constitution was "colorblind." But if he had truly read Article IV, Section 2, Clause 3 of the very document he swore to uphold, he would know otherwise. That clause gave slaveholders the legal right to retrieve their "property", enslaved human beings, from free states, dragging them back to bondage in the South. That clause enshrined race-based ownership into the founding law of this nation.

The Constitution is not colorblind. It was color-coded from inception.

And so too is the American justice system. In Ventura County, in Arizona, in Georgia, in Missouri, in New York City, in Chicago, and everywhere in between, Black and Brown drivers are not simply stopped, they are surveilled, extracted, fined, incarcerated, and erased.

This is not anecdote. This is design.

From traffic stops to grand juries, from sentencing disparities to jury selection bias, the entire infrastructure of American justice has been built on the presumption that whiteness is innocent, and color is guilt.

That's not equality. That's apartheid.

That's not justice. That's American jurisprudence.

## United Nations Condemns The U.S Justice System For Racially Profiling Black And Brown People

### MICHAEL GREENBERG:

### A California Workers' Compensation Judge Who Weaponized Law Enforcement Against a Black Man

### A United Nations Case Study in Systemic Racism

On September 26, 2018, Dr. Deshay David Ford suffered a job-related injury. Like millions of other Americans, he turned to the state's judicial system for resolution, in this case, to the Workers' Compensation Office in Oxnard, California. But instead of receiving due process, Dr. Ford, a Black man, was treated not as a citizen but as a criminal suspect.

What unfolded in that office was not a courtroom drama, it was a state-sanctioned reenactment of racial intimidation.

When Dr. Ford arrived to request a simple continuance in his case, he was met not with administrative civility but with police enforcement. The information officer, Mr. Michael Avila, refused his request and claimed he would "check with his superior." That superior was Judge Michael Greenberg, a white judge who emerged from his chambers, not with an extension, not with a ruling, but with an order to summon an armed police officer to stand over Dr. Ford.

That act, calling an armed officer to confront an unarmed Black man in a government office, was not an administrative procedure. It was racial performance violence.

Dr. Ford stood still as the officer entered, stood over him, and established a line of psychological control. He was not shouting. He was not disrupting. He was not threatening anyone. He was simply asking for an extension. Yet the judge's response was to invoke the threat of state-sanctioned force, because in America, being Black and assertive is all the provocation needed.

Dr. Ford feared for his life. And rightly so.

He remembered George Floyd, murdered in 2020 in Minneapolis by a police officer who pressed his knee into Floyd's neck for nine minutes over an allegedly counterfeit $20 bill, an accusation made by a white teenager, never proven, and irrelevant to the value of a man's life. He remembered Michael Brown, a Black teenager gunned down in Ferguson, Missouri, after being racially profiled. He remembered Philando Castile, killed in front of his child. He remembered Tamir Rice, Oscar Grant, Breonna Taylor, and countless others whose names echo like tombstones in the mind of every Black man in America.

Dr. Ford knew the statistics. He knew that Black and Latino men are disproportionately killed by police in the United States. He knew the fear was real, not rhetorical.

He filed a federal racial profiling complaint in the U.S. District Court in Los Angeles, citing violations under:

- 18 U.S.C. § 241 (conspiracy against rights),

- 18 U.S.C. § 242 (deprivation of rights under color of law),

- and the 1964 Civil Rights Act, on the grounds of race, age, sex, and disability discrimination.

But the judges, Valerie Baker Fairbank and Rozella Oliver, dismissed his complaint. Their ruling? That his claims of racial profiling were "frivolous" and "without merit." These words have become judicial code for "we do not believe Black people."

In their dismissal, the judges falsely stated that Dr. Ford had filed under 42 U.S.C. § 1983, a legal technicality which allowed them to invoke the doctrine of judicial immunity, shielding Judge Greenberg from consequence. But Dr. Ford had filed under federal criminal statutes, not civil immunity ones. The mischaracterization was not merely an error, it was a maneuver.

In doing so, Judges Fairbank and Oliver did more than dismiss a case, they protected a racially discriminatory system. Their decision validated what the United Nations has documented for years: that Black and Brown citizens in America receive neither equal protection nor fair due process in U.S. courts.

In 2023, the U.N. Working Group of Experts on People of African Descent concluded that the American legal system is structurally racist, perpetuating inequality through implicit bias, procedural discrimination, and judicial disregard for Black plaintiffs' claims.

Dr. Ford's experience was a case study in that report. He was not denied justice. He was targeted by it.

THE U.S. CONSTITUTION: BUILT FOR PROPERTY, NOT PEOPLE

Those who claim that "all men are created equal" must first reckon with the document they revere.

The U.S. Constitution of 1787, particularly Article IV, Section 2, Clause 3, clearly states that if an enslaved person escapes to a free state, their "owner" has the right to retrieve them. This was not the law. It was property insurance for white slaveholders. Men like George Washington, Thomas Jefferson, and James Madison, all of them slave owners, crafted a Constitution to protect their investments, not liberate the people they owned.

So when Associate Justice Clarence Thomas told a journalist that the Constitution is "colorblind," he was not quoting history—he was reciting mythology. The Constitution was never neutral. It was penned by men who believed in racial superiority and economic dominance through bondage.

PANDEMIC PROFILING AND MEDICAL RACISM

In 2020, during the COVID-19 pandemic, the veil fell again.

## Decline of America and Israel: The Last Two Racial Apartheid White Colonial Nations

Black and Brown Americans died at significantly higher rates than white citizens, not because of biology, but because of a lack of access to quality healthcare, testing, and treatment. In New York, Chicago, and Los Angeles, Black and Latino communities suffered silently while white suburbs received government PPE, vaccines, and rapid response teams.

The myth of American equality evaporated. The world saw it. The protests erupted. And white America pretended to be shocked.

But this ignorance, too, was performative. When apartheid fell in South Africa in 1994, many white Afrikaners claimed they "had no idea" how bad the racism had been. In America, the script is the same. Denial is a defense mechanism for those who have always benefited.

## THE RISE OF CHINA AND THE FALL OF THE WHITE EMPIRE

As America stumbles under the weight of its own hypocrisy, the global stage shifts beneath it.

China, once bullied by the West, now leads in economic strength, infrastructure diplomacy, and international influence. The developing world, Latin America, Africa, and Southeast Asia, now turns toward Beijing, not Washington, for trade, aid, and investment.

The U.S. Empire, like Spain in 1898, is in free fall. Once a young, ambitious nation, eager to become an imperial power through wars like the Spanish-American War, the U.S. now finds itself drowning in debt, violence, and social decay.

As historian Howard Zinn wrote in *A People's History of the United States* (1980), the American elite believed they had a divine racial destiny: to rule the darker peoples of the world. Theodore Roosevelt, Henry Cabot Lodge, and their contemporaries preached Anglo-Saxon supremacy not as prejudice, but as policy.

The U.S. military invaded Haiti, Cuba, the Philippines, Guatemala, Iran, and Chile, not for democracy, but for control of natural resources, from sugar and copper to oil and bananas.

And yes, the United States forced its way into Japan in 1854, gunboats blazing, demanding trade at cannonpoint. It joined Britain and France in the Opium Wars, turning China into a market of addicts for imperial profit. European diseases and European domination ravaged civilizations for generations.

## WHITE SUPREMACY ATOMICIZED: THE BOMBING OF JAPAN

The United States is the only nation in world history to use nuclear weapons against civilians. In August 1945, the U.S. dropped atomic bombs on the Japanese cities of Hiroshima and Nagasaki, killing hundreds of thousands. This was a strategically planned racial vengeance.

Japan was already seeking surrender through diplomatic channels, but the American military wanted to make a point, not just to end the war, but to assert racial dominance over an Asian people.

That decision haunts humanity to this day.

## THE NEW ORDER: THE BROWN WORLD RISES

Today, the monopoly on violence once held by white Western powers is gone. North Korea has nuclear weapons. Pakistan has nuclear weapons. Nations of color can now defend themselves against white militarized empires.

Jeb Bush once said, "People of color don't fear America anymore."

That is the new reality. The old fear is gone. The old empire is collapsing.

The United States and Israel, the last two apartheid states built on settler colonialism, now struggle to maintain white supremacy on a global stage where the rules have changed.

The rise of China, the resilience of the Global South, and the awakening of formerly colonized peoples signal the end of the White World Order.

We are now living in the dawn of a Brown Century

# The United Nations Findings Of Racial Profiling By America's Justice System And White Racist Police Departments

The United Nations carried out an investigation into complaints by African Americans regarding racism in the U.S. courts, justice system, and police departments. Its findings were clear: America continues to engage in racial profiling, brutality, and killings of Black people by white police officers, reinforced by a deeply entrenched racist system of policing. Michael Brown's parents testified about this ongoing racism in American law enforcement. The UN concluded that the United States had established its system of racist policing during the historical period of Black slavery.

According to Dr. Ford, the American police system has its origins in the era of slavery. President James Madison, who personally owned hundreds of enslaved Africans on his Virginia plantation, enshrined this system in the Bill of Rights in 1791. Slave owners, fearing uprisings such as the 1811 New The Orleans slave rebellion demanded protection. Madison's Second Amendment declared: "A well-regulated militia being necessary to *the security* of *a free state*, the right of the people to keep and bear arms shall not be infringed" (Wilson, 1998). These "militias" were in fact slave patrols, organized to hunt down, torture, mutilate, lynch, decapitate, and punish enslaved people who resisted the institution of slavery (Ford, 2024). The Constitution itself legitimized slavery in Article IV, Section 2, Provision 3. Of the first nine presidents, all but John Adams owned enslaved people (Ford, 2024). Even Chief Justice Roger B. Taney, a slave owner, ruled in the infamous Dred Scott case of 1857 that Black people had no rights under the Constitution of 1787.

California, often idealized as a progressive state, also bears a history of racial genocide. As Benjamin Madley has documented in An American Genocide (2017), the United States, in cooperation with California, perpetrated genocidal campaigns against Native peoples from 1850 to 1853. This legacy of state-sanctioned violence continued into modern times. In 1991, Los Angeles erupted into riots after police brutally beat Rodney King, exposing the deep racism of the LAPD.

In October 2022, Deshay David Ford himself was racially profiled at the California Workers' Compensation Court. Judge Michael Greenberg ordered an armed officer to profile Ford, who had simply requested a continuance to introduce California labor codes—specifically Section 11762, which prohibits employers from falsifying income statements to reduce disability payments. Ford's employer, Gary Lavagna, had deliberately underreported his income. Judge Greenberg's actions, Ford argues, would never have been taken against a white or Jewish litigant. But as a Black man from an oppressed community, Ford faced discriminatory treatment (U.S. District Court 2-22-cv-08339-VBF-RAQ; 9th Circuit Court of Appeals, San Francisco, CA; CA Workers' Compensation Case No: ADJ11994903).

The injustice deepened when U.S. District Court Judges Valerie Baker Fairbank and Rozella Oliver, both white women, dismissed Ford's racial profiling claims as frivolous. In their courts, they declared that all such allegations should be considered without merit. The UN's findings stand in stark contrast, affirming that America's justice system is historically and systematically racist (2-22-cv-08339-VBF-RAQ).

The United Nations found that the U.S. legal system is as systemically racist toward Black and brown people as the apartheid system of Israel is toward Palestinians in Gaza and the West Bank. Both states share a legacy of racial apartheid directed against Indigenous peoples (Brown, 1970). Yet California's Attorney General, Rob Bonta, refused to act on Ford's complaint under the California Racial Profiling Identity Act of 2015, which mandates investigation of such allegations. By failing to act, Bonta reinforced the reality that Black and brown people in California—and in the United States—are denied rights under both state and federal constitutions. In this, Judge Taney's infamous declaration from 1857 remains hauntingly true: people of color have "no rights which the white man is bound to respect."

Decline of America and Israel: The Last Two Racial Apartheid White Colonial Nations

This hypocrisy extends beyond America's borders. The white colonial powers of NATO committed genocides against Indigenous populations across Africa, Asia, and the Americas. Japan too perpetrated racial violence and oppression in its colonies, though China, as Kishore Mahbubani (2020) emphasizes, did not. Unlike Western powers, China's civilization was not built by enslaved Black labor nor by genocidal campaigns against Indigenous peoples. In contrast, Israel today embodies the most brutal aspects of racial colonialism, more vicious even than Nazi Germany under Adolf Hitler. Prime Minister Benjamin Netanyahu bombs hospitals in Gaza as acts of racial genocide, motivated not by security but by the pursuit of gas and oil resources off the coast of Gaza—resources granted to Palestinians under the Oslo Accords of 1995. The U.S., providing Israel with weapons, enables this genocide.

African Americans recognize this war for what it is: a European and American race war against brown people in the Middle East. Having themselves endured 450 years of racial genocide in America, Black communities see their own struggles reflected in Palestine. Under Donald Trump's 2024 candidacy, the flames of white supremacy burn hotter still. Yet history shows that the oppressed endure and resist. Vietnam in 1975, Iraq in 2008, and Afghanistan in 2021 all revealed the limits of American empire. Today, the U.S. is a finished empire, eclipsed by the rise of China in 2024.

The war between Hamas and Israel in 2024 is not only a political conflict but a race war. Netanyahu has targeted hospitals and Palestinian infants, carrying out genocide under U.S. sponsorship to seize Gaza's oil and gas wealth—valued in the trillions. Whoever controls these resources will command global influence. Yet Israel, a settler colony of white Europeans from Russia, Germany, Poland, and Britain, cannot endure in a region of brown peoples. It stands as a military fortress of whiteness in the Middle East, much as apartheid South Africa once did in Africa. Just as Nelson Mandela and the ANC brought down South Africa's regime in 1994, so too will the peoples of Palestine and Lebanon bring down Israel's apartheid system.

Decline of America and Israel: The Last Two Racial Apartheid White Colonial Nations

China and Russia watch these events with celebration. They know the racist extermination campaigns of Israel and the U.S. are doomed. History is not on the side of empire but of the oppressed.

And history also testifies that white settlers in Israel cannot claim to be descendants of Abraham. In ancient Mesopotamia around 2320 BCE, the people of the Middle East were brown and dark-skinned, living in climates of 120 degrees Fahrenheit where pale-skinned populations could not survive. Skin color, determined by environment and evolution, ensures that white Europeans cannot be the biological descendants of Abraham (Ford, 2022). Only in northern climates could white skin develop. The gene for melanin, the genetic *shield* of color, protects dark-skinned people from the sun's destructive rays. White Europeans, lacking this genetic defense, cannot credibly claim to be the authentic heirs of the Jewish patriarch.

# Section VIII:
# Media, Culture & Religion (Propaganda, Hollywood, Evangelical Politics)

# Hollywood The Propaganda Machine For The American Empire

In the modern American empire, where bombs fall in silence and drones kill with precision, the most dangerous weapon is not launched from aircraft—it is broadcast from a screen. Hollywood, the global epicenter of film production, has become what Joseph Goebbels was for Adolf Hitler's Nazi regime: a machine of mass consent, constructing false realities to justify wars, glorify military conquest, and dehumanize those who stand in the way of empire.

Joseph Goebbels, born October 29, 1897, in Rheydt, Germany, was Hitler's master of propaganda. He famously persuaded the German public that Poland had invaded Germany in 1939, a lie designed to justify the Nazi invasion that started the Second World War. He glamorized the German military's campaigns across Europe and the Eastern Front, including the June 22, 1941, invasion of the Soviet Union. Goebbels didn't just manipulate the truth—he obliterated it. And in doing so, he turned propaganda into performance art.

Hollywood plays the same role for the United States.

During George W. Bush's war in Iraq, the American media establishment—Fox News chief among them—parroted official lies with cinematic flair. Films and television shows portrayed the U.S. military as liberators, painting the invasion as a righteous campaign to free the Iraqi people from the grip of a so-called "mobster" dictator, Saddam Hussein. The truth, however, was that Bush's administration sought to gain control over Iraq's oil reserves, as noted by Dr. Deshay David Ford in *Decline of America: The Last White Man's Empire and Rise of China the Brown Empire* (Ford, 2022). The pretense of Weapons of Mass Destruction was a manufactured lie, a deception that not only justified a catastrophic war but enriched U.S. oil companies and defense contractors (Ford, 2022).

Goebbels created his lies through radio, speeches, and newspapers. But Hollywood brought imperial fantasy to life on screen. During the

Decline of America and Israel: The Last Two Racial Apartheid White Colonial Nations

Bush years, Hollywood films and military-sponsored productions such as *American Sniper*, *The Kingdom*, and *Zero Dark Thirty* reinforced the narrative that U.S. soldiers were heroes, the enemies were savages, and the violence was necessary. These weren't just movies. They were cultural conditioning.

Just as Leni Riefenstahl, Hitler's favored filmmaker, crafted *Triumph of the Will*—a visually stunning piece of Nazi propaganda to elevate Aryan supremacy and militarism—Hollywood created its own masterpieces of nationalist cinema. These films made Americans proud of their wars. They celebrated soldiers, glorified war, and dehumanized entire nations with a flick of a script.

But this imperial propaganda did not begin with the War on Terror. It began with the 1915 film *The Birth of a Nation*, directed by D.W. Griffith. The film depicted Black men as savages, rapists, and threats to white womanhood. It glorified the Ku Klux Klan as heroic defenders of the white race. The film was shown in the White House to President Woodrow Wilson, who, as a committed white supremacist, found the film "like writing history with lightning." Wilson's presidency (1912–1920) oversaw the re-segregation of the federal government and coincided with the lynching of thousands of Black Americans in the South.

*The Birth of a Nation* wasn't an anomaly. It was a blueprint.

According to Ford (2022), the American film industry has long portrayed Black and brown people as criminals, rapists, degenerates, and burdens on society. Hollywood crafted these stereotypes and exported them globally, shaping how entire civilizations perceived people of color. Black men were criminals. Latino men were drug lords. Arab men were terrorists. Asian men were emasculated or mysterious. Indigenous people were savages. These weren't just characters—they were policies in waiting.

And just as Goebbels used the media to build support for genocide, Hollywood built support for incarceration, war, and structural racism.

Decline of America and Israel: The Last Two Racial Apartheid White Colonial Nations

Fox News and Hollywood remain twin pillars of white supremacist propaganda in the United States. Together, they manufacture fear of Blackness, criminalize poverty, and create the conditions for state violence. Meanwhile, they ignore the white perpetrators of mass shootings across the country—from the Las Vegas shooter who killed 58 people, to the young white man who drove 600 miles from Fort Worth, Texas, to El Paso just to kill Mexican shoppers at a Walmart. As Ford (2022) notes, most violent crime in the U.S. is committed not by immigrants, but by homegrown individuals—white men radicalized by racial anxiety and right-wing propaganda.

Yet Hollywood and Fox News never center this reality. Instead, they blame immigrants, Muslims, and Black communities for America's decline. They don't tell the world that the U.S. has more people in prison than China, Russia, or North Korea—a system of racialized incarceration built on stereotypes born in movie studios and newsrooms.

Hollywood does not merely reflect American values. It creates them.

Through its imagery, language, and characters, it elevates whiteness, normalizes war, and promotes capitalism. Its films don't just entertain, they instruct. They teach audiences who are worthy of life, and who are disposable.

That is not art. That is indoctrination.

And that is what Goebbels mastered nearly a century ago.

Let the record show: Hollywood is the propaganda ministry of the American empire.

Its movies are weapons. Its scripts are blueprints for domination. And its legacy is soaked in the same ideological blood that once stained the swastika.

Hollywood did not invent racism, but it perfected its performance.

And the world still pays the price.

# Donald Trump's White Male Evangelical Southern Baptist Christians Are Sodom And Gomorrah Of Sexual Molestation Of Children

At the heart of America's largest white Protestant denomination, a crisis of moral collapse festers beneath a veneer of piety. The Southern Baptist Convention (SBC), the spiritual home to nearly 13 million members across the United States, including over 370,000 in Arkansas alone, stands exposed as a haven not only for hypocrisy but for widespread sexual abuse, particularly against children. As of 2024, reports across the nation and within the Convention's own internal task forces reveal that the SBC has harbored hundreds of sexual predators, many of them white male pastors, deacons, and church officials, whose crimes have been systematically covered up, ignored, or dismissed.

The comparison to Sodom and Gomorrah is not hyperbole, it is tragically accurate. Churches across the SBC hierarchy have been revealed as unsafe spaces for children, with widespread molestation cases taking place in congregations, camps, and youth programs. The magnitude of this crisis has stunned even devout Southern Baptists, many of whom now fear for the safety of their children every time they step into the sanctuary. According to a June 16, 2024 front-page report in the *Arkansas Democrat* titled *"Church Group Ends With Its Job Undone"*, task force leader Josh Wester admitted that the Convention failed to post an online list of abusers, despite months of work to compile verified reports of misconduct.

This is not a new failure, it is part of a broader historical pattern. The Southern Baptist Convention, formed in defense of slavery before the American Civil War, was founded on the theological justification of white supremacy. Its members were slaveholders, segregationists, and later, among the most aggressive opponents of the Civil Rights Movement. Many in their ranks were affiliated with the Ku Klux Klan, opposing school integration, interracial marriage, and voting rights for Black Americans. And today, the same denomination that once blessed the noose and fire now blesses Donald Trump, a convicted sexual abuser and serial moral transgressor.

The connection is more than symbolic—it is spiritual alignment. White evangelical leaders, particularly in the South, have consistently defended Trump despite his legal convictions and moral failures. They defend him not in spite of his behavior, but because of it. His conduct mirrors the culture of concealment that has defined their leadership. In SBC churches, many pastors and their administrative staff have themselves been accused or convicted of child molestation. Rather than excommunicate abusers or protect children, many churches chose to protect their reputations, shielding predators from consequences and reassigning them to other congregations.

One of the most public examples occurred at Immanuel Baptist Church, the largest Baptist church in Arkansas, where Pastor Steven Smith faced criticism for mishandling sexual abuse claims. He eventually announced his resignation in March 2024, effective April 7. Still, no complete list of predators has been released, even after years of investigation by the SBC's Credential Committee, of which mental health therapist Kelly Lammers was a member. Lammers voiced deep frustration that despite gathering credible evidence, the Convention's leadership refused to publish the names of known abusers. As she said in her statement to the *Arkansas Democrat*, the failure to act has left millions of children in Southern Baptist churches vulnerable to sexual violence.

According to the SBC's own internal report, 80% of all recent cases before the committee involved sexual abuse of minors, a staggering figure that implicates the Church as an institution fundamentally broken at its core.

That brokenness extends to politics.

It is no coincidence that the white evangelical base of the Southern Baptist Church remains one of Donald Trump's most faithful voting blocs. Their moral collapse mirrors his. Trump has been found liable for sexual assault, named in civil litigation tied to Jeffrey Epstein's Island,

and convicted of falsifying business records to conceal an affair with an adult film actress. And yet, he is celebrated by many white evangelical leaders as a chosen instrument of God.

This alignment speaks volumes about shared values. As the saying goes, people support those who reflect their moral worldview. The Southern Baptist leadership and Donald Trump have created a coalition of denial, where abuse is normalized, truth is suppressed, and power is protected at any cost. Trump's values are rooted in misogyny, racial grievance, and predatory entitlement, and have become the values of the political religious right.

This moral decay was foreseen. In *The End of White Christian America*, Dr. Robert P. Jones warned that the influence of white evangelicals is waning, and with that decline, their desperation grows. In *American Fascists*, Chris Hedges similarly described the fusion of Christian fundamentalism with authoritarian nationalism, predicting that the final act of this movement would not be revival, but collapse.

And collapse may be near. If Donald Trump is re-elected on November 2, 2024, the United States risks entering a terminal decline. Professor Alfred McCoy, a leading historian of empires, has projected that the U.S. could cease to exist as a global power by 2030, splintered by internal division, corruption, and the erosion of democratic institutions. Much like the fall of Rome, brought on by decadence, economic inequality, and moral decline, America now teeters on a precipice. Trump's election would not merely be a setback, it could be the death knell of American democracy.

Let the record show: a nation cannot be saved by men who prey upon its children, nor by churches that cover their sins in scripture.

If America falls, it will not be because of enemies abroad, but because it placed its fate in the hands of predators, liars, and cowards cloaked in the garments of religion.

231

# Section IX:
# Conclusion &
# Meta-Analysis

# Observations Of Dr. Deshay David Ford As A Citizen Of America

I was born on January 14, 1948, in the small, racially-strangled town of Scott, Arkansas. A dot on the American map, yet a profound reflection of the racial apartheid that defined the American South long after the Civil War had ended. My very birth was within a state where the air still smelled of Confederate pride, and the black body remained chained, not in visible iron, but in policy, poverty, and prejudice. In Arkansas, as in much of Dixie, the Constitution of 1787 was not a document of liberty for all—it was a contract of exclusion for us.

America's founding law, enshrined in Article IV, Section 2, Clause 3, did not see my ancestors as human beings. It legalized the trafficking and enslavement of Black people, codifying a hierarchy that placed white men above the law and Black men beneath it. In 1948, nothing had fundamentally changed. My parents, Juanita Robinson and Maurice Harold Ford, could not vote freely. They had no access to the wealth, privilege, or protections that white Arkansans inherited at birth. My family lived on the outskirts of American democracy, in its shadows, in its fields, in its forgotten shacks.

Growing up in the Jim Crow South was not merely a personal experience. It was a national indictment. The conditions for Black Americans in Arkansas mirrored those of apartheid South Africa before the 1994 election of Nelson Mandela. Segregation was not just a social inconvenience; it was an institutional weapon. We were denied entry to restaurants, barred from voting booths, and hunted by white mobs with impunity.

I recall a school field trip during my senior year of high school. We visited Vicksburg, Mississippi, the site of one of the most decisive battles in the Civil War, where General Ulysses S. Grant delivered a fatal blow to the Confederacy in 1863. I was one of three Black students on that trip. When we stopped for lunch, our teacher, a white woman named Mary Martin, entered a local restaurant to inquire if the establishment would serve us. She returned with the cold truth: the restaurant refused to allow Black students inside. We were permitted to order our food from a hole in the side of the building, as if we were diseased dogs begging for scraps.

I refused.

I would not debase myself to eat from a hole carved in a wall of hate. I stayed on the bus while my two Black classmates accepted the humiliation and ordered their meals. Miss Martin, with genuine concern, returned and offered to bring me a sandwich. I declined. Even in hunger, I knew my dignity was not negotiable. I chose pride over sustenance.

Miss Mary Martin was not like most white teachers. She was an angel in human flesh. She saw in me a spark that the system had tried to extinguish. She placed me in advanced academic classes and encouraged me to pursue higher education, an audacious suggestion for a Black boy in 1960s Arkansas. Her belief in me was a lifeline. More than a teacher, she was a moral witness in an immoral time. I remember her with reverence. Decades have passed, but her kindness remains unforgotten.

My parents raised nine children in a world where the economic system was designed to crush them. They struggled as sharecroppers, modern-day slaves, tied to a system where white landowners dictated every aspect of Black existence. We picked cotton from sunup to sundown. When it rained, we were allowed to attend school. When the skies were clear, our education stopped, and our labor began. This was the cycle: work, hunger, work again. We were children of the field long before we were ever allowed to be children of the classroom.

Literacy came late to my siblings and me. Our early schooling was fragmented by labor, by poverty, by neglect. It was my great-uncle, Desha Robinson, who gifted me my first set of encyclopedias. They became my salvation. I read them relentlessly through the night, during breaks, whenever I had light and silence. Knowledge became my rebellion. My teachers noticed. They allowed me to study during lunch and recess. In a system built to keep me ignorant, I found allies who gave me space to grow.

Even as the 1954 Supreme Court ruling in *Brown v. Board of Education* declared racial segregation unconstitutional, change did not come to Arkansas overnight. I was seven years old when that ruling passed. But I did not enter an integrated classroom until 1966. The law said we were equal. The culture said otherwise.

During my teenage years, I was recommended by a white supervisor to the plantation owner where my family sharedcropped. That man, John Robert Alexander, took a peculiar interest in me. He arranged for me to work at the Little Rock home of his college friend, Dr. Graham Roots Hall, former U.S. Consul General to both Australia and India during the Eisenhower Administration. I was not merely tending a garden. I was absorbing the behaviors, conversations, and intellect of a world I had never seen. It was there I began to understand what power looked like, and how far away it was from the cotton fields of Scott.

I graduated from Scott High School in 1968 and enrolled in Philander Smith College that same year. It was a historically Black institution committed not just to education, but to liberation. The students I met there were visionaries in the making; young, defiant, and determined to transform America, not beg for entry into it.

Philander Smith College saved me. It took a boy bent by labor and made him into a man sharpened by knowledge. I earned my bachelor's, then a master's, and finally a doctorate. Every page I turned, every lecture I attended, was a blow against the system that said I would never make it. I am not the product of personal genius. I am the product of a collective will: of parents, teachers, mentors, and strangers who lifted me when I was down and demanded that I keep going.

I debated Muhammad Ali in 1969. Yes, the Greatest of All Time. He won the debate, of course. But I walked away knowing that even the sons of sharecroppers could stand on the same stage as legends. That moment wasn't just personal triumph. It was prophecy. A testament to how far we had come, and how far we still had to go.

Decline of America and Israel: The Last Two Racial Apartheid White Colonial Nations

My skin tone and the color of my siblings were often a topic among white observers. One white man once remarked how we all looked different, some lighter, some darker. I explained: African Americans carry the genetic imprints of the world because of slavery. We were raped and trafficked across continents. We bear the DNA of every empire that violated our ancestors. That is not a weakness. That is proof of survival. Even Michelle Obama's great-grandfather was a white man. Thomas Jefferson himself fathered children with enslaved Black women. This is America, not a land of purity, but of contradiction.

I was the first in my family to attend college. I was not the last.

My parents, Maurice and Juanita Ford, labored not only under the hot sun of Arkansas's cotton fields but beneath the weight of a system built to break them. They struggled to provide for their children in a region where the air reeked of Jim Crow and the ground had been fertilized with the blood of generations of enslaved Black labor. In the Apartheid South of the United States, there was no margin for error. For a Black family to survive was a triumph. For one to dream was an act of revolution.

Under the so-called Constitution of 1787, celebrated by white America as a symbol of liberty, Black people were nothing more than chattel. Article IV, Section 2, Clause 3 enshrined slavery into the very DNA of the American experiment. The Founding Fathers, that venerated pantheon of white statesmen, George Washington, Thomas Jefferson, James Madison, James Monroe, and South Carolina's Pierce Butler, were not moral visionaries. They were slaveholders. They wrote laws not to expand liberty but to protect their wealth, which at that time was counted not in currency but in Black bodies.

Andrew Jackson, America's seventh president, carried this barbarism further. In 1830, he signed the Indian Removal Act, initiating what would become the first coordinated campaign of racial genocide on American soil. The Trail of Tears, as it came to be known, was not a forced migration. It was an extermination route. By the 1890 massacre at Wounded Knee, the U.S. military had all but completed the ethnic cleansing of the continent's original inhabitants. And even those Native warriors who fought back, such as Crazy Horse and his men who defeated General George Armstrong Custer's 7th Cavalry at Little Bighorn in 1876, were vilified, not honored, in America's textbooks. As historian Dee Brown so powerfully documented in *Bury My Heart at Wounded Knee* (1970), this was no accident. It was design.

The only reason African slaves were not annihilated outright is because they were considered property—investments too valuable to destroy. As Dr. Nikole Hannah-Jones of the *1619 Project* notes, slavery in America was not simply an institution of racial hierarchy; it was a business model. The goal was not to civilize, nor to integrate, but to extract, to work slaves to death and profit from their suffering. America was not founded on high ideals. It was founded on the commodification of human life.

Take, for example, the 1772 case of James Somersett in Britain. A Black man enslaved by an English official named Stewart, Somersett sued for his freedom upon arriving in London. Chief Justice Lord Mansfield, in a historic ruling, declared that slavery was unsupported by English Common Law. Had America still been under British rule, Washington, Jefferson, Madison, Monroe, and other southern elites would have been legally compelled to free their human property, destroying their wealth overnight. Thomas Jefferson, in his infinite hypocrisy, concocted a brilliant scheme to protect his assets: revolution. American independence was not born of tyranny; it was born of greed.

The July 4th celebration that white Americans hold sacred is, in fact, a commemoration of their right to continue enslaving African people. Independence was not a protest against oppression. It was a declaration of economic self-preservation by the slaveholding elite.

In 2024, the legacy of that economic decision still haunts the U.S. Congress. The majority of sitting Senators and Representatives are direct descendants of slave owners. The structures they uphold are mere echoes of a slave state, dressed in modern attire.

By contrast, China's historical path reveals a strikingly different foundation. The Chinese civilization, dating back over 10,000 years, was not forged on the backs of enslaved people. China was not born through racial genocide. It was built on familial unity, agricultural ingenuity, and philosophical depth. It was not a nation founded for profit, but for survival, continuity, and community. The Chinese people began their civilization not by enslaving a darker race, but by cultivating land, raising families, and developing governance systems rooted in harmony and self-discipline.

America is the only modern empire to be physically constructed by enslaved laborers. Yes, Athens and Sparta had slavery. But their slaves were prisoners of war, not victims of racial ideology. America, however, institutionalized slavery based explicitly on skin color. The "land of the free" was founded by men who believed freedom was the exclusive right of white men. The buildings of Washington, D.C., the railroads of the West, and the cotton wealth of the South, all were created by people denied even the recognition of their humanity.

And in 2024, the racial fault lines remain. America is just as segregated now, economically, socially, and politically, as it was in 1950. The schools may no longer have "Whites Only" signs, but the zip codes, funding disparities, and police brutality speak for themselves. The nation has not evolved—it has only rebranded its apartheid.

Like South Africa before the election of Nelson Mandela in 1994, the United States now stands at a crossroads. A society cannot claim moral superiority while maintaining systemic injustice. A government cannot call itself a democracy while disenfranchising its Black and brown citizens.

And yet, my parents still believed in education. Despite every obstacle, they instilled in us the conviction that learning was liberation. We lived on a large plantation in Scott, Arkansas. The soil beneath our feet was soaked with the memories of slavery, and yet we dreamed of books, not bondage.

## Decline of America and Israel: The Last Two Racial Apartheid White Colonial Nations

According to Pulitzer Prize-winning journalist Douglas A. Blackmon, author of *Slavery by Another Name* (2008), no people in human history—none—have emerged from such a brutal past to accomplish what African Americans have. Our race has endured chains, whips, burnings, lynchings, false imprisonments, and still given the world unmatched contributions in every field of human endeavor.

Take jazz, for example, a music born in the cotton fields and juke joints of Black America, now studied in doctoral programs across Russia, China, Iran, North Korea, and Vietnam. That which was birthed from our pain is now a global treasure. From Harlem to Hanoi, the trumpet of freedom still echoes.

And yet, white Americans continue to define their national greatness not by culture, but by conquest. I once heard two white men boast that America invented the atomic bomb. Not Beethoven, not brushwork, not philosophy, but the bomb.

It was a Jewish-American physicist, J. Robert Oppenheimer, who led the Manhattan Project. And it was the United States, the only nation in world history that deployed atomic weapons against civilian populations. On August 6 and 9, 1945, the cities of Hiroshima and Nagasaki were vaporized. Over two million Japanese people were incinerated in seconds, along with American prisoners of war held captive in those cities.

The bombs were dropped not out of military necessity, but as racial vengeance. According to declassified military reports, the timing was deliberate: market day, when civilians, mothers, children, and the elderly were most exposed. There were no leaflets, no warnings, no mercy.

(Ford, 2022, *Decline of America: The Last White Man's Empire and the Rise of China, the Brown Empire*, Dorrance Publishing).

In the fall of 1968, I began my freshman year at Philander Smith College in Little Rock, Arkansas, a historically Black institution whose legacy continues to shine as a sanctuary of intellect, resistance, and excellence. By 2024, the institution has rightly earned its recognition as Philander Smith University, but even then, in 1968, it was a beacon. A place where the children of sharecroppers, domestic workers, and laborers could enter the world of letters and law, debate and dignity.

It was at Philander Smith that I first felt the rhythm of academic ambition beating in my chest. The faculty there did not simply teach; they molded. They challenged. They uplifted. It was not merely a college; it was a forge. I remain forever indebted to the professors and fellow students who walked alongside me on that path of transformation. It was there, on that humble campus, that I encountered brilliance, resistance, and camaraderie. Philander Smith College was my launching pad, not just into education, but into the world.

After completing my undergraduate studies, I pursued graduate work at the University of Central Arkansas. My advisor, Dr. Paul Witherspoon, was a true Southern gentleman, an honorable man of scholarship and fairness, rare in those days and still rare now. He mentored many, including me, with compassion and academic rigor. May he rest in eternal peace.

It was also during this time, around 1970, that I had the honor of meeting Muhammad Ali. The Greatest. He visited both the University of Arkansas and Philander Smith College as a guest speaker, and his presence was electric. Charismatic, unapologetic, and brilliant, Ali did not simply speak—he prophesied. His words carried a cadence that echoed through the bones of Black men like me, reminding us that white systems did not determine our value, but by our birthright as human beings.

During my educational journey, I also worked for Graham and Louise Boaz Hall at their home in Pine Knoll, Little Rock. Graham Roots Hall had once served as the United States Consul General to both Australia and India during the Eisenhower administration (1952–1956), and through that experience, their household became a revolving door of diplomats, intellectuals, and world travelers. In their employ, I met a remarkable African-American woman, Elizabeth Minor, their longtime housekeeper and companion in travels around the world. Mrs. Minor was a model of quiet dignity, and her presence in the Hall household offered me an intimate view of global diplomacy through Black eyes. She had seen the world, not through a television screen, but with her own vision—and she taught me that no matter where I came from, I belonged anywhere I chose to go.

I remained connected with the Hall family in some capacity until 1984. And along my path, God placed other angels. One of them was my dear friend, Robert W. Lewis, a U.S. Navy Administrator and lifelong civil rights activist. He was a brilliant, committed African-American man whose love for justice was matched only by the love he shared with his wife, Mrs. Doree Lewis. Married for over 50 years, they raised a beautiful family, each child a reflection of strength, purpose, and pride.

And then, there are my sons, Daniel Deshay Ford and Edward Maurice Ford. Words fail to capture the pride I feel when I speak of them. Both pursued education, both live productive, meaningful lives, and both carry the fire of our family legacy. I look at them and see proof that we are not what America tried to make us. We are not bound by slavery, poverty, or silence. We are testimony.

My brothers too walked the path of dignity. They labored under the weight of a racist world, yet emerged as strong African-American men who gave their families reason to be proud. In their struggles and triumphs, I see the enduring power of our people, a power that no system could erase.

In 1972, I completed further studies at the University of Arkansas at Little Rock. The institution I encountered in 1969 and 1972 was not the diverse and inclusive campus it is today. Back then, it was still grappling with the weight of its own segregated past. The shadow of the 1957 Central High School crisis still hung over the state like smoke from a burning cross. The integration of the "Little Rock Nine" had placed Arkansas at the epicenter of America's racial battle, and the scars were still fresh.

In 1969, the University of Arkansas at Fayetteville had not yet accepted Black athletes onto its celebrated Razorback football team. The myth of white athletic supremacy still gripped the institution. When Jon Richardson, an exceptional Black athlete and graduate of Horace Mann High School, became the Razorbacks' first Black football player, it marked a milestone in Arkansas sports history. He died in 2010 at 63, but his courage cracked the walls of segregation that had long dominated Southern college athletics.

In 1972, I enrolled at the University of Arkansas Law School. The experience was anything but welcoming. The school's discomfort with Black students was palpable. I did not feel embraced, I felt endured. And so I left.

But the future, like history, moves forward even when institutions do not. Over fifty years later, I returned to the University of Arkansas at Little Rock and found a different place, one almost unrecognizable. A campus filled with Black, white, Latino, Muslim, Asian, international, disabled, and LGBTQ students. A multicultural, multiracial, multifaith university that no longer resembled the narrow halls of the old Jim Crow South.

It brought tears to my eyes.

The transformation was profound. The very institution that once resisted my presence had now become a mirror of the America we had always fought to create. And while we are not there yet, while racism still rots the foundation of this nation, it is undeniable that the seeds we planted decades ago have begun to bear fruit.

I am proud to be a graduate of the University of Arkansas at Little Rock. I am proud of Philander Smith University. I am proud of the Black men and women—named and unnamed—who refused to bow.

But I am most proud that I kept going.

From the cotton fields of Scott, Arkansas to the debate stage with Muhammad Ali, from Jim Crow classrooms to diverse campuses, from a child born in a nation that considered me three-fifths of a person to a scholar bearing witness in the twilight of empire, I have walked the long road of America.

# Conclusion

We now face the great historical question: *When* will the *American empire* fall?

Some historians argue that the fall has already occurred. They point to 2016, when the American people elected Donald Trump as president, as the turning point. That election, more than any other moment, exposed the deep moral and structural decay at the heart of the nation. Trump himself embodies what the Romans once represented at the height of their decline—immorality, corruption, and the normalization of debauchery. Rome, before its collapse, was consumed by decadence. America, in its modern decline, has followed the same path.

Trump's degeneracy is not merely personal; it is symbolic of a wider crisis. The support he receives from white evangelicals, many of whom preach morality yet tolerate or conceal abuse, reveals the hypocrisy of American religious life. Reports such as the *Arkansas Gazette* (July 2024) expose widespread child molestation within white evangelical congregations, including the prominent Immanuel Baptist Church in Little Rock. Families live in fear of the very institutions that claim to guide them spiritually. This collapse of moral authority is a hallmark of empire in decline: when corruption spreads not only through politics and economics but also through faith and family life.

At the same time, the demographic balance that once underpinned white supremacy is shifting. For centuries, the growth of the white population in America coincided with the destruction and decline of Indigenous populations. Today, the trend is reversed. White birth rates are falling, deaths now outnumber births, and immigration ensures that white Americans will soon be a minority. The same demographic pressures exist in Europe, where aging populations foreshadow a loss of dominance. History moves in cycles. Just as white settlers once overtook Indigenous peoples, now the descendants of those settlers confront their own decline.

# Decline of America and Israel: The Last Two Racial Apartheid White Colonial Nations

What comes next? Martin Jacques, in his influential work *When China Rules the World* (2009–2012), argues that China will become the global hegemon of the 21st century. Yet Jacques warns that Chinese dominance will not usher in an era free of racism. On the contrary, he predicts that China, like every empire before it, will assert its racial and cultural superiority over others. Race, Jacques concludes, will remain the central factor in relations between dominant powers and the peoples they subjugate.

History bears this out. Every empire: the Egyptians, Assyrians, Babylonians, Persians, Greeks, Romans, Muslims, Mongols, Spanish, Portuguese, French, British, Russians, and Americans, has justified its rule with claims of superiority. The white American empire, in particular, rested on the ideology that whites were destined to rule over Blacks, Indigenous peoples, Asians, and Latinos. Will China be any different? If history is our guide, then Jacques is correct: racial superiority will remain at the heart of imperial power.

For my family and my people, the story of empire has been one of pain and survival. Our existence within the American empire has been a brutal nightmare of racist hate, lynching, injustice, and murder. From the daily harassment of police to the denial of basic humanity, from the Tulsa Race Riot of 1921 to the thousands of lynchings that scarred the South between 1877 and 1970, from the denial of rights under the Constitution of 1787 to the systemic inequalities in health care, education, and employment—our story has been one of resilience under oppression.

Gunnar Myrdal, in his landmark study An *American* Dilemma (1944), made it clear: the system of white racism in America was created by the white man, and it is the white man alone who has the power to end it. Yet, as history shows, those who profit from empire rarely dismantle it voluntarily. Collapse comes when the weight of corruption, inequality, and resistance becomes too heavy to bear.

## Decline of America and Israel: The Last Two Racial Apartheid White Colonial Nations

The American empire was built on slavery, genocide, and exploitation. It now faces its twilight. Whether the final collapse comes swiftly, as with Rome, or slowly, as with Britain, the outcome is inevitable. What remains is the question of how we will endure it. And whether a new world, one more just than the old, might one day rise from the ruins.

# Bibliography

Balfour, A. J. (1917). *The Balfour Declaration*. British Foreign Office.

Brown, D. (1970). *Bury my heart at Wounded Knee: An Indian history of the American West*. New York, NY: Holt, Rinehart & Winston.

Ford, D. D. (2022). *Decline of America: The last white man's empire and rise of the Brown's empire*. Pittsburgh, PA: Dorrance Publishing.

Ford, D. D. (2024). *Why Muslim people hate Donald Trump and America*. [Publisher not identified].

Hourani, A. (1991). *A history of the Arab peoples*. Cambridge, MA: Harvard University Press.

Madley, B. (2018). *An American genocide: The United States and the California Indian catastrophe, 1846–1873*. New Haven, CT: Yale University Press.

Mahbubani, K. (2020). *Has China won? The Chinese challenge to American primacy*. New York, NY: PublicAffairs.

Rosen, R. (2006). *The Jewish Confederates*. Columbia, SC: University of South Carolina Press.

The Constitution of the United States of America (1787). *Primary legal document*.

U.S. Court of Appeals for the Ninth Circuit. (2023). *Deshay Ford v. Judge Michael Greenberg, Case No. 23-55699*.

U.S. District Court, Central District of California. (2022). *Deshay Ford v. Michael Greenberg, Case No. 2-22-cv-08339-VBF-RAQ*.

U.S. Health Services. (2022). *[Report referenced regarding opioid epidemic]*. [Publisher not identified].

Zinn, H. (1980). *A people's history of the United States*. New York, NY: Harper & Row.